D0333956

Journey into God's Heart

Also by Jennifer Rees Larcombe

Turning Point
Unexpected Healing

Journey into God's Heart

The True Story of a Life of Faith

Jennifer Rees Larcombe

Hodder & Stoughton
LONDON SYDNEY AUCKLAND

Copyright © 2006 by Jennifer Rees Larcombe

First published in Great Britain in 2006

The right of Jennifer Rees Larcombe to be identified as the Author
of the Work has been asserted by her in accordance
with the Copyright, Designs and Patents Act 1988.

1

All rights reserved. No part of this publication may be
reproduced, stored in a retrieval system, or transmitted,
in any form or by any means, without the prior written
permission of the publisher, nor be otherwise circulated
in any form of binding or cover other than that in which
it is published and without a similar condition being
imposed on the subsequent purchaser.

British Library Cataloguing in Publication Data
A record for this book is available from the British Library.

ISBN 0 340 86157 6

Typeset in Bembo by Avon DataSet Ltd,
Bidford-on-Avon, Warwickshire

Printed and bound in Great Britain by
Bookmarque Ltd, Croydon, Surrey

The paper and board used in this paperback are natural recyclable
products made from wood grown in sustainable forests.
The manufacturing processes conform to the environmental
regulations of the country of origin.

Hodder & Stoughton Ltd
A division of Hodder Headline
338 Euston Road
London NW1 3BH
www.madaboutbooks.com
www.hodderbibles.co.uk

To Sandra Wheatley and all the other people who have shown me what intimacy with God really means.

> *I stretch out, reaching for you, and daily add praise to praise. I'll write the book on your righteousness, talk up your salvation the livelong day, never run out of good things to write or say.*
>
> Psalm 71:14–17, *The Message*

All the people whose names I have mentioned in this book have generously given their consent; this is important to me, because I would never have published it without their blessing and consent.

With special thanks to Tony Larcombe for his helpful comments and advice.

Acknowledgements

Unless otherwise indicated, Scripture quotations are taken from the HOLY BIBLE, NEW INTERNATIONAL VERSION. Copyright © 1973, 1978, 1984 by International Bible Society. Used by permission of Hodder & Stoughton. All rights reserved. 'NIV' is a registered trademark of International Bible Society. UK trademark number 1448790.

The following abbreviations have been used to indicate where other Bible versions are quoted:

AMP   **Amplified Bible**
                Scripture quotations taken from the Amplified® Bible, copyright © 1954, 1958, 1962, 1964, 1965, 1987 by The Lockman Foundation. Used by permission (www.Lockman.org).

GNB   **Good News Bible**
                Scriptures quoted from the Good News Bible published by The Bible Societies/HarperCollins Publishers Ltd, UK, copyright © American Bible Society, 1966, 1971, 1976, 1992.

KJV   **King James Version**
                In the public domain.

The Message	**The Message**

The Message

Scripture taken from *The Message* copyright © 1993, 1994, 1995, 1996, 2000, 2001, 2002. Used by permission of NavPress Publishing Group.

NKJV — **New King James Version**

Scripture taken from the New King James Version copyright © 1982 by Thomas Nelson, Inc. Used by permission. All rights reserved.

NLB — **New Living Bible**

NRSV — **New Revised Standard Version**

Copyright © 1989, Division of Christian Education of the National Council of the Churches of Christ in the United States of America.

Introduction

'If God can heal people as dramatically and unexpectedly as he healed you, then why doesn't he do it more often?' That's a question I am often asked. The reply is simple: 'Being healed suddenly and completely after eight years in a wheelchair is such a traumatic experience that God is far too merciful to do it very often!'

It is now some years since that afternoon in June 1990 when I was speaking from my wheelchair at a ladies' conference near Guildford. I had been disabled by a brain virus that had left me with constant pain, weakness and a whole clutch of other physical problems; but at the end of the conference a new Christian called Wendy prayed for me and I have never once sat in a wheelchair since! I was instantly and permanently healed, but also given far more energy and strength than most other people I know.

At first I was a nine days' wonder, hitting the headlines in the secular media as well as the Christian press, and I was invited to tell my story all over the world. People argued endlessly about what had happened, dissecting the experience. Some rejoiced with me while others rejected the whole thing as a fake or a publicity stunt. Since then people have often asked, 'With the benefit of hindsight, what do you *really* think happened that day?' Others want to know, 'Has your healing lasted?' Many also demand, 'How did the instant change from a disabled housewife into a woman with a popular ministry affect your personal life and your marriage?'

My main aim in writing this book was not to answer questions like that, even though you may form your own conclusions if you decide to read it. The book was 'conceived' many years before I was disabled, during a rainy holiday in Devon. I was browsing round a junk shop when I found a battered paperback by my favourite author, Catherine Marshall; it was called *Meeting God at Every Turn*. I had already enjoyed several of her books in which she described various dramatic incidents in her life, so I wondered why she had felt the need to write yet another book about herself. I soon discovered the answer. This book was more like a love story than an autobiography, as she described the gentle unfolding of God's grace from her childhood to her old age and the way he had gradually made himself known to her through the various people she met along the way. As I read, I sensed my own spirit was being drawn closer to the God she obviously loved so much. 'One day,' I thought as I reluctantly reached the end, 'I'd love to write this kind of a book.'

Three years ago, when I finally plucked up the courage to begin, the job proved far more difficult than I anticipated – perhaps because the moments when I have experienced God most intensely have been during times that I would much rather forget and would least like to share with others! One of the other problems I faced when I sat down to write was that, while describing my journey with God, I realised, as Catherine Marshall must also have done, that I would have to mention briefly some of the events I have already written about in other books. While I did not want to relive the pain of them all over again, I knew I needed to look at them from a new angle and with the perspective which only time can give.

One of the things that kept me going was a quote I found in a book by Frederick Buechner, *Telling Secrets* (HarperCollins,

1991). He says that nothing is more important, 'than that we keep track, you and I, of who we are and where we have come from and the people we have met along the way because it is precisely through these stories, in all their particularity, that God makes himself known most powerfully and personally'. Another quote from Henri Nouwen also helped: 'We are called to lay down our lives for . . . people. This laying down . . . means first of all making our own lives – our sorrows and joys, our despair and hope, our loneliness and experience of intimacy – available to others as sources of new life' (*Bread for the Journey: Thoughts for Every Day of the Year*, Henri Nouwen, Darton, Longman and Todd, 1997).

While I know that my healing was a quite remarkable intervention on God's part which he has used to strengthen my own faith and to bless thousands of other people, seen in retrospect it does not seem nearly as significant as other events which I have never yet been able to put into words. Of course, it has been wonderful to be fit and active once again, and during the last fifteen years I have tramped thousands of miles over hills, moors and Kentish footpaths, enjoyed my full-time job and revelled in being an energetic grandmother. However, on a personal level there have been times when my healing has actually seemed so destructive that I wished it had never taken place. Some of what I say may well surprise or even shock you, and that is another reason why working on this book has been so hard; but I knew I could not be selective with the truth when I was writing in God's presence. The Jesuit priest John Powell once wrote a book called *Why Am I Afraid to Tell You Who I Am?* (Zondervan, 1999). It was subtitled 'I am afraid to tell you who I am because you may not like who I am and it's all that I have'. You certainly may not like the person you find behind the warts on this self-portrait, but you might also be encouraged to see how God continues to love and use the most unlikely of people! Some of the mistakes I have made could also warn other people, particularly those with a public ministry, and prevent them from stumbling on to the same landmines that blew up in my face.

In August 1980, two years before I became ill, I felt that God called me to be a prophet; at that time I thought he meant I was to become a preacher, like my parents, but I have since realised that it was the *lives* of the prophets that spoke to people far more clearly than their *words* ever could. So this book is really my way of handing on to others all that I have personally discovered about the goodness and faithfulness of God. As I am no theologian but just an ordinary granny, the only way I could communicate my discoveries was by telling you how they have impacted my own private journey into God's heart.

1

*Yes . . . let us be zealous to know the LORD, to appreciate, give heed to
and cherish Him.*

Hosea 6:3, AMP

'I'm home!' I shouted as I opened the front door. No one
answered, which was hardly surprising since I'd lived alone for
seven years – but family habits die hard! Kicking off my smart
shoes I gingerly opened the sitting-room door, bracing myself for
the avalanche. Three large dogs hurled themselves at me with
wildly wagging tails.

'Anyone would think I'd been away for months,' I said as I
pushed them out into the garden before their excitement ruined
my carpet. 'I've only done a Ladies' Breakfast; and if you're
interested,' I added, 'it went really well.' They weren't remotely
interested, but when you come back from doing something you've
been dreading it's nice to tell someone how it went.

With a huge sense of relief I peeled off my best working suit
and replaced it with gardening clothes. 'It came to pass,' I
muttered thankfully, quoting one of my father's favourite Bible
verses (King James Version, of course!). Although I usually speak
at several churches or Christian events every week, this outreach
breakfast had been the first I'd done for a while. Just a few

5

weeks before, I had held the little body of my granddaughter, Cerian, in my arms and dressed her in the clothes we'd all made for her so carefully. I had prayed for months that this child would live, but as I looked down at her dear little face I knew my hopes had just died with her. Everything in me had been crying out ever since, 'God, why didn't you heal her?' I had been so sure he *could*. Only twelve years earlier he had healed me suddenly one day after eight years of life in a wheelchair. I had been telling people ever since about his power and had often seen him responding to my prayers on their behalf. Yet he seemed to have ignored all my agonised prayers for Cerian, even though I would willingly have given up my own healing for hers. When your grandchild dies you not only grieve for them but you also have to watch your own child grieving.

Maybe I could have handled that double-edged misery a little better if it had not come as the climax of six other major losses that had hit in rapid succession. I felt punch drunk and was almost afraid to pray because it seemed that everything I asked God to do, he promptly did the opposite! A nasty cold feeling often seeped through me early in the mornings: suppose I had been deluding myself all my life? Perhaps God was actually powerless after all and it was only coincidence when he appeared to respond to our prayers.

It is extremely unnerving to have a diary full of engagements where you are supposed to stand up and share your faith when you don't seem to have any left! As a bereavement counsellor, I knew that a temporary faith loss is normal when a lot of things go wrong all at once, but somehow I had lost my nerve as well as my faith. I had cancelled a whole string of invitations, but you can't go on running away for ever and that breakfast felt like the crunch point, a 'now or never' moment – so I had decided to risk it and go. I knew I would have to be totally honest with those ladies in Tenterden because Christians who pretend make me cringe, but I had dreaded the prospect of making myself so vulnerable.

Facing the ordeal on my own didn't seem sensible so I had rung round all my friends, hoping that one of them could come with me, but for some strange reason every single one of them said they were busy that day. So, early in the morning I had set off alone to tell a whole room full of strangers that sometimes you can't feel faith in your heart or reason it out logically in your head – you just have to choose to keep holding it tight by willpower, like a flickering candle in the dark.

'Now that's safely over,' I thought happily, 'I'll get the last of those wallflowers in, and finish up with a huge bonfire.'

My foot was halfway into a Wellington boot when I remembered that my relief was premature. I had been fool enough to say yes to a second invitation that day. The local Baptist church had invited me, months before, to give an address at a dinner to mark the completion of their building project. I knew I should have wriggled out of it – they could easily have found someone else – but I like and respect Derek, their minister, too much to do that.

So reluctantly I pulled off my gardening clothes; I would have to spend the afternoon preparing instead of planting. My father always used to say, 'For every hour you stand speaking or preaching you need to spend at least three praying and preparing beforehand.'

'Bad luck, dogs,' I said crossly as I called them in.

By six that evening I was terrified. I had been speaking regularly in public for forty-two years, but that horrible 'abdominal-cement-mixer' feeling never gets any better. That evening it was worse than usual because, however hard I prayed, I simply could not seem to hear what the Lord wanted me to say.

'Lord, you know I can't do this kind of thing without you!' I told him crossly as I squeezed back into my speaking outfit. 'I'm not the kind of person who can think up clever little talks with six points all beginning with P.' In the end I printed out a few opening ideas from my computer and fervently hoped that, once I had rattled through them, he would take over.

'Sorry, dogs,' I sighed, as I shut the door on their drooping ears and reproachful eyes. Hiding my scanty notes in the largest Bible I could find, I set off. I still hated going to social things like this without my husband, even after seven years, but my last-minute efforts to get a friend to come with me had all ended in the sound of their answering machines. Wherever were they all?

The minister was waiting for me in the church car park and steered me firmly into his vestry.

'They're not quite ready yet,' he said, and I couldn't help thinking he looked oddly furtive.

'Oh good,' I replied brightly, 'that gives us time to pray, and perhaps you could tell me a bit more about your vision for this evening?' But for the next ten minutes he evaded my questions, waffled endlessly and firmly avoided prayer. 'Why isn't he helping me?' I thought desperately.

'I'll just pop and see if they're ready to serve the meal,' Derek said at last. Left alone, I struggled not to remember my recurring nightmare where I stand up to speak to a huge crowd and dry up completely or, worse still, realise I am stark naked! I hastily did up my jacket buttons and clutched my large Bible for support. 'I could have been home by the fire with the dogs,' I thought bitterly.

When I was finally ushered through the doors of the newly decorated hall I was confronted by darkness and total silence. Before I'd had time to suspect murder or kidnap lights blazed, balloons floated from every direction and I was surrounded by crowds of smiling faces and a deafening chorus of 'Happy Birthday to You!'

A week before, I had been sixty. All my six children, and their spouses and children, had come for the day, but I hadn't asked anyone else because there simply wouldn't have been room!

They say your life flashes before you as you die, and I certainly felt mine was doing that as I began to notice individuals in the blur that surrounded me. Some of their lives had crossed and re-crossed my own right back since my babyhood; others had walked beside me for a short stretch of the journey and then disappeared. Their faces brought back memories, good and bad. There was the minister who had prayed for me when I was at the point of death back in 1982; the nurse who had come in to bath me during those wheelchair years; friends who had cared for my children when I was too ill to do it myself. There were the colleagues who had worked with us in the hectic years that followed my healing, and the faithful friends who had comforted and advised me after I lost Tony. I almost choked when I realised how far some of them had travelled, and when I caught sight of my brother Justyn, trying to hide behind a screen in the corner, I was quite unhinged! He had flown all the way from Canada.

Before I had time to blow my nose my best friend Barbara was frogmarching me towards the stage and I heard the fateful words, 'Jennifer Rees Larcombe – this is your life!'

Fortunately there were no TV cameras, just friends and relations popping out from behind the screen to recount their own humorous recollections. It was impossible to concentrate on what they were saying because of the carousel of emotions that was spinning round inside me. There was gratitude to all these people who had enriched my life in so many different ways; but there was also a terrible sense of loneliness. This kind of thing happens to couples on their golden wedding day but I sat there alone; these people were not only 'my' friends, they were 'our' friends, Tony's and mine. They had loved us *both*, and many of those joint relationships went back forty years – yet no one mentioned his name. I missed him badly, and the gap beside me, where he should have been, felt gigantic.

There was also another uncomfortable feeling that was hard to define. The words 'This is your life' were making me wonder what those sixty years had really been all about. In the final analysis, the things I had done, said or written would taste like stale sawdust if I never managed to fulfil my secret vow. No one in that crowded room knew about the most important moment of my life, when I had made that vow, sitting on a tree stump, at the age of seven.

The desire to fulfil it had become the hidden engine that had driven me through life, but I realised, with a pang of regret, that I had come closer to abandoning it during the last few months than ever before.

However, when the moment finally came for my brother Justyn to spring out of hiding in order to recount some of my most embarrassing moments, I forgot all those gloomy thoughts and thoroughly enjoyed the rest of the evening.

At a hideously early hour the following morning Justyn woke me with a mug of coffee in his hand.

'Don't waste any more time sleeping!' he said. 'Get up quick and let's go for a walk.' I did not need to ask *where* he wanted to go before I took him to catch his plane back to Canada later that morning. Neither of us could resist this unexpected opportunity to revisit our childhood home. We knew we were trespassing but we hoped it was too early for anyone else to be in the grounds of what is now a private hospital. Our parents had once run the place, Hildenborough Hall, as a Christian conference centre, providing us children with thirty-six acres of garden – and we still loved every inch of it!

Dawn was just breaking as we pushed our way through the undergrowth in what had once been a large shrubbery.

'Where on earth are you taking me?' protested Justyn, as brambles tore at our clothes.

'I'm looking for a tree stump,' I replied. 'It really matters to me.'

We finally discovered its crumbling remains, half-hidden among the long grass, and as I stood on it I savoured all over again that moment, fifty-three years before, when God's presence had suddenly enveloped me. It had felt as if warm cotton wool had been wrapped all round me, and I had been afraid to move, or even breathe, in case it went away.

'I want to know you,' I had managed to whisper at last. '*Really* know you – that's what I want most in my life. I'll do anything, *anything*, so long as I can know you!'

Suddenly, the beauty of that moment had been ruined by a large figure in a starched white apron and frilly cap. Nanny had obviously been searching for me all over the garden and her neck had turned turkey-red with exasperation; but she must have noticed the tears pouring down my face, because her scolding petered out as she asked,

'Whatever's the matter?'

'I want to know God,' I replied.

Her evangelic soul sprang into action instantly. 'You can ask Jesus to be your saviour right now if you like, dear — I'll help you.'

'Oh no!' I said quickly. 'I did that three years ago when I was four! I want to *know* God, really know him.'

Mystified, she hastily marched me back to the nursery for tea. It might well have helped her to understand what I meant if I could have explained to her that the previous day I had climbed into my mother's bed, early in the morning, and found her reading her battered old Bible. She must have been looking at Hosea chapter 6, because I vividly remember her repeating, several times over, '*Then shall we know, if we follow on [press on] to know the LORD*' (v. 3, KJV). Then she looked up at me and added: 'Jen-Jen, you'll meet lots of people in your life who ask Jesus into their hearts, go to church every week or even spend all their lives working for him, but only a small handful of them will "follow on to *know* him". That is the most important thing you can ever do in your life. Follow on to *know* the Lord.'

Nowadays she would probably have talked about 'intimacy with God' to explain this kind of close, dependent relationship of love, but whatever words she used I doubt if I could have grasped her meaning when I sat on the tree stump the following day and made my vow. What I had picked up from her went far beyond words: I had 'caught' her passionate, insatiable desire to press into God himself and her total determination to abandon herself to him and him alone. The look of ecstatic love I saw in her eyes that day profoundly influenced me for the rest of my life. It launched me off on a voyage of discovery; I not only wanted to be one of the 'small handful' of people that she had mentioned but I wanted to study them and find out what made them different.

When someone first asks God to deepen their relationship with him to the point where they know him in the fullest and most intimate way possible, he takes their request far more seriously than they do! Most people forget they ever made it – but God never does because it delights him so enormously. He spends the rest of that person's earthly life trying to draw them deeper and deeper into his heart. During the previous evening my friends had described the important occasions of my life; but none of them had realised that the times I treasured most, in retrospect, were the secret moments alone with God when I felt my spirit had touched his and, for a brief moment, we had merged completely. The memory of those special encounters seemed to have been buried, lately, under a rubbish tip of doubts and disappointments.

Justyn was still looking mystified so I told him about my vow, then added with a sigh,

'If I had known, when I was seven, just how hard the journey into God's heart really is, I wonder if I would ever have dared to make that vow.' Throughout my sixty years I had definitely identified a 'handful' of people who shared my mother's kind of passion for intimacy; they had all taught me different aspects of what it means to know God, but I had also observed that their quest had not made life comfortable for any of them.

'Just recently,' I told Justyn, 'I've felt like St Theresa when she said to God, "If this is the way you treat your friends then I'm not surprised you have so few of them!"'

'Yes,' he replied, 'it's quite a dilemma, isn't it? The more you come to know a God who is full of tenderness and compassion, the harder it is to accept that he allows people who really love him to experience the same kind of "nasties" that hit the guys who are quite indifferent towards him.'

'Well, sometimes I feel I've been hit harder and more often

than anyone else I know!' I said rebelliously. I knew Justyn would understand how I felt because he had once experienced the same bewildering scenario himself; and his response did not irritate me as it might have done if it had come from anyone else.

'Perhaps *really* knowing God is a lonely business because he has to keep on unplugging us from everyone and everything that we trust and rely on *more* than on him for our security and happiness,' he said thoughtfully. 'It isn't that he doesn't want us to have other people in our lives, but knowing him means realising that he is the only one who can meet all our human needs, both physical and emotional, rather than us always trying to meet them through other people.'

'You're right, of course,' I conceded reluctantly. 'I suppose the only way he can teach us that kind of dependency is by allowing us to lose all our human props.'

'Yes, but that sure does hurt!'

Justyn always reminds me of a huge shaggy teddy bear, stuffed with nothing but love. Because he had already emerged safely on the far side of his 'dark night of the soul' he was exactly the person I needed right then. 'None of us can ever figure out, at the time, what God's trying to do,' he said, with his crooked smile. 'It's only later, when we look back, that we realise he's allowed all this suffering because he wants us to discover that it's only when our need for him is paramount that we really know him.'

For a while we stood there silently, looking down at the rotting stump; Justyn was probably praying for me! Although my heart was still screaming that God just isn't fair, my brain was struggling to remind me that knowing God is not only a journey into his heart: *he* is also travelling deeper and deeper into *our* hearts, too. It is definitely a two-way affair, but the hard, outer shells of our hearts often impede his progress. It is only when our hearts are broken open by grief and loss that we are able to receive more of his love than at any other time. I did not want to accept all that, just then – it took many more months to work it all through –

but that was the moment when I realised I had been closing my heart against him rather than opening myself to his love.

'The trouble is,' said Justyn, as we walked away to find our other special corners of the overgrown gardens, 'when you turn your back on the Lord, you find there isn't anywhere else worth going!'

2

For I [the Lord] desire and delight in dutiful steadfast love and goodness, not sacrifice, and the knowledge of and acquaintance with God more than burnt offerings.

Hosea 6:6, AMP

'She should *never* have attempted a pregnancy, not with a heart condition like hers!'

'We're going to lose her, she's going into heart failure!'

'Where's the father? Send him out to the hospital for oxygen – quickly!'

My grandmother told me the story of my dramatic birth so many times that I could 'see' it happening, like a scene from a stage play in which I was definitely cast as the villain. My arrival in this world almost precipitated my mother's departure!

Just before my parents' wedding in 1936 my mother had become seriously ill with rheumatic fever, which had left her with a permanently damaged heart. The doctors had told her firmly that she would be a virtual invalid for the rest of her life, and naturally babies were right out of the question.

'Never walk when you can ride, never stand when you can sit, never sit when you can lie,' was their gloomy advice, but she never took the slightest notice and always seemed to have five times more energy than anyone else I ever met, except for my father!

He had only one ambition in life and that was to introduce people to God; when he first met my mother he was working at that full-time, surviving without an income but with a great deal of faith. It must also have taken a great deal of courage for this penniless young evangelist to ask my grandfather, who was an extremely wealthy businessman, if he could marry his favourite daughter.

Before cigarettes were discovered to be a health hazard most people smoked, and my grandfather had built up an international tobacco empire. He lived in one of the finest houses in Hampstead but preferred riding round his large estates in the southwest of Scotland. He was a leading member of the Brethren Church and quite the most terrifying man I have ever encountered. When he walked into a room all remarks were automatically addressed solely to 'The Chair', but he adored his second daughter, Jean. She had one of those sparkling personalities that draws people like pins to a magnet. Not only was she brilliant, witty and beautiful but she was also a highly gifted painter. When her older sister Kathleen went to London University, Jean asked if she could go to art college. Grandpa admired her gift enormously, but when he went to inspect the college he was horrified to see a nude model posing in a classroom. Needless to say, his precious Jean was *not* allowed to study art! She did not appear to mind; she just went on painting anyway while developing her other great gift – evangelism. While Kathleen worked for her degree Jean spent her time running meetings for women and children in the poorest parts of London's East End. In her spare time she helped her mother organise her numerous maids, played hilarious games with her five younger brothers and sisters and sat through interminable tea parties in Granny's sumptuous drawing room.

In the summer of 1935 she was helping to run a holiday club for children when she took a violent dislike to the bumptious young man who was leading the proceedings. Everyone who ever met my father either loved him on sight or totally loathed him – he never caused a neutral reaction. He was the first man my mother had ever met who had an even larger personality than her father's, but gradually she realised that he also possessed enormous, but quite unconscious, charm. Perhaps it was no wonder that she gradually revised her first opinion of him and fell deeply in love. It was just as well that she loved him, because living with a man who is 'larger than life' is definitely *not* easy. Actually she was larger than life herself and equally difficult to live with, so it is a good thing that he adored her too!

To everyone's amazement Grandpa gave his consent to the wedding, perhaps because he was a shrewd judge of character, but my father must have rapidly discovered that he was engaged to marry an entire family, and not just his fiancée. They were an extremely close clan and Jean was the hub of their existence so, quite naturally, they viewed the monster who threatened to take her away with great suspicion. Perhaps it is always difficult to 'marry into' a large family – at least, I have been told as much by my six sons- and daughters-in-law. It says a lot for my father that he very quickly won, from all of them, their lifelong respect.

In order to make sure Jean remained close enough to visit every day, Grandpa bought, furnished and equipped a nearby dream house as their wedding present. Sadly, they lived there for only a few months before she became seriously ill again and had to go home to be nursed by her family. They were all delighted to have her back, but the next three years must have felt like the worst-case scenario for my poor father!

When at last my mother became a little stronger, some wise person must have told them both that their only chance of making their marriage work was to move as far as possible from Jean's family. So they escaped by renting a tiny cottage in the Somerset village of Banwell. In her book *His Name was Tom* (Hodder & Stoughton, 1971) my mother describes the next three years as the happiest of her entire life. Father became the minister of the Baptist church. It had only five members when he arrived, but he soon increased that to over a hundred and set the whole district rocking on its spiritual heels. So many people 'fell in love' with God that a pungent sense of his presence hung over the village; strangers passing through would suddenly start to long for God and could not be satisfied until they found him.

Their salary was less than Grandpa paid his parlourmaid, but they made ends meet by buying derelict cottages, doing them up and selling them on. However, all that stopped abruptly when war was declared.

Now for the mystery that has bothered me all my life. Why didn't my father join up, when everyone else seemed to be going off to war? He was physically fit and only in his mid-twenties. I suspect he was a pacifist – the thought of killing anyone would have been totally abhorrent to him – but it was something my parents never talked about. Whenever I broached the subject my mother always said he was not called up because he was a minister, but I suspect that his unfashionable convictions troubled and embarrassed her. She had grown up during the First World War, when women gave white feathers to men who refused to go to war, and like her father she was a passionate patriot – they would both willingly have died for Winston Churchill.

However, my father did not sit out the war twiddling his thumbs. A huge Royal Air Force camp was built just outside the village and scores of trainee airmen began to flood into the already overcrowded Baptist chapel. He also began to conduct evangelistic missions. In those days 'missions' were the big thing in the Christian world. Most large towns staged regular 'campaigns', organised by people from all the local Protestant churches who invited an evangelist to preach the gospel every night for two or even three weeks in the largest available hall in town. Church members would be urged to invite their 'unconverted' friends and neighbours, for whom they would pray earnestly in the early morning prayer meetings. My father ran numerous such missions and they soon became so successful that he handed his church over to a trusted friend and became a full-time travelling evangelist.

Early in 1942 he returned from one of these missions in Northern Ireland; his face positively shone as he told my mother the stories of some of the people who had been 'saved'. She later wrote, 'I was so glad to think that my baby's father had a face like that', but she had not liked to spoil his joy by telling him I was 'on the way'.

'The thought of this baby depresses me,' he wrote in his diary when she finally dared to tell him she was pregnant. It was probably no wonder: he was afraid of risking her newfound health by going against her doctor's advice. She, however, was totally delighted; being one of seven children made the thought of staying childless quite unbearable, even if it did mean risking her life.

★ ★ ★

I doubt if anyone could have had a more idyllic babyhood than I did. For eighteen months, while my father was away preaching, my mother and I lived in complete bliss in the Somerset cottage with my mother's youngest sister, Geraldine, for company. My first memory is of the garden, a riot of colour that only an artist could have created. How she loved that garden, and the paintings it inspired are among her finest. I also remember collecting the eggs from the hens she kept with enormous enthusiasm to supplement our meagre wartime rations.

She was a most unusual mother; she knew intuitively what we needed without us ever having to explain, but she was totally unable to meet those needs herself. She would never have remembered to change a nappy or wipe sticky fingers after a meal; in fact she probably would not have provided the meal in the first place if she had been in the middle of painting a picture or writing a book! Fortunately for my survival, there was Gom. Molly Neads was the fifteen-year-old village girl who came and 'did' for my parents when they first arrived in Banwell. For the following seventy years she was a deeply valued member of the family, and apart from the Lord himself no one has ever loved me as unselfishly as Gom. My parents wouldn't have been able to pay her so I guess it was Grandpa who provided the thirty shillings (£1.50) a week she received in exchange for her twenty-four-hour seven-days-a-week devotion.

She had short, straight, wispy hair, which she held back from her face with 'Kirby-Grips', and peered out at the world through thick rimless glasses. Her fat lumpiness made a delightfully secure lap on which children always spent as much time as possible. My mother was one of those people who everyone else loves looking after, and Gom did everything for her, leaving her free to evangelise not only the airmen from the nearby camp but most of Somerset as well. People came to the house in floods, and she had a charming way of keeping them there until she discovered whether they had 'met the Lord'; if not, she made the necessary introductions so gently that no one was ever embarrassed. I am sure that if Hitler himself had arrived on her doorstep she would have made him a batch of her magnificent scones and explained the way of salvation before he finished the first! Both her mother and her grandmother had the same gift of one-to-one evangelism; I am not sure it is hereditary but I know it is highly infectious.

★ ★ ★

Early in 1944 my father conceived twins, or at least he felt God gave him the two great commissions that became his life's work. While he was successfully leading hundreds of people to the Lord in Ulster he began to yearn for the opportunity to run similar missions for the people of London and the Home Counties. For five years they had endured bombing on a scale it is hard to appreciate nowadays. My first memories of London are the bombsites; in some areas almost every second building was nothing but a gaping hole, like someone who has had half their teeth pulled out. People were worn and spiritually starved. Many churches were also lying in ruins, and regular habits of church attendance had been disrupted. Many had lost the faith they had once known through the horrors they had witnessed, and a new generation of young people were growing up without any faith at all. This deeply troubled my father and he decided to book the Central Hall, Westminster, seating four thousand people, every night for the month of September. He had no money and no church or committee to back him, but, egged on by his outrageous wife, he put all they had saved from their cottage development project into paying the £300 deposit on the hall. I will describe his other 'twin' later.

My parents were both as bad as each other and their enthusiasm for organising this daring venture knew no bounds; they sold the Somerset cottage and went back, yet again, to stay with my grandparents. Fortunately for me, Gom came too, because my mother took on all the secretarial side of the planning, which involved pounding her old-fashioned typewriter from dawn until late at night.

The slogan they chose for the campaign was 'This is the Victory', which was perhaps a little premature because the war still had a year to run, and their flood tide of enthusiasm was balked by Hitler and his deadly flying bombs. This new threat made any kind of mass event in London totally impossible and 'This is the Victory' had to be cancelled a few weeks before it was due to begin.

So there they were back at square one, jobless and homeless – and even Grandpa's imposing house in Hampstead was no longer a safe place in which to live.

Perhaps I ought to be grateful to Hitler for extending my safe little existence for one year more. One of the grey granite farmhouses on Grandpa's Scottish estate was conveniently empty so my parents, Gom and I made a hasty withdrawal to this bleak sanctuary. I loved it, but I was the only one who did! Gom complained that it never stopped raining in Scotland, but she must have exaggerated slightly because I can remember sitting in my pram in the garden watching her pegging out the washing as the flocks of seagulls circled the blue sky above the black slate roof.

The estate covered a large slice of the outstandingly beautiful Solway Firth and became the backdrop for every holiday throughout my first twenty years. But a holiday was the last thing my father wanted in 1944! He was like a huge express train suddenly halted as it thundered towards its destination and shunted off into a siding, still hissing steam. (Trains did hiss in those days!) Right from his conversion in 1927 he had sensed God had placed a very special calling on his life – a destiny that had to be fulfilled at all costs. When you feel like that you can't ever settle back and enjoy a peaceful life. When he first met the Lord he was working in the city of London and he used to eat his lunch on the steps of St Paul's Cathedral. He was fascinated by the sound of the biggest bell, 'Great Tom', and discovered that it has these words of St Paul engraved on it: 'Woe is me if I preach not the gospel.' He approved of the apostle's sentiments because he felt exactly the same.

So he roamed round Grandpa's Scottish estate, restlessly beating the heather with his walking stick, too frustrated to notice the magnificent scenery that surrounded him. Then one day he came back from a long wet walk a totally different man.

'The Lord showed me that this time up here is his gift to me,' he explained to my astonished mother (and probably to Gom, who always listened in to their conversations from outside the door). 'This is the last time that I will ever have the chance to study and prepare sermons, so that is what I am going to do.' As it turned out, that year in Scotland *was* the last time he ever took extended leave; he was always far too busy for the rest of his life.

So he buried himself in his little study at the back of the house and was totally content while my mother got on with evangelising the women from the cottages that nestled in the hills – and their numerous offspring. She also wrote the first of her thirty-five books, and I remember one day sitting under a table while she thundered out a torrent of words on her battered old typewriter.

Perhaps Gom had gone out because I remember asking my mother for a drink. 'Hush, dear,' she murmured absently, 'don't break my chain of thought.' So I went to my father's study and asked him for a drink. He was also writing *his* first book, the fruit of all that study, and he said, 'Don't bother me now, I'm writing.'

Fortunately for me, Gom seldom went out and never wrote a book! She acquired her lifelong nickname because my father always affectionately referred to her as 'Good Old Molly' so it seemed easier to shorten that to G.O.M.! The two of us went out into the cobbled farmyard every morning after breakfast to feed the chickens, which Gom always referred to as 'chuckers'. I always saved my toast crusts for my favourite, who we christened 'the Old Black Hen'. She was huge and a superb broody. Gom would put a clutch of twelve eggs at a time under her warm breast, and the old hen would sit on them almost continuously until they hatched into a brood of delightful balls of yellow fluff. Then she would strut round the yard with them, chuck-chuck-chucking proudly; but if I went too close her clucking became urgent and the chicks would scuttle from all directions to hide under her outstretched wings. Before my bedtime Gom and I would check all the hens were safely in the hen house (which still stands in that same farmyard, now owned by my uncle). It was my job to pull the rope and shut the door, and I can never read the story of Noah and how God shut the door of the ark without thinking of that nightly responsibility.

One morning, when Gom and I went out with our scraps, the Old Black Hen didn't strut out of the chicken house with the rest of her fluttering relations. We could hear the chicks peep-peep-peeping contentedly from inside so we assumed she was having a lie-in. Later in the morning, when we opened the nesting boxes to collect the eggs, she was still sitting in her warm bed of hay, while her chicks scrambled all around her.

''Ang on a mo,' said Gom, who never remembered her 'Hs', and she gave the hen a poke. She didn't move; she was stiff, cold and very dead. During the night a weasel or stoat must have got into the chicken house; all the other hens would have fluttered up to the high perches but the Old Black Hen had stayed where she was, covering her chicks with her wings. She remained there, protecting them, while the intruder latched on to her neck; it sucked every drop of blood from her body, but all her chicks were saved.

I've told that story so often to audiences all over the world, because it so beautifully illustrates the way Jesus was willing to give his last drop of blood to save us. And tears always run down my face when I read the story of how Jesus stood, weeping over his beloved Jerusalem, because he could foresee what the Romans would eventually do to it. The bit that triggers my tears is when he says, '*How often I longed to gather your children together, as a hen gathers her chicks under her wings, but you were not willing!*' (Luke 13:34). The chicks always came running when the Old Black Hen warned them of danger, but I've so often turned for comfort to someone or something else. Looking back now I can see this has been a lifelong struggle for me; in fact, I've often wondered if God ever regrets that gift of choice that he gave us. I know he did not want us just to be robots, programmed to love and trust him automatically, but down the centuries most of us – most of the time – choose to turn away from him. How that must hurt him! When you love someone enough to die for them but they reject you, the pain is agonising. I know that from bitter experience. God could have spared himself so much pain if he had withheld that gift of choice.

3

Now Samuel did not yet know the LORD: the word of the LORD had not yet been revealed to him.

1 Samuel 3:7

In the spring of 1945 three things happened that radically changed our lives. First we moved back to Grandpa's house in London. At last the war in Europe had come to an end and the September mission in London was given the green light, one year late. My parents were in their element, both working round the clock, surrounded by enthusiastic volunteers. Gom and I missed the chickens and both felt rather lost in what Gom called 'this posh 'ouse'. I guess, from my adult standpoint, that Granny's three smart, well-trained maids would have looked down on her as an untidy country bumpkin, but she used much ruder words to describe them!

One day, three months before the mission, while my mother was typing a promotional article for the Christian press she was violently sick into a nearby plant pot. She was delighted! She recognised the cause of her nausea – but she didn't dare tell my father. In spite of vomiting on average fifteen times a day she just carried on typing.

The third event was really my father's other 'twin': the second part of what he felt was his Grand Commission. I can remember sitting in the back of my parents' ancient car as we chugged up an imposing avenue of towering trees and stopped in front of a huge sprawling mansion.

'This is where we are going to live when the mission is over,' my father told me brightly. The prospect definitely did not appeal. The Scottish farmhouse with its four bedrooms had seemed too big for my liking, after our cosy West Country cottage, but this place had far more bedrooms than a three-year-old could possibly count. I remember feeling completely diminished by the high ceilings and the wide expanses of polished wood floors, not to mention the great sweeping staircase. It smelt musty, too. The house had been left almost derelict through wartime neglect: magnificent specimens of fungi grew out of the walls, while in other places the lavishly decorated plasterwork had crumbled away revealing the laths underneath.

'We'll soon put this to rights,' said my father, probably remembering all those Somerset cottages he had renovated. But I can still picture the long, eerie corridors that stretched away into the far distance and the muffled sounds of mice in the wainscoting. I loathed it, wet my pants and cried for Gom.

'You'll love playing in that garden,' persisted my father, looking out across the terrace. 'Just think, thirty-six acres for you to enjoy.' In his mind's eye he had already restored the gardens to their former Victorian glory, but it reminded me of Sleeping Beauty's castle engulfed by impenetrable brambles.

I was far too young to understand *why* they wanted to live there, but looking back now I can see what a marvellous venture it was. My father was never satisfied with just making converts — he longed to transform them into disciples. (How he would have approved of Nicky Gumbel's Alpha courses!) His idea was to take his new baby Christians away from the depressing ruins of London to a beautiful, peaceful place in the country. There he planned to give them residential courses, teaching them how to pray, read the Bible and win others for Christ. Between the end of the war and the beginning of the 1960s there was definitely a huge desire, in this country, to move back to the moral values that the war had disrupted, so my father's vision fitted well with a contemporary need.

'We'll give our guests good country food,' he said enthusiastically when we discovered the old walled garden. 'We can grow all our own vegetables; and just look at those fruit trees in the orchard!'

'And the peaches and grapes in the greenhouses,' put in my mother.

'We'll have our own cows, too, out in the meadows, so we can give them lashings of cream with everything.'

'And lots of chickens!' murmured my mother dreamily. 'We'll make these gardens so beautiful they'll mend people who've seen nothing but ugliness and destruction for six years!'

At that crucial point in the conversation Mr Walster suddenly emerged from the potting shed, wearing a green baize apron tied round his waist with twine. It is strange how you can remember people from your childhood so much more clearly than someone you met last week! I can still see every wrinkle of his face and recall the way his moustache curled into the corners of his mouth. He had been head gardener in Lady Fladgate's time, he told us. 'Worked here man and boy,' he added proudly. He and his wife lived in a flat over the stables, and in the coming years going to have tea with them would be one of my greatest treats. Mrs Walster's stories of life 'in service' in Lady Fladgate's time would make a book in themselves!

As Mr Walster showed us round the ruins of his beloved glasshouses, he described, in gory detail, the night when a German Messerschmitt had crashed, setting them on fire, while its pilot parachuted into the middle of the tennis court.

'We'll soon put it all to rights,' smiled my father, while tears of joy poured down Mr Walster's walnut cheeks. 'But you'll have to help me get every detail of the gardens just like they used to be,' he added, putting his hand gently on the old man's shoulder.

'I never thought I'd live to see the day ...' choked Mr Walster, wiping his nose on the back of a knobbly hand. 'But, Sir, it used to take eight of us gardeners to keep it up!'

'We'll *have* eight,' promised my father, 'so long as you stay on and help me organise them!' but Mr Walster was crying too much to reply.

★ ★ ★

The evangelistic rallies during that September in the Central Hall, Westminster, were a sensational success – packed to capacity every night while hundreds were turned away disappointed. Countless young people made the choice to follow Christ and have been serving him all over the world ever since. The crowds became such an embarrassment that my parents booked the Royal Albert Hall, Kensington, for the last night of the mission. It seats 10,000, but still that was not large enough to hold those spiritually hungry people. The slogan 'This is the Victory' must have been prophetic because, at the end of the war, it caught the mood of the moment exactly.

When the mission finished, Christians from all denominations clamoured for a second series – all in the Royal Albert Hall this time – so it was duly booked for every Saturday night during February and March. However, all the tickets were sold out long before Christmas!

What I didn't realise, as I played with my rag doll Zola, was that my parents had suddenly been rocketed to spiritual stardom. Churches hired coaches and sent parties up to the rallies from every corner of the country: Devon, Manchester, Aberystwyth and Norwich. Squeezing into the largest auditorium in Britain on a Saturday night to hear Tom Rees was suddenly The Thing To Do, and he soon became a household name. For the rest of his life I hardly ever went anywhere with him without someone recognising him and saying, often with tears in their eyes, 'I have been so blessed by your talks, books or radio programmes.' Fame made no difference to him: he persistently refused to benefit financially from the work he did for the Lord. He saw his popularity merely as something the Lord had arranged to give him greater opportunities of explaining the gospel to even more people. Children, and particularly teenagers, quickly detect the slightest hint of hypocrisy in their parents. I can honestly say that my father was exactly the same person when he was 'off duty' with the family as he was when surrounded by admiring crowds. He showed me, rather than taught me, that integrity matters if you want to know God intimately.

★   ★   ★

On a cold, foggy day in November 1945 we moved into Hildenborough Hall. I remember how my footsteps echoed as I ran about, searching for familiar bits of furniture from the Somerset cottage. They were now scattered incongruously around the huge rooms, looking like doll's house miniatures in their new lofty surroundings.

My father paid £6,000 for the mansion and its thirty-six acres of garden, which may not seem much now but was a considerable sum in those days. And when he had no money whatsoever it must have been quite a faith challenge. My father was highly relieved not to have to ask his father-in-law for a loan because, to his vast surprise, his own father offered him the money. Richard Rees had always dismissed his second son as a total failure, but Tom's sudden rise to success altered his father's view just as an insurance policy matured. My mother's father, who had always shared the same opinion of Tom, was somewhat nettled when his suddenly famous son-in-law did not come to him for help!

Odd little memories, like faded snapshots in an old album, are all I can recall of that first winter – except that it always seemed to be night-time and bitterly cold. An army of volunteers came to help set the house and gardens to rights before the first guests were due to arrive the following June. They were all young and wildly enthusiastic; most were newly demobbed from the services and had been blessed by my father's preaching.

I can remember watching a group of them, on their knees, restoring the beautiful parquet floors with huge tins of brown wax 'Mansion' polish. I offered to help them but soon discovered what a marvellous art material the polish could become if you daubed it on the wall. Unfortunately my early masterpiece was lost to the nation – rather rapidly.

I can never read the story of Moses in the bulrushes without thinking of German prisoners of war. For some odd reason there were still some in the neighbourhood in the spring of 1946 and a working party was sent in to help us. Their assignment was to dredge the marshy swamp that I could see from my bedroom window. Mr Walster assured everyone it had once been a magnificent lake, but I was so sorry for those prisoners as I watched them wading round in all that ice-cold mud. I knew all about crocodiles after hearing the story of Peter Pan and I was sure there must be lots of them waiting to bite off their legs. 'Good job too,' said Gom. 'They're Germans!'

In spite of these terrible hazards the bedraggled young men soon transformed the swamp back into such a beautiful lake that I still 'walk beside it' in my imagination whenever I sit in a dentist's chair. The ploughed field that sloped down to the lake was also restored to the great sloping lawn it had once been, and when the towering banks of brambles that flanked it had been cleared, enchanting rhododendron and azalea walks were revealed, which I have always considered far better than any at Kew Gardens. Nearly sixty years later I often dream I'm playing there – perhaps a part of us never grows up.

One afternoon I remember my father driving up to the front door in a large van he had borrowed for the occasion. Gom said he had been to an 'ock-shun' but she probably meant auction sale! The volunteers helped him unload all kinds of furniture before he drove off, with his usual enormous enthusiasm, to collect some more. You could pick up all kinds of treasures for next to nothing just after the war, and he had a sixth sense when it came to finding bargains. The last thing to come out of the second vanload was a huge Victorian doll's house, taller than I was. It was left in the hall, where I gazed at it longingly. My father had bought it for me specially; admittedly it only cost him two shillings, but he was oddly shy of small children and could not quite manage to say it was for me. He had it put in an outhouse where I happily played with it for many years. My mother, who was heavily pregnant by that time, created a whole set of dolls for it, made quite brilliantly out of pipe cleaners and odd scraps of fabric. I still have several of them but I often wonder what became of their house – it would be worth a fortune now!

It was fortunate that military camps were being disbanded all over the country in 1946 so buying 200 iron beds and utility lockers to go beside them was no problem at all, particularly as my father was granted £4,000 for war damage and dilapidation on the property. This money provided him with just enough to furnish and equip Hildenborough Hall before the guests were due to arrive.

The first rally in that second series took place on 2 February. The Royal Albert Hall was packed right up to the top gallery, as it was on fifty-two subsequent occasions, but to her great annoyance my mother was not there. It was the only RAH rally she ever missed, but two days earlier she had given birth in the Middlesex Hospital to a son, this time without any complications. For days before one of those huge rallies my father was so spiritually burdened that he hardly ate or slept. Hour after hour he paced his study praying, totally oblivious to anything that happened around him. In my mother's book *Putting Ten Thousand to Flight* (Marshall, Morgan and Scott, 1952) I found this fascinating extract.

Two nights before the first rally, on 31ˢᵗ of January, just after ten o'clock, Tom received a telephone call.
    'Hello,' he said, 'who is that?'

'It's me, Jean,' I said ungrammatically. 'We've got a son.'
'What?' said Tom. 'Whenever did that happen?'

It was typical of her not to disturb his preparation with trivial details like the onset of labour!

★ ★ ★

During the last months of her pregnancy I suspect that my mother faced a major dilemma which will be familiar to many families in ministry. She had always longed for children, and because she put 200 per cent into everything she did she would have wanted to be the best mother in the world. On the other hand, she was endowed with just as many natural and spiritual gifts as her husband and shared his vision with equal passion. Her sparkling charisma and love for people were Hildenborough's greatest assets and she longed to organise the residential courses, which were to run throughout most of the year. A full-time job like that left little time for hands-on motherhood!

Now, with hindsight, I can see she had no alternative but to engage a highly trained nanny; after watching Gom happily spoiling my own children I realise she could never have taken sole charge of a new baby and a three-year-old. So my mother created a nursery out of the old housekeeper's sitting-room, hastily painting huge portraits of our favourite fairytale characters all over the walls. But when she had finished she went away, beyond the green baize door which in Lady Fladgate's time had separated the servants from the family, and suddenly I was on the wrong side of that door. Gom had vanished, too, to be replaced by a stranger in a starched apron and a head full of the rigid rules of nursery discipline.

The loss of Gom was a shattering blow for me, but she stubbornly refused to desert me and joined the permanent community as one of the cooks. Nanny disapproved of her and only permitted her to wave at me from a distance, but when I was settled in bed at night Gom used to creep upstairs to say goodnight and share chocolate bars from her precious sweet ration. However, when Nanny found sweet papers in my bed she firmly put a stop to Gom's nocturnal visits.

I remember standing at the nursery windows, feeling like a prisoner, confined by Nanny's nursery routine. I hated her – simply because she was not Gom. Old photographs that I discovered recently show me wearing a hunted expression on a thin, white face, and I remember always feeling afraid. As a nanny myself, and then a foster mother, I have so often seen disturbed children who desperately need love but for some reason make themselves so obnoxious that they repulse the love they want so badly. I guess I was angry with my parents for abandoning me, but I was so afraid of displeasing them that I took out my rage on poor Nanny. One evening, while she was bathing me, I could feel the hate surging up inside me like sick. I ground my teeth and, screaming furiously, I tore at her fat bare arms. The intensity of my own anger frightened me. I literally saw her through a red haze. She flung herself backwards on her haunches, wailing, 'Oh God, oh God,' and I thought my anger must have killed her when I saw the blood pouring down her wet arms.

Just at that unfortunate moment the door of the bathroom opened ominously and my father stood on the threshold. Throughout my whole life I can never remember him raising his voice or hitting either of us; he simply said calmly, 'Jen-Jen, in our family we never get angry.' Then he disappeared; but such was the power of his personality that I never dared to be angry again for many years. Of course, that is not really true: all human beings get angry. I simply learned to hide my anger behind a sweetly smiling face. I often wonder if the months of depression that followed the two worst experiences of my life might have been avoided if I had been taught how to express anger more appropriately. Anger that is denied a hearing gets trapped inside us and often turns into depression or triggers a physical illness. Worst of all, it affects us spiritually, because the best way of being rid of anger is to give it to God and, in exchange, receive his forgiveness as well as his power to forgive those who hurt us. While we are busy pretending that we are not at all angry we allow a barrier to form between ourselves and God. Looking back, I can see that my journey into God's heart has often been impeded by unacknowledged resentment and bitterness.

Going to bed at night terrified me, particularly after Gom's visits were banned. Our night nursery lay at the top of the house at the far end of a long dark corridor. The idea behind this was probably to provide us with quiet, well away from the noisy laughter and singing of the guests below. Once baby Justyn was asleep and Nanny had gone downstairs for a well-earned rest, the house felt anything but quiet to me. The parquet floors creaked as if monsters were creeping up to my door; the antique plumbing knocked, or even wailed like demented ghosts; but worst of all were the mice. Thousands of them must have lived happily under the floorboards and emerged to play games all over my floor. My mother insisted that Nanny left the light on, but there were so many power cuts in the late 1940s that I used to lie there stiff with fear, waiting to be plunged into darkness.

One night I woke up to find myself in the dark. I was too afraid to move and no sound would come out of my mouth when I tried to call. Then I remembered how my mother had tried to help me over my sleeping problems by saying, 'You never need to be frightened in the night, because Jesus always sits on your bed, all night long.' I decided to see if she was right, so inside my head I cried out to him for help. Instantly, something wonderful happened. Outside the wartime blackout curtains it must have been getting light, but I could not have realised that. Suddenly a blackbird began to sing on the wisteria outside my window; then a thrush joined in and another answered it. All at once the sinister silence of the night was replaced by all the familiar daytime sounds of sparrows chirping and cuckoos calling cheerfully from the woods. Of course, it was only the dawn chorus, which still delights me every morning, but I had never heard it before and for years I was quite convinced that God had arranged for his orchestra to play – just for me!

Happily I drifted back to sleep, not realising that I had just learnt one of the most important lessons of my life. If Gom and my parents were too far away to help me when I was in trouble, Jesus was always there for me and he never ever went away (Psalm 27:10, KJV).

It makes me smile sometimes when I think how anxiously we parents try to protect our children from any hardship, and struggle to provide a perfect environment for their development. When things do not turn out as we hoped, we suffer from nail-biting remorse. Yet if we faithfully pray for them and constantly let them know they are loved and valued, even the situations that we would never have chosen for our children can be reversed by God until they become their greatest assets. Our parents may have been busy but they both prayed earnestly for us, and a couple of years after we first arrived at Hildenborough God really did rescue me from the pit of misery into which I was sinking. It happened the day my parents took me to London.

I felt very grand sitting on the soft leather seats of the old Daimler, which belonged to the community and was used to meet guests from the station. My father, although he remained virtually penniless throughout his life, always contrived to look like a millionaire. That day he had some business in Jermyn Street, and in the happy days before yellow lines, parking meters and traffic wardens you left your car where you liked. So my mother and I sat and waited for him, and because I so seldom had her to myself, I managed to ask the question that had been burning into my soul for many months.

'Why do we have to live in a horrid big house with hundreds and hundreds and hundreds of other people?'

'Because we want to help them ask Jesus into their hearts,' she replied simply.

'Why?'

'Because Jesus makes people feel happy and safe when he lives inside them.'

Feeling 'happy' and 'safe' were the two things I had been missing so badly so I said hopefully, 'Can I do that?'

She could easily have said, 'Yes, dear, when you're a big girl,' but typically she replied, 'Let's do it now!' Then she helped me pray a simple little prayer that I have never forgotten, 'Come into my heart, Lord Jesus, come in today, come in to stay, come into my heart, Lord Jesus.' I said the words after her, parrot fashion, but I meant every one of them.

Something supernatural took place in Jermyn Street that day. When a human being, of whatever age, chooses to invite God Almighty into the centre of their existence, he comes and then proceeds to make a difference. My parents both told me in later life how totally I changed from a frightened, tense little shadow into a happy outgoing child. I even overheard Nanny telling the housekeeper that I was 'vastly improved – at long last!'

★　★　★

For the first couple of years after my parents became spiritual superstars they were so busy that I guess they were less than 'good enough' parents. However, I am sure it is possible to serve the Lord effectively and still give your children the love and security they need, and I believe the Lord helped them to realise that before it was too late. At first they always ate their meals with the guests, but suddenly my mother made a decision for which I shall always be grateful. Each day she joined us in the nursery for breakfast and tea. While Nanny pushed porridge into Justyn's mouth and cut my toast into soldiers, Otty, as we had begun to call her, told us Bible stories. She got so carried away she would act out the adventures of Daniel and David all over the nursery, climbing on the furniture and crawling under the table. Nanny was not amused – and the doctors who had told Otty she would be an invalid for life would have been astounded! At teatime she read aloud from *Robinson Crusoe*, *Gulliver's Travels* or *Wind in the Willows*, but we always thought the Bible stories were best. Both Justyn and I agree that whenever we are Bible teaching or writing Bible notes, we can still hear her telling the story in our heads!

Otty also realised how afraid I was at night, so for two blissful years I slept in the corner of my parents' bedroom while Justyn was left to Nanny's mercy in the next room. This gave me the delicious opportunity of sliding into Otty's bed early in the morning, while she read her Bible. Watching the way she enjoyed communicating with God did far more for me than a thousand lectures on the importance of regular daily devotions.

In spite of sharing his bedroom I continued to have no contact whatsoever with my father. He came to bed hours after I was asleep and always rose hours before anyone else to pray downstairs in his study. However, our relationship was changed completely after a disastrous experience in a Scottish forest. Nanny used to take Justyn and me to stay in Grandpa's house in Scotland for the whole month of August each year. Once, I remember managing to pluck up enough courage to tell Grandpa how much I loved the place, but my efforts to please him were a disaster. He was extremely proud of this rather imposing house, set high on the crags above the bay, but in comparison to the vastness of Hildenborough Hall it seemed delightfully small to me, and I envied him.

'Grandpa,' I said, 'you live in a much much *much* smaller house than we do.'

Highly chagrined, he replied acidly, 'I know that, but at least I don't have to take two hundred lodgers!'

It must have been on one of these annual summer holidays that my father was prompted to take fatherhood more seriously. Occasionally, when his brother, the Rev. Dick Rees, could be persuaded to take over the running of the conferences, my parents would come up to Scotland to join us for a week. I can remember the joy of knowing that my father was actually in the house because, although he didn't often talk to me, he was the centre of my universe. To my utter amazement he announced one day that he was going to take me for a walk to buy an ice cream. That was a very rare treat so soon after the war, but the shop was three miles' walk through the forest.

'Isn't Kippford rather a long way away?' protested Mother. 'She is only five, remember.' But we had never done anything together before and I wanted to go so badly that I assured everyone I could manage fine – not realising we would also have to walk back! He strode off, swinging his walking stick, while I struggled hard to keep up, intoxicated by the joy of being with him.

All would have probably been well if we had not got lost in the forest. After what seemed like hours of walking in circles he abandoned the track and struck off into the dark trees in what he hoped was the direction of the ice-cream shop. For him the slippery granite boulders and giant anthills were easily negotiated, but I kept falling over, skinning my knees and grazing my hands, as I battled along in his wake. I was terrified of getting lost because forests, in my favourite fairy stories, were the haunts of bears, trolls and monsters – not to mention Red Riding Hood's wolf! Through my tears of pain and fear I could 'see' them lurking behind every tree. Then suddenly a huge hand descended from high above my head, gripping my own. It was so big that the fingers reached right up to my elbow.

'Come on, Jen-Jen,' said my father. 'We'll only manage this if we hold on to each other.' I can't remember him ever touching me before, though I suppose he must have done, but that was the moment when we bonded – and bonded for life. The tree stumps and rocks no longer bothered me – he just lifted me clean over the top – and who cared about trolls and wolves with such a big man beside me? We also began to talk and even laugh together as we slithered and slipped among the pine needles. We did reach the shop eventually, and never has vanilla ice cream tasted better, even if it was only made of chalk and wartime egg powder! We finally drove home in the only taxi in the district, and he insisted on pulling out all my splinters himself rather than letting Nanny loose on me with her tweezers.

Probably, for most of us, there is a single moment when we first bond with God and our journey into his heart really begins. I am not sure it always happens at conversion: he can be there in our lives for years, too distant and unconnected to be more than an vague object of worship – rather like my father during the first few years of my life. Then, perhaps during a difficult experience, you suddenly feel his hand taking hold of yours and a personal relationship of mutual friendship begins to grow.

When we came home after that holiday my father asked Nanny to bring me to his study every day after lunch for exactly half an hour of what he called 'fathering time'. He was such a busy person that outside his study door he installed a little set of traffic lights. If someone knocked when he was in the middle of something important he pressed a button on his desk and the red light told them it was no use waiting. If they saw an amber light they could try again in a minute or two, and a green light meant, 'Come right in, I'm expecting you.' Waiting to see that green light appear, after Nanny had knocked on the heavy oak door, became the best moment of my day.

We would listen to his numerous gramophone records or he would read aloud a children's version of *Pilgrim's Progress*. To me, it really didn't matter what we did, it was just being with him that was so wonderful and knowing that for those thirty minutes I had his undivided attention and anyone else who knocked would be dismissed by the red light!

Quite often nowadays, through my work as a counsellor, I meet fathers who fear they will not be able to maintain their relationships with their children because of the demands of work or after a marriage breakdown. Because those half-hours with my father were so enormously influential in my life I can reassure them that it is the quality of the time they spend with their children that matters far more than the quantity.

★ ★ ★

The witch came to see us one evening in February 1948. I don't think she was *quite* a witch but Justyn and I thought she was at the time. Occasionally during midweeks in the winter there would be no guests in the house, and how Justyn and I loved having the whole place to ourselves. We were taught to answer the guests' repetitive questions politely and to smile into their endless cameras, but it was so lovely not having to keep on dodging out of their way. Both Justyn and I still quite often meet elderly people who produce photos of 'the Rees children' they have treasured for years.

'You were such good little children,' they say as they gaze at our dutifully smiling faces; but little do they know what we were calling them under our breath!

On one particular winter evening, when the community had probably seized the rare chance of a night out and even Nanny must have gone too, we were having a family evening in my father's study. The memory remains vivid because it was so unusual.

A cosy fire cracked in the grate, sending shadows dancing around the panelled walls and the old oil paintings of Fladgate ancestors. Outside a terrible storm was raging and we could hear the rain lashing against the french windows on the far side of the faded velvet curtains. It was in the middle of a Royal Albert Hall series, so both our parents were utterly exhausted, lying back in two leather armchairs on either side of the fire. When the gramophone record finished, the Boss (as everyone called my father) groaned and said he was too tired to turn it over. It was well past our bedtime but Otty never remembered dull things like that, so we played very quietly on the floor hoping she would not look at the clock.

Abruptly the shrill ringing of the doorbell broke the spell. I followed Otty across the shadowy expanse of the great hall, and watched her fumble with the bolts of the massive front door.

Outside stood the forlorn figure of a woman; she was so thin she reminded me of the skeleton I'd seen in Nanny's textbook of child development. Her face certainly looked as lifeless as a skull, glassy white with two black holes for eyes and hair plastered flat by the rain.

'I've walked from the station,' she said and even I knew what a long way that must have seemed through all those dark country lanes. 'Help me!' she added, clutching Otty's hand appealing. 'I've got all mixed up in witchcraft, and I'm so afraid. I came to the Albert Hall last Saturday because I want so much to belong to Jesus but I wasn't sure if he would have me – after all I've done.'

Something extraordinary happened to my mother. Instantly all her tiredness was forgotten. 'Come right in,' she said. 'I'll run you a bath and you can wrap up in some dry clothes while I make a cup of tea.'

The arrival of this 'lost soul' had exactly the same resurrection effect on the Boss; he loved nothing more than explaining the love and limitless power of Jesus. Later, while he talked to the visitor in the far corner of the room, Otty astonished Justyn and me by kneeling beside her armchair, Bible in one hand while she stabbed and thrashed at the air with the other. She looked as if she was wielding a sword.

'What *are* you doing?' we whispered at last.

'I'm fighting the Devil by prayer,' she whispered back, 'so he has to let his prisoner go free.' As we watched her, fascinated, we did not realise we were receiving our first lesson in spiritual warfare! Prayer for Otty was not the 'hands-together-eyes-closed' version. She used her whole body to express her feeling to God, stamping out her fury at the works of the Devil, dancing with joy or punching her way into God's presence through spiritual flack.

My most vivid memory of that evening is the sight of our visitor's face when the Boss had finally led her to Christ. As they came back to the fireside she looked a completely different person, and I concluded that having God inside a person changes them on the outside too (2 Corinthians 5:17).

'We'll drive you back to the station,' said the Boss. 'The last train goes in half an hour.' We all went, and I wondered ecstatically what Nanny would have said about us being out so late! On the way home the Boss suddenly stopped the car and looked round at the two of us, bright-eyed, in the back seat.

'Jen and Just,' he said, 'remember this: there is nothing in the whole of life more enjoyable than introducing people to Jesus. When you grow up, don't waste your time doing anything else.' And we have both been taking his advice ever since!

* * *

So many of Otty's watercolour paintings now cover the walls of my bungalow that I can hardly see the wallpaper. Her way with skies was masterly, but it was her use of shadows that makes her pictures great.

'However good you are with buildings or landscapes a picture is dull and lifeless unless you bring it to life with lots of *deep purple shadows*,' she would say while trying to teach me to paint. She always emphasised those three words by punching them out like gunshots. 'People are the same,' she would always add. 'It is the bad times we have to go through that make the good times stand out. Life would be so dull if it was flat sunshine all the time!'

While the first couple of years at Hildenborough Hall were very darkly shadowed for me, the following two were bathed in contrasting sunshine. Not only was I seeing a lot more of my parents, but Nanny decided to leave and her replacement did not keep me tied so tightly to her apron strings. Suddenly I was free to roam the gardens alone, and for hours I would wander among the flowers and trees telling myself stories. Having a vivid imagination is a definite hazard in the middle of a dark night, but during the day, particularly with a huge Victorian garden at your disposal, it becomes a wonderful asset. The beauty of it all sank deeply into my soul, and I remember one day crying with joy as I stood under a cherry tree frothing with pink blossom; the inexpressible beauty gave me a physical pain. How vital it is to fill our children's memories with natural beauty so they have a 'bank account' to draw on during ugly times in later life.

It was not only the space and solitude that I recall with such gratitude, but the people. The members of the community were like loving aunts and uncles who always seemed to have all the time in the world for us. Norman was a Yorkshireman, and I never once saw him without an old cloth cap on the back of his head and a matchstick stuck between his teeth (the Boss never allowed anyone to smoke on the estate). I thought Norman must even go to bed in his cap! His job was looking after the livestock, two Jersey cows and hundreds of chickens, ducks and turkeys.

For me it was a case of love at first sight with Billy. He was one of the 'day-old chicks' Norman raised under a light bulb in one of the disused wine cellars. By the time he was two Billy was the most gigantic turkey I have ever seen, and was the undisputed ruler of the poultry field as he strutted up and down, gobble-gobbling his supremacy. But I never understood what Norman meant when he kept saying, 'He'll make thirty-five pounds, plucked and pulled.' Enlightenment came in early December when Billy's naked body was hung upside down from a hook in the larder next to our nursery, definitely putting me off the thought of Christmas! Norman is nearly ninety now and living in Yorkshire, but he still wears a cloth cap and sucks a matchstick.

Chris and Ken were gangling fourteen-year-olds, apprenticed to Mr Walster. The stories they told me about life in their orphanage made me hastily revise my opinion of nannies! I don't think those two lads learnt much about gardening; all they seemed to do was stoke the voracious greenhouse boilers and follow the three Land Girls round like adoring puppies.

Alic Duffus was always referred to as 'the Handy Man'; for years I thought this was because of his badly crippled hands. He was too shy to speak to other adults but he loved children, and I spent so long listening to him talking about his home in Ireland that I developed a rich Belfast brogue that horrified our new Norland-trained nanny.

Of course, being in the kitchen with Gom was always my preferred option, watching as she and the other cooks miraculously stretched the wartime rations from the books all guests still had to bring with them.

Smells are so evocative! Petrol always makes me feel desperately sad because it reminds me of the awful day when Mr Hill dropped dead in the garage. We used to love visiting his oily workshop, which had once housed Lady Fladgate's carriages. He maintained all the cars, tractors and trucks belonging to the estate, but when he changed his greasy boilersuit for a chauffeur's uniform he looked like the original Jeeves, driving off in the Daimler to meet guests from the station. To my enormous embarrassment, he insisted on wearing his uniform when he took me to school. I would plead with him to take off his cap as we drove up the drive, but one terrible day my passenger door got stuck, so, right in front of a group of my classmates, he walked round the car to open it for me. Too late, I realised he was still wearing his cap! I never told him that I was taken straight into the cloakroom to be kicked and punched for being a stuck-up rich girl.

For many years after Mr Hill's sudden death, the Boss used to take me to visit his widow; he had sat up with her all night after the awful day when he had had to break the news to her that her husband would not be coming home at teatime ever again.

'Your father arranged everything for me,' she loved to say, 'just as if he'd been the son I never had!' The Boss's endless tenderness and concern towards sad and broken people made a very deep impression on Justyn and me.

In those early postwar years, surviving fighter pilots were placed on very high pedestals, and I remember Nanny telling me breathlessly that Bill, a very handsome young member of the community, had shot down more German planes than any other pilot in the whole war.

'He must be such a brave man,' she sighed. However, she revised her opinion when she asked him to kill a mouse that had got itself trapped in the nursery bread barrel. I can remember his white terrified face to this day!

One afternoon I was out walking with Nanny in the grounds when we met the Boss, strolling through the trees with a man in a cowboy hat.

'This is my friend Dr Billy Graham,' said my father, as I looked up into a most remarkable pair of blue eyes. It was 1946 and he was making his first visit to the UK, at my father's invitation. He later became the most widely known and respected evangelist of our time, but I can personally vouch for the fact that in spite of his fame he and his wife Ruth always remained just as 'ordinary' as ever. Ruth and my mother became very close friends and visited each other often, comparing notes on the horrors of living with an evangelist. Their anecdotes were hilarious and mostly unrepeatable. During their great Wembley Crusade my mother popped in to see Ruth in her London hotel and found her cutting her own hair with a pair of nail scissors. 'Just take a look at the back, Jean,' she said, 'I can't see if I've got it straight.'

'Ruth!' protested my mother. 'You and Billy are going to tea with the *Queen* this afternoon! Why on earth don't you go to a proper hairdresser?'

'Oh, no,' laughed Ruth. 'They might make me look all sophisticated and Billy would hate that. He just likes to keep things simple.'

That night my mother went to Wembley with Ruth and her daughter Ann (who is now following in her father's footsteps and bringing blessing throughout the world). Ann wanted to sit in the front row because the seats were softer. 'No, dear,' said Ruth, looking shocked. 'Those seats are only for important people.'

I guess it was that quality of humility that has always impressed me most about the Grahams. They are both among my 'small handful of people who *really* know God', and they showed me that humility is vital if we want real intimacy with him. So many successful people have had their private relationship with the Lord destroyed by pride and self-confidence (Jeremiah 9:23–4).

On one of my mother's visits to their simple country home in Montreat, North Carolina, Ruth met her from the airport in her battered old car. As they drove along my poor mother was horrified to see a mouse eying her suspiciously from the dashboard. 'Oh, take no notice of her,' laughed Ruth. 'She made herself a nest in my glove compartment and she's raising a family in there so I didn't have the heart to move her out.'

My mother liked dogs even less than mice and the Grahams had a large Doberman Pincher to protect themselves from intruders. One morning, when Billy and Ruth were out, my mother was in their lounge when this huge dog walked in and advanced towards her chair. She was in the middle of taking the medication for her heart condition, and in her panic she dropped the whole bottle of water pills all over the floor. The dog thought they were 'treats' and licked them all up eagerly. Horrified, my mother ran out of the room, shutting the door behind her. For over an hour she frantically tried to find help, quite convinced she had killed the dog Ruth adored. By the time she eventually dared to peep through a crack in the door the dog was fine, but the Persian hearth rug never recovered!

On another occasion Nanny, after hastily teaching me to curtsey, marched me towards the study, explaining in a hoarse whisper, 'You're going to meet an Emperor.' The only Emperor I had ever heard of was the one in my fairy storybook who didn't wear any clothes. So I was mildly disappointed to see a small man in a black suit sitting, stiffly upright, in my father's leather armchair. Emperor Haile Selassie of Ethiopia had come to see if Hildenborough was a suitable place for his granddaughters to visit. When they arrived a few weeks later I was disappointed yet again, because I thought all princesses had long golden hair!

Of all our fascinating visitors, Gladys Aylwood was quite my favourite. When she came I was always allowed to sit at the back of Lady Fladgate's ballroom, now the conference hall, to hear her recounting her amazing adventures as a missionary in China. The film that was made about her, *The Inn of the Sixth Happiness*, is tame in comparison!

★ ★ ★

It was a summer afternoon when I made the second of those vows which have shaped my life ever since. My father decided to use our thirty minutes of 'fathering time' to take me for a walk round the terrace rose garden. I had recently been a bridesmaid and was proudly wearing my pink frilly dress, and Nanny, much to my disgust, had brushed my long golden hair until it shone. As I looked up at the vast white bulk of Hildenborough Hall towering over the terrace I was reminded of a picture book I had just been given. It was about a princess who lived in a great white palace; she too had long golden hair and wore pink frilly dresses.

'Daddy,' I asked, 'am I a princess?'

He roared with laughter and hastily explained: 'Daddy and Mummy are only servants, not a king and queen. Jesus owns this house and lets us live here so we can rescue people for him, people who've got lost and feel scared and lonely.' Then he added the quick giveaway sentence that proved to be so damaging: 'We can only do that important job if you are always very very good.' Because I so much wanted to please him I inwardly vowed that I would always be 'very very good'.

On the surface, being 'very very good' may appear like an ideal life goal, but I think it made me grow up so anxious to please the significant people in my life by apparently perfect behaviour that I covered the real me with a mask made of sweet, fluffy, pink candyfloss. It took me half a century to realise I was wearing this mask in all my relationships. It made me unable to 'rock the boat' in any conversation or situation; I could not disagree, cause conflict, say what I really thought or refuse any request, however inconvenient. I might boil inside over things that were happening to me but I hid my feelings behind my smiling mask.

These secret vows are often made by children between the ages of five and seven who have no idea how greatly they will affect their future lives. One child might say, 'When I grow up, I won't be pushed around like my dad, because I'll make lots of money.' Another might promise herself, 'I'll make sure I always look beautiful so everyone will admire me,' while a third may decide, 'I must always be in control so I can feel safe.' These vows, that most of us can't even remember making, can develop into a whole clutch of goals, attitudes and mindsets that form themselves into the kind of strongholds I believe Paul was talking about in 2 Corinthians 10:4–5. They can drive us through life relentlessly like little motor engines, but God has the power to render them harmless once we realise their destructive power. The vow I made on that tree stump, to know God, was the best I could have made (Psalm 65:1), but not only did the other two, made around the same time, work against that central vow, but the engines they installed headed me off down the road to endless disappointment. For instance, you soon realise that being 'very very good' all the time is quite impossible and only results in a terrible sense of failure simply because your personal standards are too high. Of course, it was many years before I worked all that out and discovered finally that the only person I needed to please was God, and perfect behaviour would never make him love me any more than he already did! Only then was I able to throw away all that disgusting candyfloss.

4

I count everything as loss compared to . . . the possession of the over-whelming preciousness, the surpassing worth and supreme advantage of knowing Christ Jesus my Lord and of progressively becoming more deeply and intimately acquainted with Him, of perceiving and recognizing and understanding Him more fully and clearly.

Philippians 3:8, AMP

The third vow must have been made a few months later, when life had suddenly plunged back again into those 'deep purple shadows' which, at the time, looked more black than purple to me. Perhaps Grandpa had decided, about that time, to make things a little easier for my mother financially, because in 1949 she decided to send me to the 'best' private school in the district as she said the local school wasn't 'pushing me'. As far as I was concerned she could have invested her money much more wisely!

Dressed in a navy gymslip and a beret with a yellow tassel, I was deposited, one morning, in hell. All the other neat little girls in their rows of sloping wooden desks could read, but I could not even recognise words like 'the' or 'and', and at seven I still could not write my own name. They certainly 'pushed me' at this new school, but I realised as quickly as they did that something was terribly wrong with me.

In the days before dyslexia had been recognised, children like me were quickly labelled 'stupid' or 'lazy'. The trouble is that most dyslexics are far from stupid, which makes their disability all the more frustrating. I loved the sound of words and played about with them endlessly in my head, but when I tried to transfer them into my exercise book the result was a jumbled mass of letters, most of which were written backwards. Other girls were given merits for their boring efforts, while the teacher wrote 'Gibberish' across mine. Worse still, she often held up my book to give everyone else a good laugh.

It is not only letters that defeat dyslexics: numbers are also a problem. Miss Mitchell, my teacher, shook me like a rag doll in her bewildered rage when I could not take two away from three or tell her if five was more or less than seven. We can't tell our left from our right, either, so poor Miss Mitchell was even more exasperated when we did 'drill' in the Big Hall. One horrendous day she yelled, 'To the right – turn!' and ninety-nine girls turned right and one turned left, causing chaos – and terrible humiliation.

When I had been there for a year, far from making progress I had actually gone backwards. I was so afraid of Miss Mitchell that I became a gibbering idiot whenever she came near me. My mother was summoned to the school, and for some reason I had to accompany her to the headmistress's study. I knew only really bad girls ever went there so I expected nothing short of a death sentence.

'We're sorry to have to inform you but your daughter is backward,' rasped Miss Mitchell, who was never one to soften a blow – any kind of a blow! 'She is hopelessly behind, educationally subnormal; we can't seem to teach her anything.' My parents' approval was vital to me, so the look on Otty's face as she heard those words was the worst punishment I could possibly have received. For years I felt she was ashamed of me. Perhaps I was wrong, but a deep sense of shame and failure seeped into my soul. Children often misinterpret situations and grow up seeing themselves as defective and therefore a disappointment, when actually that was not the case.

> *I am not what I think I am;*
> *I am not what you think I am;*
> *I am what I think you think I am.*
>   Selwyn Hughes

'I'm sure she'll improve if you can give her a good grounding,' Otty told Miss Mitchell brightly, and turning to me she added reproachfully, 'You'll just have to work a lot harder than the others because you're not as clever as they are.' Once again it was a casual sentence that caused me to make another vow: 'I'm always going to work harder than everyone else, because that's the way to please my mother (and probably God).' For years I had a problem with really knowing I was loved and accepted by God just as I am; to me he has so often looked like my mother in the headmistress's study, disappointed that I had not worked quite as hard as I ought to have done.

Rather grudgingly the school kept me on, but they gave me no remedial help or extra support so I just sat at the back of the class and tried to be invisible. For some reason, however, Miss Mitchell never seemed able to stop herself from tormenting me; I've often tried to figure out why she seemed to hate me so intensely. I was too afraid to be naughty or defiant, but every day she seemed driven to go out of her way to make my life a total misery, and teachers who pick on a particular child subtly encourage the rest of the class to persecute them too. Perhaps it was my parents' Christianity that she detested.

One Sunday something happened which, I can now see, formed yet another stronghold in my mind, one which the Enemy has used against me so many times! On Sundays *both* our parents had lunch with us in the nursery, which made it a very special occasion indeed, crowned by Schweppes Ginger Beer from brown glass bottles. There was always laughter and fun wherever our parents were – perhaps that is one of the reasons why half the Christian world flocked to Hildenborough – but at Sunday lunch Justyn and I had all the laughter and fun for ourselves.

On this particular day Gom had made us a very special gateau covered in cream, churned by Norman, and Mr Walster's fresh-picked raspberries. We were just about to try it when some emergency occurred with a guest and both my parents were called hastily away. Nanny took Justyn upstairs for his nap and I was left alone. I distinctly remember the sense of desolation – and then I saw the gateau sitting, untouched, in the middle of the table. 'It's all right,' I thought, 'it doesn't matter that they've all gone away, I can always eat that cake – every bit of it!' I kept going until I had scraped the plate, and I wasn't even sick! That was the day I discovered that if you feel miserable or unloved you can always cover the inner emptiness with food. Ever since that moment, times of emotional stress have triggered months of compulsive comfort eating, with the embarrassing result of a rapid weight gain.

Soon after that Sunday lunch Gom had to leave suddenly under a terrible cloud that was never explained to me. The first I knew about it was when I caught a glimpse of her climbing into a taxi, wearing her best navy suit – but I wasn't even allowed to kiss her goodbye. The loss of her was crippling, and the memory of that taxi driving away still reduces me to helpless tears. She refused to be permanently separated from me and spent most of what she earned, cooking in a boys' prep school, on a constant stream of presents and postcards. Ten years later, when my mother finally had a home of her own, she came back to 'look after us' and we were never separated again until her death in 1994.

Perhaps all the chocolate bars she gave me also made me associate love and security with eating sweet things; my eating problem definitely grew a lot worse after the day she had to leave me so suddenly. I was allowed to come home from school alone on the bus, but on the way to catch it I passed a sweet shop. Otty was always lavishly generous with pocket money and sweets were no longer rationed, so I dulled the horrid memories of the day with toffees and chocolate. Nanny provided a massive old-fashioned nursery tea and, with the larder and the kitchen both so close to the nursery, it was easy for me to go on 'nicking and picking' until I went to bed. In one year the skinny child in my first school photo was replaced by a gross version of Miss Piggy. My being fat gave Miss Mitchell and the rest of my tormentors even more scope for derision, and by the time I was eleven life was intolerable.

Why do children who are being bullied and abused keep silent for so long? I suppose my self-esteem was so low that I assumed I deserved the treatment I received, but every worm turns eventually. One day I came out of school and found Otty waiting in her little car to meet me. The unexpected joy of this treat was just too much and I suddenly blurted out: 'I'm sorry but I just can't go back – ever!' To my vast surprise she never made me, and I was home-schooled from that time by a series of well-meaning but totally incompetent women; but anyone was better than Miss Mitchell.

Because I did not learn to read until I was fourteen, Otty spent all her spare time reading aloud to me. She loved it, so it was no sacrifice, but if she started a book at my bedtime she could never bring herself to stop until it was finished. I remember us enjoying *The Scarlet Pimpernel* until three o'clock in the morning, when my father put his head round the door and said, 'Have you two any idea what the time is?' She also gave me her ancient typewriter and encouraged me to learn to type. She had no idea that this was the best possible treatment for dyslexia.

*   *   *

If it had not been for an extraordinary experience I had about ten years ago I would not have been able to remember any of the events I have just described. Troubled children often cannot express how they are feeling, so they lock away painful memories in a cellar under the floorboards of their adult lives. Those four years were a complete blank to me, but the memories, and all the strong emotions attached to them, were still down there in my subconscious mind. Most nights they crept out in the form of a recurring nightmare when I was dragged back to school to face Miss Mitchell. They caused other problems, too, as buried memories and emotions often do. When we are on that journey into God's heart he longs to be allowed into all these dark cellars and he patiently waits until we are willing to give him the key. Not only does he want to bring healing into every damaged area of our lives, but he also wants to use our past experiences and make them work for our maximum benefit – even the experiences that seem totally negative to us.

Nearly forty years after I finally walked out of school I went to a communion service in a healing centre called Crowhurst. That morning, the Gospel reading was Matthew 6:14–15, and for some reason some of the words from that passage hung, suspended, in my mind: *'For if you forgive men when they sin against you, your heavenly Father will also forgive you. But if you do not forgive men their sins, your Father will not forgive your sins.'*

'Goodness!' I thought. 'Those are strong words.' My imagination clicked in and I saw myself standing at the gate of heaven while Peter sternly shook his head. 'Sorry, you can't come in! There was that person you never got round to forgiving – so your own sins are still sticking to you!'

The idea was so nasty that I shuddered and rapidly returned to earth. 'But do I have anyone I need to forgive?' I asked myself. I couldn't think of anyone who had ever hurt me so I did my best to concentrate on the sermon. This was on forgiveness, too, and the preacher talked about the man Jesus described in Matthew 5 who came to worship God at the altar with his offering.

'Jesus said it was useless for him to try to worship,' thundered the preacher, 'because he was holding a grudge against someone in his heart. He had to put down his offering and go at once to put that broken relationship right!' He glared at us severely over his half-glasses as he added ominously, 'I don't want any of you coming up here to take communion if there is someone you still need to forgive.'

By this time I was beginning to feel a bit bothered so I said a quick but risky prayer, 'Lord, if there *is* anyone I need to forgive, please show me.' Instantly, inside my head, I heard a harsh voice shouting, 'Jennifer Rees, you are the stupidest child I have ever had the misfortune to teach!'

I smiled, almost fondly. 'Surely God doesn't want me to forgive poor old Miss Mitchell?' I thought. 'I can scarcely remember her, and anyway she was quite right to call me stupid – I was!' Just to be on the safe side, however, I muttered a hasty, 'Lord, I forgive her,' as I went up for communion and then thought no more about it. I was soon to learn that I had only just begun a very lengthy process.

I am convinced that our journey into God's heart is held up not only by buried painful emotions, but also by failing to forgive the person who caused them. I've often heard people say, 'But I *can't* forgive what they did to me!'

Of course, they are quite right! When our lives have been devastated by the selfishness, carelessness or cruelty of other people we can't possibly forgive them – humanly speaking! We are often urged to do so by well-meaning friends or pastors who know how healing forgiveness can be, but however hard we try the whole thing is quite impossible on our own. First we have to ask Jesus himself to come right into the centre of the pain that is trapped deep inside our hearts, and then give him permission to perform a heart transplant. Gently he removes our old, broken heart and replaces it with a new one, through which flows his own forgiving grace. All he needs is our 'yes' and then he literally forgives *for* us and *through* us.

Many people, however, have a different problem over forgiveness. We don't forgive people in our past because we have deleted every memory of them – just as I did with Miss Mitchell. When God sees we are ready to open up our hidden cellars to his healing light he gently prompts us, as he did for me through that sermon on forgiveness. I gave him the cellar key when I prayed that risky prayer, 'Lord, show me if there is anyone . . .'

But sadly I've met a number of people who cannot bring themselves to pray like that because they are too afraid of what may be down in their personal cellar. 'I can't stand all this raking up the past,' they say. 'We need to forgive and forget!' They do not realise that we cannot forgive fully until we *remember*. Until we identify the person who damaged us, we will never be free of the damage that person caused.

After that fateful communion service my nightmares became even worse! It was as if the memories were rattling my cellar door, but I did not realise that at the time. Then two months later I had a letter. It was from the only girl who had been even remotely friendly in those four years at school. We had never met since, or even been in touch, but she had read one of my books and wrote via the publisher. 'Let's make a date and get together,' said her letter.

I enjoyed meeting her again but was rather surprised to find she no longer had pigtails or a brace on her teeth!

'Miss Mitchell was a brilliant games teacher but I don't think she liked you much!' she said.

'I can't really remember her,' I said vaguely, trying not to hear that voice shouting across the netball pitch, 'You're supposed to *catch* the ball, not stand there until it hits you! You're too revoltingly fat to move!'

'I've got a photo of her,' my friend said, as she rummaged in her bag. 'I took it last year at the school's centenary.'

I went ice cold all over as I looked down at the face I claimed to have 'forgotten' but actually remembered in minute detail. It seemed quite extraordinary that a woman of fifty could be so terrified of a mere photograph, but I felt sick with fear. I was oddly angry too. How *wicked* to make the whole form laugh at me, I thought, but hastily pushed both the fear and the anger back down among the cobwebs. 'Good job I've forgiven her,' I thought as I locked the cellar door firmly. But I had not really forgiven her, because I had not yet been able to acknowledge how much she had hurt me.

Later that year I went for some prayer ministry; life was going through a very stressful patch and I had put on so much weight none of my clothes fitted me any more. I felt out of control as diet after diet bit the dust. The people who were praying for me felt that my eating problem had been caused by people in my past whom I had not yet fully forgiven.

'But I thought I'd done all that,' I said miserably as I told them about the communion service at Crowhurst.

'There are so many layers of forgiveness!' they said vaguely, but as I drove home I felt so low I ate three bars of chocolate.

Soon after this I was doing a speaking tour in the north of England and at one event I spoke about 'the power of words'. I explained how the things people say to us as children can bind us almost like a curse, changing the very way we think and feel about ourselves. By way of illustration, I mentioned Miss Mitchell and how I had always felt like a failure because she had told me so often I was stupid. I quickly added that I had 'forgiven' her and believed forgiveness was the way to be free from the effects of harmful words. It all sounded quite good and everyone was nodding agreement, but I was in for a nasty shock. In the meeting that night was a missionary teacher called Ann, home from Kenya on furlough. We had been penfriends for years, so we arranged to meet for a coffee before I left the area.

'There is something I feel I must say,' she began awkwardly. 'You haven't forgiven Miss Mitchell at all, have you?'

I was stunned. 'Yes I have!' I protested.

'Something tells me you have only forgiven her in your mind,' persisted Ann, 'but not from the heart – because in your heart you still hate her.'

'I don't hate anyone!' I protested. 'But I do think she hated me!'

'Have you seen her lately?'

'Oh no!' I said hurriedly. 'I never want to see her again in my life!'

'That's the problem, then,' replied Ann. 'You're only in the first stage of forgiveness, the part that happens inside us, but the second part is all about moving towards the other person to offer forgiveness in a tangible way. When we have been hurt we shrink away from the person who inflicts the pain by keeping out of their way, but while we are still doing that we are only at the halfway mark. I think you should go and see that teacher of yours.'

I really could not see the point, but Ann is a persuasive lady. 'Miss Mitchell probably died years ago,' I told myself as I eventually dialled the school number. The secretary soon dashed my hopes: 'Miss Mitchell is always *delighted* to see Old Girls,' she gushed.

'Only the ones who were good at netball,' I thought bitterly.

It took me several days to pluck up the courage to ring her, and I was shaking so much I dialled three wrong numbers before I heard the familiar rasping voice that echoed through my nightmares.

'Speak up, how can you expect me to hear if you mumble like that!' Her words instantly reduced me to the quivering child I had once been – almost too afraid to remember my own name.

'I was in your form,' I managed at last, 'for four years. I wondered if I could just p-pop in and s-see you?'

'Why?'

'There's something I want to give you . . .' I wanted to give her my forgiveness even if I only intended to convey it through a bunch of flowers.

'Tuesday, eleven – sharp,' she said and hung up while I collapsed, sweating, in an armchair. I was not at all sure I could go through with this visit, and my feelings towards Ann were anything but affectionate.

My husband was away that week, and there were only three of my six children left at home so I had more time to think than usual. Isaiah describes Jesus as a 'Wonderful Counsellor' (Isaiah 9:6) and he definitely became that to me during the next six days.

If someone else were writing this I would have a problem believing that so many extraordinary things could possibly happen spontaneously in just one week – but I know that they did because I kept a detailed record in my journal.

First I began to realise just how many of my lifelong problems could be traced back to those four years in my childhood and how, subconsciously, I had always held Miss Mitchell responsible. One morning I felt drawn towards Luke 6 in my Amplified Version. '*Pray for the happiness of those who curse you, implore God's . . . favour upon those who abuse you, who revile, reproach, disparage and high-handedly misuse you*' (Luke 6:28, AMP).

'*Pray* for her!' I protested. 'Surely you can't expect me to do that!' I was beginning to feel overwhelmed by all the hate that was surging out of my cellar at an alarming rate, but if Jesus said I had to pray for her, then pray I must, though I have to admit I did so through clenched teeth! I soon discovered that praying for someone you detest has the most remarkable effect. First it kills hate. When you pray you take the other person with you into God's presence and allow the light of his love to pour down on them as if you had stood them in the beam of a great lighthouse. To pray for them means you have to stand next to them, and the shaft of light penetrates your own heart too, like a laser beam, cauterising all the anger.

Praying also helps you to get inside the other person's skin and you begin to understand why they behaved as they do. That week, for the first time in years, I just 'happened' to meet another teacher from my school, Miss Howe. She had been the only member of staff I had liked, because she taught art and I was reasonably good at that! I mentioned that I was going to see Miss Mitchell in a few days' time and she said, 'Poor thing! Such a bitter woman – but no wonder when you know what happened to her as a child.' I knew nothing about her past but Miss Howe enjoyed enlightening me, and by the time she had finished I began to see the reason why Miss Mitchell might have been such a bully.

There is an old French proverb that says, 'To understand all is to forgive all.' I am not sure I fully agree, but understanding definitely helps.

During that week I read everything Jesus said about forgiveness and dug around in my father's old commentaries for further information. I soon made the slightly unnerving discovery that I was not being asked to go to Miss Mitchell in order to offer her some grand gesture of forgiveness; the main purpose of the visit was for me to ask for *her* forgiveness! I began to see that it is a terrible thing to hate someone for so many years and to put on them all the blame for all your personal weaknesses and failures. One commentary said the word 'forgiveness' means 'to set free' and is the Greek word which Jesus used at the grave of Lazarus when he emerged all bound up in his shroud like an Egyptian mummy. Jesus said, 'Loose him and let him go!' (John 11:44). But his words could also have meant, 'Forgive him and let him go.' By not forgiving Miss Mitchell perhaps I could have bound her spiritually by the grudges I held against her, and I felt even more sure of that when I read: '*if you forgive anyone's sins, they are forgiven. If you refuse to forgive them, they are unforgiven*' (John 20:23, Living Bible). I was not sure that I wanted God to let Miss Mitchell off the punishment I felt she so richly deserved, but I had to face the fact that I had sinned by hating her for so long and blaming her for so much.

The climax of this extraordinary week came during the night before the Dreaded Visit. At two in the morning I sat bolt upright, feeling sure it was the Holy Spirit who had woken me. I asked what he wanted me to do, thinking he would bring to my mind someone who needed urgent prayer; but all I could think about was Miss Mitchell. The memories, long suppressed, suddenly became so vivid that I felt they were reality and I was a child again. I could not 'see' myself because I was inside the child who clutched a grimy arithmetic book, full of sums I knew would be wrong – yet again. The familiar school smell engulfed me: stale sweat, disinfectant, old plimsolls and a dash of cooked cabbage.

In the distance I could hear Miss Mitchell, shouting as she

came up the corridor towards me. Like a giant bat she was finally looming over me as I cringed away in terror; all around us were the taunting voices of the other girls: 'Fat moron ... thick idiot!' When you are an adult living a reasonably happy, successful life, it is hard to remember how helplessly vulnerable a child can feel, but at that moment I became a child again, feeling her emotions intensely. When I heard my own adult voice shouting out in the darkness, 'Lord, help me!' I suddenly sensed Jesus really was there, standing beside that frightened child with one big hand on her shoulder. As the face of the monster loomed closer, distorted with rage, I could feel his hand tighten reassuringly. Then, just as she raised her bony fist to strike, Jesus stepped between us taking the pain, abuse and jeers while I hid safely behind him. '*Surely he has borne our griefs and carried our sorrows*' (Isaiah 53:4, NKJV) and '*the insults which are hurled at you have fallen on me* (Romans 15:3, GNB).

I sensed that there was something very important that he wanted me to do next, and I heard my child-self saying, 'Miss Mitchell, I forgive you freely for everything you did or said to me. I let go of all the blame and set you free from the grudges I have carried against you. And please forgive me for hating you and binding you up for so long.'

Ever since that moment I have firmly believed that it is the child inside us who has to express forgiveness to an adult who hurt us in the past.

As I felt myself standing there behind Jesus I became conscious of the enormous love he had for Miss Mitchell. It poured out of him in waves, and he understood all the unhappy reasons which had caused her behaviour.

'Please forgive her, Lord,' I whispered. 'Delete every cruel thing she ever did from your files!'

Sometime later that night I felt that he wanted to bring me even more healing, and I saw my child-self sitting on his knee. I kept wriggling restlessly, constantly trying to slide off and run away. I sensed this behaviour distressed him because he wanted to comfort and reassure me but I was refusing to let him. I knew only too well that he was showing me how it made him feel when I ran to the biscuit tin for comfort rather than going to him when I was stressed out or upset. For a while after that extraordinary night I hoped that food would never ever be my god again, and that by forgiving Miss Mitchell the root of my eating problem had finally been dug out for good. Sad to say, I have to admit that when a major tragedy hit my life a few years later my compulsion to binge came back for a while, but one of the things that helped me to regain my healing was the realisation that I also had to forgive my mother for allowing me to gain so much weight – in spite of our doctor's entreaties.

Parents so often let their children become obese because giving them food is their way of showing love or a substitute for their time – a salve for their guilty conscience. They do not seem to realise that they are crippling their child both physically and emotionally, often for life. Had my parents abused, neglected or ill-treated me, the need for forgiveness might have been obvious much earlier in my life. However, I had grown up convinced that they were perfect! Admitting that they had failed me, even in the smallest way, felt disloyal and ungrateful. Perhaps it is easier to forgive people for the bad things they do to us rather than for the good things they failed to do. Even the best human parents need our forgiveness if we want God to make us completely whole.

The following morning at eleven (sharp) I stood on Miss Mitchell's front doorstep clutching a gigantic bunch of flowers in my shaking hands. I was so terrified I could not help thinking that the first stage of forgiveness, the part you do in your head, is much easier than the second, when you have to demonstrate it tangibly! By one minute past eleven I was sitting nervously on the very edge of an uncomfortable chair in Miss Mitchell's front room. I could hear myself chattering like a nervous eight-year-old and tried hard to remind myself I had six children and had published sixteen books! Fortunately Miss Mitchell cut into my infantile giggles by saying: 'So why *did* you come?'

'To lay some ghosts,' I answered awkwardly. 'I wasn't very happy at school, you see.' She raised her eyebrows, so I added, 'If you remember, I couldn't read – or write either. I guess nowadays I'd be labelled dyslexic.'

'We used to call children like that thick or lazy,' she replied with a dismissive shrug, but perhaps she saw me wince because her face changed as she added, 'Maybe we didn't know much about that kind of thing in my day. I suppose we were sometimes rather cruel.' I felt this was her way of saying sorry and the conversation began to flow much more easily after that.

When she finally showed me out, something very significant happened on the doorstep. She said, 'I'm sorry you were unhappy at school.'

I reached out and took the hand that I had been so afraid of as a child – and held it for a moment. 'That's all all right now,' I replied. 'You couldn't have known how I felt, could you?'

The transaction was complete; we had both offered and received forgiveness, and we kissed each other warmly before parting with promises to meet again.

Miss Mitchell actually taught me more about forgiveness than I could have learnt from a thousand books! All those lessons not only helped me on two further occasions when I faced much bigger forgiveness challenges, but I have since shared them with thousands of people right across the world and been allowed to see the healing that has come to them as they released forgiveness themselves. God's ability to make 'all things work together for good' (Romans 8:28, NKJV) never ceases to amaze me!

I always laugh whenever I remember the only other time I visited my school after that day when I left so abruptly. In 1997 I was invited to Founder's Day in order to make a speech as a 'local author' and then to give out the prizes. That kind of occasion is definitely not my thing, but I decided to go because the school had relocated to new premises built in the grounds of my old home, Hildenborough Hall. The governors' invitation felt like a perfect excuse to visit old haunts and, to the disgust of the staff and delight of the pupils, I said that being a dud at school did not necessarily make you a failure for life. With a sigh of relief I finally escaped after presenting a copy of my *Children's Bible Story Book* to the school library. I had used special gold ink to write the name of the school and the date on the flyleaf, but as I drove out, past the school crest emblazoned on the gates, I realised to my horror that I had spelt the school's name completely wrong! Dyslexia had the last word after all, and I laughed so much I nearly crashed the car.

5

*Then you will seek Me, inquire for and require Me (as a vital necessity)
and find Me when you search for Me with all your heart. I will be found
by you, says the LORD.*

Jeremiah 29:13–14, AMP

One golden evening early in September 1954 I was sitting in
my favourite spot by the lake. It was nine years since those
German prisoners of war had dredged it, but I always thought
about them as I sat by the sluice gate they had built. The shadow
of the great cedar tree lay long over the sloping lawn and a
solitary moorhen chugged across the polished surface of the
water. I was trying to pack every detail of the scene into my
memory because I knew that, by the following morning, I would
have lost it all for ever. My parents had decided to sell up and
move the conference centre into a hideous Edwardian hotel on
the front at Frinton-on-Sea, Essex. To this day Justyn and I still
cannot understand why they did it! The Boss said people wanted
seaside holidays now that all the wartime barbed wire and
landmines had been removed from the British coastline, but
Justyn and I couldn't see how anyone would want to have a
holiday in a *town*! When Otty had taken us down for a preview,
the heaving crowds that thronged the promenade made me want

65

to run for cover and the flat, treeless expanse of Essex depressed me.

'We can't play in that tiny garden,' had been Justyn's doleful comment when we were shown round the hotel, 'there's nowhere to hide.' It reminded me of a park, with its neat rows of flowers stiffly standing to attention. My mother explained that Kaiser Wilhelm, Mrs Wilson and George Bernard Shaw had all once stayed in the Esplanade Hotel, but she did not mention that the furnishings and décor had been left untouched ever since!

That evening, as I listened to the birds singing their 'settling-down-for-the-night' songs in the familiar trees around me, I thought, 'I'll never be able to come here again.' Actually I've 'walked' round that garden every single day since – in my imagination; and I know Justyn does just the same. All our memories of the house and grounds form the wallpaper that frames everything we think about each day. Every time Justyn comes to visit me from his home in Canada we always climb over the fence near the lake to scrabble around the dense undergrowth looking for buried rockeries and overgrown paths that no one else knows are there. I believe you can mourn for a lost place just as deeply as you mourn for a beloved person.

Our parents had made another unfathomable decision that was making me even more miserable: Justyn was going to be sent away, aged eight, to board at an exclusive prep school a hundred miles away. Nanny, who was leaving too, had been crying continuously for days as she sewed quantities of name labels on to his uniform before packing it all into a huge wooden trunk.

Otty took me with her when she drove Justyn to school on that dreaded First Day of Term. He sat white-faced and rigid in the front seat, clutching his favourite teddy bear. After we had abandoned him in a barrack-like dormitory Otty and I cried all the way back to Frinton, and we became hysterical when we arrived, only to find he had left his precious teddy behind on the floor of the car.

★ ★ ★

Left alone in a bustling seaside town I soon began to feel like a bird in a cage with nowhere to hide. The beach might have been an adequate replacement for the garden if I had not been so embarrassed by my enormous size. I felt like a freak as I tried to disguise my fat inside layers of clothes while everyone else was wearing bathing costumes. So I withdrew into my bedroom, claiming I was too shy to face all the staff and guests who constantly thronged the new Hildenborough. Enormous meals were sent up to me on trays, cooked specially by Lucien, the new French chief who ruled the hotel kitchens, and I 'pigged out' in solitary state.

Without school or nanny I was left very much to my own devices. Perhaps my increasing girth was also an embarrassment to my parents; it was probably also humiliating for them to keep explaining to each new houseful of visitors why I did not go to school like a normal teenager. So it was easier for us all if I stayed out of sight, and my bedroom became my safe hiding place while I waited for Justyn to come home for the next holidays – for some reason I never minded going outside with him.

One Easter holiday something happened which still makes us laugh. Justyn had an airgun, of which he was enormously proud, but finding space to practise shooting was a real problem in that genteel town. One evening at dusk we went down to the beach hoping no one would be around to hear him firing at the wooden breakwaters. Unfortunately someone must have complained because we suddenly saw a policeman scrambling down the bank, heading towards us. However, to our surprise, instead of telling Justyn off, the policeman apologised. 'I was told some children were playing with a gun down here,' he said, 'but I didn't realise you had your mother with you,' and off he went. In the fading light my size and shape had fooled him completely, so just for once being fat was an asset. How we laughed.

Frinton is full of retired lady schoolteachers, and a string of these dogged females visited my bedroom regularly and made unsatisfactory attempts at teaching me to read. My one companion was a little sausage dog called Fossil; I used to take him out for long walks on the beach early in the morning or after dark at night when I could be sure no one was about to see me.

For many years I never even considered that my existence in Frinton was abnormal and I was totally content — so long as I didn't have to go out. I spent my time creating hundreds of little woollen dolls, dressing them in all kinds of intricate costumes and making up endless stories about them that sometimes went on for days. My parents just accepted and loved me the way I was, probably thinking that was the way 'backward' children were supposed to live. They each spent as much time with me as they could and I grew very close to them both during those years; they did their best to provide as much education as I seemed able to absorb, but the idea of taking me to a psychiatrist or an educational psychologist would never have occurred to them in those days.

Yet I probably did need help, because during those years shame became even more firmly embedded in my soul. Shame is quite different from guilt. The Holy Spirit causes us to feel guilty when we have done something wrong in the hope of making us so uncomfortable that we will repent and come back close to God again. Shame never comes from the Holy Spirit, but is frequently used by the Opposition! It is not triggered by some specific thing we have done wrong, but is a vague sense of general worthlessness that pervades all our thinking. We always feel sure we are going to fail, say the wrong thing or not quite measure up to the standards or expectations of other people. Our whole attitude towards ourselves is one of dislike and condemnation; and it feels like walking through life wearing a permanent grey shawl over our heads. We are not aware of it, and we don't realise how it stops us from becoming the people God intended us to be. We want to obey him but the invisible grey shawl trips us up.

About four years ago I was sitting with my friend Jean, drinking coffee as I watched her knitting dolls' clothes. For some reason Frinton was mentioned and, perhaps because Jean is a very wise and highly trained counsellor, I found myself telling her about those four 'prison years' as her needles clicked on soothingly. On the table between us lay the naked teenage doll that she had bought for 50p in a charity shop the previous day. Why she wanted such a disgusting-looking thing I couldn't imagine. Its hair was matted and filthy and its body was stained with mildew. I was quite startled when Jean suddenly asked casually, 'As you look back at that girl, hiding in the bedroom, how do you feel about her?'

'I suppose I was a bit of a mess,' I said avoiding her question. 'Rather like that doll of yours!'

'Would you do something for me?' asked Jean. 'Give the doll a bath and a hair wash while I finish her outfit. While you're doing that, I want you to pretend that she is *you* aged about thirteen.'

Just to humour her, I reached out to pick up the doll, but recoiled, astonished by my reaction. 'I don't want to touch her!' I said, 'She revolts me.' (I still had my candyfloss mask on so I said it very sweetly!)

'What *do* you want to do with her, then?' said Jean mildly.

'This!' I replied, and picking the doll up by the hair I beat her body against the table. Jean made no response – she appeared to be counting stitches – so I threw the doll on to the floor and stamped on her until I was breathless with the effort. Jean knitted on peacefully like a spectator beside a Paris guillotine.

'Do you know why you want to treat her like that?' was all she said.

'I hate her,' I muttered. 'She's a disgusting coward who ran away from school and hid inside her own fat. I despise failures!'

'So what are you going to do with the doll now?' asked Jean. Without a word I took it outside and chucked it in the dustbin.

By the time I sat down again I was beginning to feel rather silly and not a little panicky, as I always did when my mask had slipped. Jean, however, kept on knitting – rather pointlessly, I thought, seeing the doll no longer needed clothes. At last she said thoughtfully, 'I've quite often seen people "throw away" a period of their lives like you just did then. Sometimes it's the years when they sowed their wild oats and got up to things they're ashamed of later; or maybe they regret the time they wasted when they let themselves be trapped in a disastrous relationship. They just can't forgive themselves for doing the things they did, so they let shame control their lives. I think you need to forgive yourself for your attitude towards yourself during those years.'

The Miss Mitchell affair had already taught me how destructive long-term resentment towards someone in the past can be, but I had not realised that a bad attitude towards *yourself* can be equally harmful. For some reason it is usually easier to forgive other people than it is to forgive ourselves!

'Jean, I'm *so* sorry about your doll!' I said ruefully. 'I'll go out right now and buy you a brand new one!'

'No,' smiled Jean, 'I just want you to go and fetch the old one from the dustbin and give her a bit of cherishing. She's "Young Jen", remember, so tell her you forgive her and don't want to leave her buried in rubbish because she's too special.'

It took a lot of Jean's best bath foam to get rid of Young Jen's dustbin smell, but something began to happen to me as I dried and brushed out her hair, and her new outfit was ready by the time I had tied it back with pretty ribbons. Finally, clothed and in her right mind (Luke 8:35), she sat on my knee while Jean and I got down to the business of praying away all that shame and self-hatred.

There is one school of thought that holds that when we first come to Christ all the sins we have ever committed are totally forgiven through the power of the cross, and all the wounds and scars others have left on our souls are instantly wiped away. I believe God works that kind of a miracle for some people but not for everyone. Many of us live happy, busy Christian lives for many years in spite of the odd little problems that keep cropping up. Then, quite suddenly, the Holy Spirit will shine a spotlight on some period of our lives in which lies the root of these problems, because he wants us to be rid of them for good. He was doing that for me when he brought to light my attitude of resentment and hate towards Miss Mitchell, but shame does not come from our attitude towards others but from our attitude towards ourselves.

'We ought to be getting on with the job of caring for others, not endlessly navel-gazing!' some people say, but they fail to realise that the Holy Spirit only shows us these dark areas because they are making us *less able* to care for others. Responding to him quickly means we can serve him with renewed energy.

Recently I was on a retreat with several others who are all in the ministry of healing. During the week the Lord did all kinds of deep and painful things for each of us, but by the last day we all felt wonderfully released and free.

'Wouldn't you think,' said someone, 'that after all the years we've all known and served the Lord he might have given us a bit of a break this week? But every time I go away with him like this he shows me yet another person he wants me to forgive or something else he wants me to repent of! Why do you suppose he goes on at us like this?'

'Perhaps we all spend too much time helping people dig into their pasts to find healing,' suggested someone else. 'It's our job that makes us introspective.'

'No!' cut in another person emphatically, 'it's *because* we're in the healing ministry; the Lord has to keep on at us because he knows we can only bring healing to others to the extent that we have been willing to receive healing ourselves.' I believe she was right; there are far too many Christian leaders and ministers who keep on damaging their relationships with others because of their own unresolved pain.

It probably will not surprise you to know that since that coffee with Jean I have used dolls and toys to help a lot of other people to find inner healing. There is often, however, an unexpected snag in taking people back to some painful place in their memory. If they know that Jesus has always been with them they find it hard to understand why he did nothing to protect them when they were being abused, neglected or attacked. This can lead to a deep sense of disappointment or even anger if it is not handled sensitively. As I sat there with Jean's doll on my lap the exact opposite happened to me. I suddenly saw Young Jen through the eyes of Jesus. He had not written her off as 'backward' or been ashamed of her ugly shape; to him she was enchantingly beautiful. Finally he helped me understand how he had used those apparently wasted years to deepen our relationship; and this is how he managed to do that.

When we first moved to Frinton I saw very little of my parents; they were both terribly busy during the first year, but later I discovered they were also having major personal problems. No one can continue indefinitely speaking all over the world, writing books and sharing their home with a continuous stream of needy people without showing signs of strain – particularly if they never take a day off! Late one night I found Otty crying alone in her bedroom, and she finally admitted that she felt totally dried up inside and empty. 'I just can't face all those guests coming here week after week, when I don't feel I've got anything left to give.'

The next day she made the decision to take some time off and come with Justyn and me during our August holiday at Grandpa's house in Scotland. It was not until years later that I discovered that it was not only overwork that was making her so unhappy: her marriage was also under huge strain. Sharing such a public ministry must have felt like living in a goldfish bowl – or a vicarage-cum-manse! Because Otty always gave everybody one hundred per cent of herself, she expected one hundred per cent in return, and that could be extremely draining. The Boss, who was also feeling burnt out, needed space and solitude in which to recharge his batteries, but the more of his time and attention Otty demanded the less he was able to give. When we set off for that holiday her frustration was rising to a dangerous level.

The three of us had Glenluffin to ourselves that year because

Grandpa had just bought a farm in Sussex and had temporarily lost interest in his Scottish estate. The summer days slid by delightfully; Justyn and I had all those bracken-covered hills in which to fire his airgun, which left Otty free to thunder away on her typewriter. The thought of relaxing would have been out of the question in days when the Protestant work ethic ruled the day. So she used the time to research a book about religious revivals. Her publisher hoped it would appear in time to celebrate the centenary of the 1859 spiritual awakening that had spread round the world like a forest fire.

She worked away, surrounded by a wall of dull-looking tomes, but it was not long before we noticed that something quite extraordinary was happening to her. The more books she read about these supernatural times of refreshing (Acts 3:19), the more parched she felt her own soul had become. Among the pile of books on her desk was one by the great nineteenth-century preacher Charles Finney, in which he said that anyone could have a personal revival in their own soul – just for the asking. One afternoon we found her sitting with this book open on her lap, weeping copiously. I still have her dog-eared copy, tear stains and all!

'What's the matter, Otty?' we asked nervously.

'I'm just so happy!' she gasped. For the rest of the month she floated round in a 'drunken' daze. Nowadays we are more used to seeing people 'zapped' by the Holy Spirit, but then traditional evangelicals related to 'Our Heavenly Father' or to 'Christ our Saviour'; only children talked about 'Jesus'. I never heard anyone even mention the Holy Spirit! Miracles, speaking in tongues and prophecy were considered to have died out with the first apostles. Whether Otty approved of any of those things I am not sure, but the Holy Spirit was certainly alive and active up there in Scotland that summer!

The kind of ecstasy I had seen her enjoy when I was a small child had returned, and once again I longed to experience it too; so early one morning, long before breakfast, I went up the Back

Hill behind Grandpa's stables and sat down on a large slab of granite. It is hard to find words to describe what happened without cheapening the experience. At that stage of my life I felt myself to be such an ugly, frightened failure, but suddenly Jesus himself came to me on that hillside. He stood beside my granite boulder and I felt I was being drowned in his love, lost in it – yet found and held so safely. It was like the experience I had on that tree stump, but even more intense.

I went on feeling his presence for the rest of the holiday and spent hours wandering up and down on the beach, praying. Poor Justyn was heartily bored! The thought of going back to Frinton filled me with dread; I was sure it would mark the end of the most beautiful thing that had ever happened to me.

Now, fifty years later, whenever I go back to Glenluffin to see my uncle I always make a hasty pilgrimage up the Back Hill to stand again on that slab of granite. I am sure it is important to revisit special places where we have met with God in the past, just as Jacob returned to thank the Lord at Bethel (Genesis 35:1–3).

Otty never wrote her book about revivals – she was too busy having her own! Years later she told me that her renewed relationship with the Lord satisfied her so completely that she stopped pressuring my father for all his time and attention. Once he was free of her nagging demands their marriage became much closer. Since then I've observed others who seem to demand that their spouse should meet all their emotional needs and become very frustrated with them when they are unable, or unwilling, to do so. Once they allow the Lord to meet their unmet needs they often discover that their spouse can release the love that could not be given on demand.

When we returned to Frinton Otty was so full of her 'revival' that the Boss asked the Lord for one, too. The reality of the Holy Spirit is so attractive that the desire for him is as catching as flu – and a great deal more fun! The Boss had always spent the first three hours of the day praying, but suddenly that did not seem long enough so he lengthened it to five, and made it a lifelong rule never to sit down to work at his desk before eleven in the morning.

Seeing my parents getting up early to pray with such apparent enjoyment made me want to do the same, but I could never manage to wake up! Then a sudden cold snap made the hotel's central heating necessary by mid-September. At an early hour each morning my radiator sounded as if two armies of rats were fighting to the death inside it. Finding myself wide awake a full hour and a half before breakfast, I formed the habit of spending that time with the Lord. Probably my parents' example helped me realise that knowing God is not about lovely feelings of ecstasy on Scottish mountains but forming the habit of spending time with God regularly. My father had given me a Bible for my thirteenth birthday and a Scripture Union reading plan to go with it. Since I still could not read, the present had not been a great success, but during those early mornings I used to sit with the Bible open on my lap just chatting to Jesus, enjoying his company. Then, quite suddenly one morning, the words that told a story about him healing a blind man began to make sense, and to everyone's surprise I was able to read the Bible long before I could cope with the simplest of secular books. I owe that radiator an awful lot!

* * *

After that August in Scotland I began going with Otty to the Brethren Assembly on Sunday mornings. My father preferred the parish church because he liked to know what was going to happen next – and that certainly was not the case in the Brethren! They had no minister to lead the Morning Meeting, nor was anyone else asked to preach or read a lesson. Any of the men who were present could announce a hymn, read a passage or give a devotional talk. Musical instruments of any kind were banned, so if some unfortunate little man pitched his chosen hymn too high or low everyone soon ground to a ghastly halt and had to start all over again. Women were not allowed to take part, but one horrendous day Otty took one of the Hildenborough guests with us to the meeting. She had only become a Christian a few days before and in her wild enthusiasm she jumped up, announced a hymn and then stood beaming radiantly round at all our horrified faces. She had also broken the other iron rule by not wearing a hat! My mother had lent her a beret, but she had taken it off, leaving her flaming red hair uncovered.

'What must the angels be thinking!' (1 Corinthians 11:10) hissed the dignified dame on my left as Otty, scarlet with embarrassment, pulled her unfortunate protégé down on to her seat and squashed the beret back on her head. I laughed so much I had to invent a cough so I could make for the door – and Otty thankfully escaped too, followed by the girl still asking when they were going to sing her favourite hymn.

In spite of all the stuffy rules and the appalling singing I loved those Morning Meetings because of Mr Luff. He was definitely one of my 'handful' who really *follow[ed] on to know the LORD* (Hosea 6:3, KJV). I understand what the Bible means when it says that Moses' face 'shone' because he had spent so long with God – Mr Luff's face shone for the same reason. He even looked like my idea of God, with his pure white hair and silky beard to match; but it was the way he worshipped that hangs in my memory. It is difficult to appreciate nowadays just how dreary most church services were in Britain back in the 1950s – before the renewal movement made so many changes in the following decade. In pre-renewal days people of all denominations bowed their heads and reverently closed their eyes when they prayed, and looked stern and serious until they were safely on their way home from church. Not Mr Luff! He sat smiling up at the ceiling throughout the Morning Meeting as if God was up there smiling back at him. When he stood up to 'give a word', love positively oozed out of him as he repeated his favourite theme: 'Seek the Lord for himself and not for what he can do for you – keep your eyes focused on his face and not on his hand. He's looking for people who are desperate for him, consumed by desire for him, obsessed by his love. Not people who fit him into their lives, but people who fit their lives round him.'

Before the First World War Mr Luff had been a footman in a grand London house. After he was converted he travelled the country in a horse-drawn caravan, preaching wherever he went. His life had been so packed with adventure that when Otty wrote his biography it rapidly became a bestseller.

Mr Luff taught me that you do not have to be highly educated to know God; he is not an academic subject but a person. Mr Luff *enjoyed* God in days when fearing him was more fashionable. There was no church youth group for me to attend because I was the only person under thirty who worshipped there, but I can only describe those Sunday mornings as sheer delight, because the Lord himself just poured through Mr Luff's whole personality. As Christians grow older I think we sometimes forget how much we can help younger people simply by infecting them with our own enjoyment of the Lord.

It was not until my own children were all in their teens, with lives full of friends, sport, exams and parties, that it dawned on me what an extraordinary adolescence mine had been. Perhaps when the Lord sees our desire is for intimacy he places us in the kind of situations that will make us cling to his presence to make up for all the other things that we lack.

★ ★ ★

My father had his next major idea when I was sixteen. He had an extremely low boredom threshold and he always maintained that God has the same! He would often say, 'The Lord must get so sick of our church traditions and "we've-always-done-it-this-way" mentality. I think he just moves out of some churches and leaves them to get on with it. Mostly they're so busy with church politics they don't even notice he's missing!' He was an innovator by nature, constantly having some new creative idea for introducing people to Jesus, which made him a front-runner in Christian fashions. Hildenborough Hall had been the first Christian conference centre of its kind, but by the early 1960s he realised that Christians would soon demand holidays abroad so he closed the conference centre at Frinton and began running holidays in Switzerland and Austria. While the rest of the Christian world was still organising mass evangelistic rallies, he had already foreseen their demise and had written a book (*Break-Through*, Hodder & Stoughton, 1970) about home-based cells being the best way to win people for Christ. This was long before house groups became the vogue, and Alpha was not even a twinkle in Nicky Gumbel's eye!

The idea he casually mentioned one morning at breakfast in 1958 was so outrageous even Otty was shocked – and I'm surprised all his office staff did not resign en masse! He had preached many times in all the big cities of the British Isles, but his heart kept going out to people who lived in the more remote parts of the country, which were seldom visited by evangelists.

'I want to preach the gospel within fifty miles of everyone in England, Ireland, Scotland and Wales,' he told us one morning at breakfast, as casually as if he was asking for more toast.

'That would take years,' objected my mother.

'No, we could do it in nine months,' he replied enthusiastically, 'if we organised a meeting in a different centre every night of the week, in two or three key centres in each county. You could do rallies in the afternoons for women,' he added; and then, looking at me, 'You should come with us, Jen-Jen. It would be a great education for you.' Fortunately I'd just been very ill for three months and had lost enough weight to give me the courage to say yes, because he was right: the Mission to Britain was the best education I could possibly have had.

Planning a venture as crazy as that was an organisational nightmare but, as usual, Otty was right at the heart of it; she no longer used a typewriter but dictated letters and promotional articles at a phenomenal rate to her long-suffering secretary, Clare.

Otty's secretaries never stayed with her long: she ran through twenty-one in as many years. They didn't resign because they disliked her but because she was a born matchmaker – they all left to get married! However, my father's PA, Joyce Silcox, worked for him faithfully for twenty-five years, withstanding all Otty's schemes. Joyce and two other remarkable women, Elizabeth Smith and Frances Hay, were really the engine behind everything my parents ever achieved. They were always known as the Old Contemptibles, which is an extremely poor way of describing their hard work and amazing patience! I've often noticed how quick Christians are to put people who achieve great things for God high on pedestals, but how often we fail to notice the even more remarkable people whose hidden industry actually made it all possible.

So the Old Contemptibles, with my mother and Clare, planned the Mission to Britain, and the whole thing was so novel that it caught the imagination of Christians everywhere. St Paul's Cathedral was packed for the valedictory service on 5 October 1958. There were eight of us in the party that set off that night in a minibus, a blue Ford saloon and a motor scooter to visit every corner of Britain. We slept in a different home every night and met a kaleidoscope of fascinating people.

The whole adventure taught me a lot about the British Isles and gave me my lifelong passion for evangelism, but it never quite cured my shyness. In one Welsh town we were entertained to tea by the Mayor himself, complete with gold chain. Usually people were only interested in speaking to my parents and left me in peace, but just as I had bitten into a cheese sandwich the Mayor asked me a friendly question. I was so terrified I choked and nearly died – of embarrassment – as I was vigorously banged on the back. I've given mayors a wide berth ever since!

Wherever we went, huge crowds gathered in town halls, churches or schools. Instead of the usual sombre hymns and funereal organ music that people in those days expected in church, the Boss 'warmed them up' with half an hour of vigorous community singing which he led himself with huge enthusiasm. He was considered even more outrageous when he made people laugh until they cried, but he used to say that it was the tears which opened their hearts. I never got tired of hearing him preach the gospel night after night. He explained the cross so clearly I could never understand how anyone could possibly reject the love of Jesus. At the end of his sermon he always asked anyone who wanted to respond to Christ for the first time to walk up to the front during the last hymn and shake his hand. Sometimes no one moved at first and I would suffer agonies thinking how embarrassed my poor father must feel, standing there waiting all alone. My agonies were usually short-lived, because in most places people poured to the front in such large numbers that there were not enough people to talk and pray with them individually. I will never forget the first night when the Boss came and pulled me out of the pew where I was hiding and asked me to help. Of course I was terrified, but he knew exactly what he was doing when he introduced me to a girl a few years younger than I was.

'My auntie brought me here,' she explained. 'She's lovely because she's got Jesus in her heart. I would so like him to come into mine too.'

When we finally walked out of the building that night, after everyone else had gone home, the Boss asked me: 'How did you get on with that little lass?' I burst into tears as I tried to explain the feeling of intoxicating joy I had felt as I watched her opening herself up to the Holy Spirit.

'There's nothing like it!' he said, beaming at me. 'Even after thirty years it still makes me want to leap eight foot off the ground!'

Not every evening was fruitful, however; some areas of the country were so spiritually hard that, night after night, few responded during the appeal. Wales was particularly difficult, I remember. It was only a few decades since the great Welsh revival, and many people could still remember it so vividly that it was as if all their spiritual clocks had stopped when the revival had ended, as abruptly as it had begun. Back then, in the 1950s, people were still talking endlessly about the wonderful experiences of the past rather than allowing themselves to enjoy God in the present. 'Disappointing meeting,' they would say dolefully after my father had preached his heart out. 'Not like the old days.'

My mother soon became so frustrated with this 'revival fixation', as she called it, that she told an astounded group at one women's meeting it was time they all stopped praying for another revival and started praying for their friends and neighbours instead. 'It's no wonder you're always complaining no one's been converted round here for years!' Like most teenagers I was often deeply embarrassed by my mother!

One of the most important things I learnt from the Mission to Britain was just how vital prayer really is. Each evening we could always tell, before the end of the first hymn, if local Christians had really been interceding. However efficient the organisation had been, without prayer the Lord just did not speak to people and draw them to his heart.

Up in the north of Scotland we had a whole run of five very difficult events culminating in the small town of Stonehaven. 'Don't try and go there,' my father had been told. 'No evangelical organisations ever survive in Stonehaven – even the Salvation Army gave up and left.' If the Boss was to complete his task of preaching within fifty miles of everyone in the British Isles he needed to go to Stonehaven, but not a single minister or layman was willing to organise an event. So he sent one of his assistants, Tony Groom, on ahead to put up posters and try and raise some local enthusiasm. Poor Tony had a terrible time and reported that all the various congregations seemed, as he put it, to be 'dying gently in their sleep while their ministers are busy fighting each other'. The meeting in Stonehaven Town Hall was the smallest and most difficult of the whole tour, and as we drove away I remember my father saying sadly, 'This is a God-forsaken hole.'

Thirty-six years later I received a letter asking if I would go and speak at an outreach event in the north of Scotland. 'We would so love to hear the amazing story of how God healed you, after those eight years in the wheelchair,' said the letter.

I always love telling that story, and their offer of a flight to Aberdeen was most tempting, so I wrote straight back saying yes before I had spent time praying over the invitation. My healing was still so recent that my enthusiasm often led me into trouble! However, as soon as I had posted the letter I began to feel uneasy. They had asked me to speak in the Town Hall, Stonehaven, and for some reason I was experiencing a nasty sense of déja vu. Then I remembered! Just to make sure, I climbed into the attic and dug out my father's diary for 1959; he always kept a meticulous journal, describing everything he did each day (modelling himself on his patron saint, John Wesley). When I found the entry he had made the night of the rally in Stonehaven I bitterly regretted my hasty decision to go back there again. His rude comments are quite unrepeatable but he must have felt considerably better after he had written them down!

When I finally arrived in the 'God-forsaken hole' I found the Town Hall packed with people who had all been prayed for, and invited, by Christians from all the churches in town. There was such an overwhelming sense of God's power and presence that people would probably have been blessed if I had simply recited the alphabet! At the end so many found faith in Christ for the first time that I thought, 'God-forsaken hole, my foot!'

Later that night I told my host and hostess about the awful things my father had written about their town. 'He was badly wrong!' I laughed.

'Oh no!' they assured me. 'That is *exactly* how it used to be when we moved here in the early 1960s. We were only just married and we wondered why God had sent us to somewhere so spiritually cold and dead.'

'Do you know what caused the change?' I asked curiously.

'Oh yes!' they both said at once. 'One day we were asked to visit an old lady no one else seemed to have time for; she was totally bedridden, crippled by arthritis, but utterly radiant. She told us that the Lord had laid a deep burden on her heart for the town and she spent hours every day praying for it. She used to spread a street map out on her bed-table and, with one twisted old finger, she would "walk" round every street praying for everyone who lived there. She would "stop" for a long time outside each church, crying to the Lord to revive the congregation and send them new leaders who were on fire for him.'

'She died before anything changed,' went on the husband. 'Only three of us went to her funeral, but *oh* how we've seen her prayers answered since then! All the churches are thriving now and working together wonderfully for the Lord.'

Sometimes I imagine the surprise we'll get one day when we arrive in heaven – those of us who have spent our lives dashing round organising church activities, running special events and feeling totally indispensable to the Almighty. When we get 'Up There' we'll discover, to our astonishment, that it was the prayers of that little old lady we hardly noticed that actually achieved far more than all our frenzied activity ever could.

Nowadays I am often asked to speak in places I remember visiting during that whistle-stop tour, and it always makes me feel excited to realise how wonderfully God has revived his Church in Britain since the 1950s. It humbles me to realise how he has brought *me* to life since then, too!

I was speaking in a church in Bath not long ago and suddenly 'saw myself', aged sixteen, hiding in the shadows at the back, hoping no one would speak to me, while my parents counselled the converts in the aisles. I had been astounded that night, walking back to our lodgings in one of Bath's regency terraces, when the Boss had suddenly said, 'Jen-Jen, the thing I most want you to do in life is to become a Bible teacher.'

My reaction was to think, 'Doesn't he realise I can scarcely read? I couldn't study all the commentaries he wades through and I'm far too shy to speak in public!' The Boss died long before I became a conference speaker or a writer of Bible-reading notes, but I guess he often sits in heaven now, enjoying the way God can use even the most unlikely people.

★ ★ ★

After the Mission to Britain I never went back into my safe prison. Instead I seemed to spend most of my life on the golf course, caddying for my mother. A few years previously Otty's doctor had suggested that she should take up golf to improve her heart condition and also to provide relaxation. It certainly kept her fit but I am not sure it relaxed her much, because she played with the same passion with which she did everything else and never reached the eighteenth hole without first having shared her faith with her partner. Once I remember wishing the bunker would swallow me when an exasperated county player exclaimed: 'Jean, for God's sake don't start converting me until we've got to the nineteenth hole!'

The Boss loathed the very thought of any form of relaxation. 'There's plenty of time for that in heaven,' he would say and he'd go on to quote Jeremiah: '*Within me there is something like a burning fire shut up in my bones*' (Jeremiah 20:19, NRSV). Perhaps it was no wonder he died of a heart attack aged fifty-eight! While he hatched his next crazy scheme for furthering the gospel I caddied for Otty until we discovered, to our joint surprise, that I was quite good at the game myself. My stunted self-esteem experienced a growth spurt when I became the Essex Girl Champion; and soon afterwards I even mustered enough confidence to start work in a day nursery caring for disturbed children.

★ ★ ★

It was the week before I started that job that I saw my first angel – but I have to admit he was heavily disguised.

Ever since the days when I could wander about undisturbed in that beautiful Kentish garden, I have always taken myself off for a

84

long, solitary walk whenever I want to talk to the Lord about something important. It's just that I feel closest to him when I am alone in beautiful places. So during a rare family holiday in Switzerland I packed a picnic and set off to hike through a lonely valley so I could chat to him about this new chapter in my life.

I was enjoying my lunch in the shelter of some rocks by a stream when I had the uneasy feeling I was being watched. Looking up, I saw the face of a man leering down at me, and I was not too naive to read the expression on his face. I sent up a quick prayer for help and scrambled hastily to my feet, but the man was moving closer. 'I wish I had a dog,' I thought, and then decided to pretend I had. I whistled and shouted so convincingly that my would-be assailant pulled back into the pine trees while I walked on down the path as confidently as I could. Naturally he soon realised I was bluffing and came up behind me – fast! Just then a large, mangy-looking mongrel came out of the trees beside the path and walked along beside me, to heel, until we were out of the forest and I caught sight of some farmers haymaking in a field. When I bent to pat my rescuer he had totally vanished.

It was that incident that led to my lifelong interest in angels (*An Angel Called Mervin*, Zondervan, 1999). I'm sure they surround us all the time, but we don't realise we can see them because we expect angels to look like potbellied babies without nappies or anorexic adolescents with long blond hair! Actually I believe they prefer to appear to us looking like ordinary human beings.

I was once driving alone to speak at a conference at Lee Abbey when I got lost in a blizzard on the top of Exmoor. It was dark when my car ground to a halt in a snowdrift, and I've often wondered if the scruffy-looking farmer in the Land Rover that pulled straight up behind me was actually an angel. I was sure no one had been following me and, once he had towed me back to civilisation, he disappeared just as suddenly. The police were adamant that not even a Land Rover could have pulled my car through those lanes to safety that night.

Perhaps angels need to help us 'incognito' because seeing one in all their splendour is so terrifying! I got a major fright quite recently when I saw one looking like a warrior with a sharp sword and rippling muscles. He suddenly appeared on the last day of the most difficult conference I have ever had to run. Numerous problems had hit us right from the start, and I felt quite exhausted as I sat, early in the morning, praying about the final talk I had to give later that day. Dawn sunlight was streaming in through the window when I saw him take shape. We didn't speak; he just stood there, head bent, leaning on his sword like a soldier returning from battle. I sensed the Lord was saying the conference had been this angel's assignment and he had been busy fighting the powers of evil on our behalf all week.

Perhaps it is more comfortable all round when God sends invisible 'ministering spirits' (Hebrews 1:14). I am still convinced it was an unseen angel who saved my life on another occasion when I was driving through the countryside. The road was so straight that I was tempted to drive far too fast as I approached a humpbacked bridge over a railway line. Suddenly I was hit by an inexplicable sense of terror and stood on my brakes, convinced I was about to have a head-on crash. I felt such a fool when I screeched to a halt on the top of the bridge and saw the road was totally empty in both directions! On the way home, later the same day, I was speeding once again, but as I reached the bridge I remembered the fright I'd had and slowed down to a crawl. At the top of the slope an idiot in a yellow sports car was recklessly overtaking a lorry, and I only just managed to stop in time to avoid the crash that would have been inevitable if I had been driving any faster.

★ ★ ★

It was while the Boss was repeating the Mission to Britain all over Canada that Grandpa became seriously ill with lung cancer and Otty and I flew home to see him. Most of his other seven children were already assembled at the farm in Sussex for what I can only describe as a Grand Deathbed Scene worthy of a Victorian novel. Grandpa had completely controlled their entire lives, but as he lay there, surrounded by his descendants, it was hard to believe he had always been so terrifying. He was a man who had once set out to know God intimately; when he was a young man, working in his father's Newcastle tobacco factory, he spent his spare time running missions for dockers and miners, leading hundreds of them to Christ, but as his success in business increased he gradually changed. He still went to the Brethren Morning Meeting but the intensity of his love for God was blunted.

His enormous wealth gave him power over most people he encountered, but my father had always been the exception. The Boss consistently refused to benefit financially because he had married a rich man's daughter, and although Grandpa was very generous to my mother, they never had a joint bank account: her money was hers and the Boss lived on fresh air and the gifts he received during his annual preaching tour in the States. His independence infuriated Grandpa, who liked to feel he had everyone under his thumb and was often scathing in his criticism of his outrageous son-in-law. I sometimes wonder if he was actually jealous. When you have enjoyed a close relationship with God, anything the world has to offer feels like second best.

God, however, has a way of never abandoning people who have once set their hearts on course to know him, and Grandpa was no exception to that rule. A few years before that magnificent deathbed scene something happened to him which always helps me to pray in faith for Christians who seem to have lost their thirst for God. I was probably about fifteen when Otty decided to take Justyn and me up to Glenluffin for the New Year. I was not at all keen to go once I knew Grandpa was going to be there too, but soon realised he had changed. Instead of being a remote, disapproving tyrant he spent hours with us playing carpet bowls up and down the vast expanse of his drawing-room floor – and he actually seemed to be enjoying himself! Later, Otty explained why he was so different. While he had been on a tobacco-buying trip to Virginia he had been taken seriously ill with pneumonia and for several days his recovery seemed unlikely. He was actually in a coma when he had a mysterious encounter with God, and as soon as he was strong enough to travel home (in a first-class cabin on the *Queen Mary*) he asked my father to come and see him. What they said to each other no one knows this side of heaven, but he became one of the Boss's most ardent admirers and enjoyed nothing better than hearing him preach. The journey he had begun as a young man may have taken a bit of a detour but he was firmly on course by the time he died a few years later.

We all know that success and financial prosperity can be Hold-Up Factors in our journey towards total dependence on God, while hardship seems to accelerate our progress marvellously. Yet, in spite of knowing that, most of us still seem to get angry with God when he allows difficult things to hit our lives!

I could never say, however, that financial prosperity *necessarily* destroys intimacy, because of Granny. Grandpa's millions never changed her one iota, and instead of playing bridge or giving cocktail parties she spent most of her time praying. As soon as she knew another grandchild was on the way she began what she called 'paying into their spiritual bank account', and it is an undeniable fact that an abnormally high proportion of her ninety descendants have lived peaceful, happy lives, and most are actively following the Lord. After she died in 1984 Justyn and I looked through her old Bible and found one particular verse she had underlined many times over: *'Arise, cry out in the night ... pour out thine heart like water before the face of the LORD ... for the life of thy young children'* (Lamentations 2:19, KJV). We knew she had always slept badly, but that day Justyn and I realised how much we, and our children, had benefited from those sleepless nights.

It has always been a mystery to me how someone as unmaterialistic as Granny survived all those years with Grandpa; but I do know that she gave away his money as fast as he made it! My aunt recently told me how Granny often went through his wallet when he was not looking, removing large wads of notes that she happily gave away the following day. Shopping with her in Highgate village was quite an experience, because every time she caught sight of a shabbily dressed woman she would surreptitiously slip a bunch of five-pound notes into her hand.

★ ★ ★

We finally left Frinton in 1963 and I can't say I was sorry! Last year I was asked to speak at a conference in Frinton's parish church. I knew there was no way I could do that until I had spent most of the previous night walking round all the roads where I had once walked my dog secretly after dark during my 'prison years'. I needed to repent of all the negative thoughts and feelings I'd had about the town in case any bitterness in me would shortcircuit the Lord's blessing. By the following morning I saw Frinton in a very different light, and by the end of the weekend I realised what a delightful place it actually is!

We moved back to Kent because my parents had decided that there was only one thing worse than running a conference centre, and that was *not* running one! So, after several years of organising holiday conferences abroad, they were busy setting up Hildenborough Mark Three. It was a smaller and much more luxurious centre, and because it was only twenty-four miles from the middle of London they hoped to run weekend retreats for professional and business people. Otty bought herself a nearby farmhouse, and at long last we had a family home of our own. I will never forget her infectious joy as we opened the tea chests that had been in store since we left our West Country cottage eighteen years before. Best of all, Gom was there to help us unpack! Otty's heart condition had become considerably worse by that time, so Gom had moved in to become her full-time nurse/housekeeper/cook and golf caddy (Otty's bad heart was never allowed to spoil her golf!).

There is no way I could possible describe how lovely life was at Shorehill Farm. Suddenly all the people I loved best were close to me again. Justyn lived at home while studying hotel management in London and my other greatly loved grandmother, Lolo, moved into a cottage next door. Coming home from work (in the nursery class of a prep school) to the comforting sound of Gom clattering around in the kitchen making a batch of cakes settled something which had been left unresolved inside me for years. We both secretly decided that nothing would ever part us again.

Justyn had hated school quite as much as I had, but he obviously had more courage because he endured prep and public school right to the bitter end. He always maintains it was his guitar that made that possible. When he was fourteen he blew all his holiday pocket money one Easter, and bought himself a battered Spanish guitar from a junk shop for four pounds ten shillings. 'I'll give you a week before you're sick of that,' I told him acidly as he shut himself in his bedroom to teach himself to play it.

However, the twanging discords that at first had set my teeth on edge improved so rapidly that I soon had to admit he had a remarkable natural gift. When other boys were swotting or playing rugby (or rugger, as it was called) he was in a soundproof music room composing songs, which he sang with the beautiful voice he had inherited from the Boss. When he came home to live I began joining in by adding little bits of backing harmony, and one day when we were practising the Boss must have heard us, because he suddenly burst into the room. We thought we had disturbed him so we both jumped up, apologising (teenagers did that kind of thing in those days), but all he said was, 'Go on – it's *lovely!*'

When the song was finished he said, 'How about you getting together a little guitar group and leading the singing at the City Temple?' His venture for that winter was a series of rallies exclusively for young people in the beautiful new church that had been built on Holborn Viaduct, just off Fleet Street.

We both looked at him in astonishment. 'Guitars? In church?'

we said. 'You can't be serious!' Nowadays, when most churches have a music group to lead at least some of the worship, it is hard to visualise a time when Christians honestly thought the *only* way to worship God was by singing Victorian hymns accompanied by an equally antique organ.

'If you use guitars for the meetings, won't people criticise you?' I asked doubtfully.

'Of course they will!' laughed the Boss. 'Didn't you know criticising other people is a Christian's favourite hobby? But their other hobby is copying other people. You'll see, they'll all want guitars in their churches soon!'

As usual, he was right, but I have to admit it was at least a year before he allowed us to risk adding drums to our group!

We called ourselves The Peacemakers, and apart from a Salvation Army quartet called The Joy Strings we were the first Christian guitar group in Britain. Justyn's songs were such a hit at the City Temple that we were soon being asked to sing all over the country at youth services, college Christian Unions and outreach events. There were five boys in the group and me, and how we managed to hold down our jobs or keep up with our studies I can't imagine, as we spent most nights in our old diesel van travelling back from gigs. There is one spot on the M1 that I can never drive past without laughing. It was well after midnight when the van's radiator boiled dry and we ground to a halt. The boys scrambled up the embankment and found a convenient pond, but they had nothing that would hold the water. So they dashed back and seized my much-loved hat before I had the chance to protest! We had been singing in a Brethren Assembly Hall that evening so I had needed it – but I never wore it again!

We used to take it in turns to introduce each song because we wanted to share our faith as well as entertain our audiences. A lifestyle like that should have cured my shyness, but I still suffered agonies when it was my turn to speak. In spite of the almost constant terror, it was in those Peacemaker days that I first tasted the joy of standing up in front of a sea of strange faces, knowing

I had nothing to say but suddenly feeling God begin to speak through me. All I had to do was be his ventriloquist's dummy as I watched the extraordinary effect the Lord's words were having on the audience.

The Beatles were all the rage then, so the boys in the group had Beatle haircuts – all except one. He was a huge blond rugby player called Tony, a student teacher, and he and I detested each other. He thought I was a pious prig and I thought he was an arrogant lout; we were probably both right! For months we travelled round the country in the back of that smelly old van, quarrelling violently.

Then, late one night after singing in the Central Hall, Westminster, we were all squashed into a friend's bedsit unwinding with mugs of hot chocolate. Tony suddenly took out his leather wallet and wrote a note on a tiny piece of paper. Rolling it into a ball he threw it across the room at me. Thinking it was yet another invitation to do battle, I opened it, and I can still hear the violins that began to play in my head.

'You look very beautiful tonight,' said the note. Most girls have received that kind of compliment before they are twenty-one but the novelty knocked me sideways. If evangelical Christians had not been teetotal in those days I might have blamed the beer!

A few days later, when he asked me out for my very first date, my wretched shyness nearly ruined everything. We no longer wanted to quarrel so I couldn't think of anything to say; fortunately the crispy meatballs salvaged the evening. They were so excessively crispy that every time we put our forks into them they shot off our plates, rolling all over the polished floor while the smart Chinese waiters ran after them, bowing their apologies.

On the way home that night something happened which convinced me that Tony was the man I wanted to marry. My mother had given me a car for my twenty-first (thanks to Grandpa) but unfortunately it broke down right in the middle of the newly opened Dartford Tunnel.

'Do you have a safety pin?' asked Tony. In those days of

elasticated knickers all girls carried a safety pin as an insurance policy, so he soon had his head in the car bonnet. How the safety pin got the engine going again before the police arrived to fine me for blocking the tunnel I still do not know, but I was deeply impressed.

After a few very successful dates I wrote him my first (and last) love letter. The following day he sent it back to me with all my spelling mistakes underlined in red pen. He said he wanted to help me, but when I remembered how much humiliation I had suffered at the hands of teachers I wondered how on earth I could ever have let myself fall in love with one!

★　★　★

One evening, when we were setting up our musical equipment in a youth club, the world began to swirl around me alarmingly, and a few days later I was lying seriously ill in London's National Hospital with viral encephalitis. Practically unable to speak, see or move, I lay wondering how Tony would feel about me now that the doctors could not guarantee a full recovery. Many young men would have abandoned a girlfriend who might have to spend her life in a wheelchair – but not Tony.

'I've been wanting to buy you an engagement ring for ages,' he said when he came striding down the ward at visiting time 'My college grant just won't run to it yet, so how about having this in the meantime?' Taking the cuff link out of his shirt, he put it into my hand and closed my limp fingers around it. I hardly put it down for weeks and always slept with it under my pillow.

His love gave me the will to live and his encouragement helped me to fight the effects of the disease – which is an inflammation of the brain, similar to meningitis but usually even more serious. I was not able to go back to work for a year, so I might well have died of boredom if Tony had not made a suggestion one day which sounded quite ridiculous to me at first.

'You always seem to be telling yourself stories inside your head, so while you're sitting about with nothing to do, why don't you write a children's book?'

'What, *me?*' I replied incredulously, thinking of Miss Mitchell's blistering words.

'You can type,' he pointed out. 'Just bash the story out, then I'll correct the spellings and you can make a fair copy.' He not only did that but also spent patient hours listening as I read my efforts aloud. 'You ought to start that chapter halfway through,' he would say, or, 'This bit's dragging, speed the pace – cut the description.' When the book was finally published I think Tony was even more delighted than I was!

One of my father's more irritating sayings was a quote from an old lady he used to visit in an almshouse: 'The Good Lord knows what 'e's a'doin' of.' He would always trot it out when Otty had lost a golf match or I'd ripped my new dress, but the saying proved true when it came to Tony's red pen! I know I could never have become a writer without his help.

6

Moses said to the LORD . . . show me now Your way that I may know
You, progressively become more deeply and intimately acquainted with
You, perceiving and recognising and understanding more strongly and
clearly and that I may find favour in Your sight.

Exodus 33:13, AMP

When we finally decided to exchange the unofficial cuff link for
a proper engagement ring the Boss was not pleased. He could not
bring himself to talk to me about it but expressed his feelings in
a letter. He had been wise enough to keep quiet about how he
felt while we had been going out with each other, but his letter
said that he felt he would be failing as a father if he let us get
married without telling me that he just did not feel Tony would
make me happy. I was travelling on the top of a double-decker
bus when I read the letter and I remember feeling as if I had been
plunged into an ice-cold bath. I was extremely close to my father,
in fact I adored him, but my love for Tony had become all-
consuming. It may be difficult to believe, but it happens to be
true, that I had never done anything to upset the Boss since the
incident in the bath when I attacked Nanny. Soon after that
unfortunate episode I made that vow in the terrace rose garden
always to be 'very very good' in order to win my father's love and

approval. Perhaps if I'd had a normal, healthy teenage I might have tested my boundaries by trying to discover what would happen if I was 'very very bad' for a change; but this disagreement over Tony was the first thing that had ever come between us.

It always strikes me as odd how we build ourselves a photo-fit picture of God looking exactly like our parents (or other adults who were important in our childhood). If they were strict, cruel or uninterested we grow up thinking God must be just the same. I am sure those inaccurate mental portraits are responsible for so many people not wanting to get too close to God, let alone burrow into his heart. However, it is not just bad parents who give us faulty concepts of the Almighty; good ones, like my father, can do it too. To me God was just a larger-sized version of the Boss, so subconsciously I still thought that if 'very very good' behaviour would win the love of my human father, the same must apply to God. As I caught the next bus home I felt I was about to lose both my earthly and my heavenly fathers in one go! Frankly, I did not care so long as I did not lose Tony.

Fortunately, I need not have worried. When I finally walked into the Boss's study, visibly shaking, he simply put down his pen and said, 'Don't worry, Jen-Jen, I'll love you just the same whatever you do, and you'll always have my help and support.' Strangely, I found it easier to accept my father's unconditional love than God's, and like so many other Christians I went on for years unable to realise that there was nothing I could do that would make him love me any more and nothing I could do that would make him love me any less.

The Boss organised the wedding with his usual meticulous care (and the help of the Old Contemptibles), even though my mother made their job slightly difficult by inviting over a thousand guests!

'Half of them won't come,' she said airily, but they did! She always loved Tony and so did Granny; but when I took him to Highgate to meet her, the State Visit was almost a disaster. For the first time in her life Granny was living alone, and it was pathetic to see her trying to manage without the help of all those efficient maids. After much frenzied pottering in the kitchen she managed to make us a pot of Earl Grey tea and even produced a Lyon's chocolate cake. I was dieting to get into my wedding dress so she cut Tony an extra large slice. As he was doing his best not to choke on the China tea, which he loathed, he realised the cake was moving about on his plate. She must have had it in the tin for months because it was literally crawling with maggots! Rather than upsetting her, he nobly besmirched his best suit by easing the cake into his pocket and then sat for an hour imagining the maggots working their way into his underpants!

On Saturday 6 August 1966 the guests who were attending the Hildenborough conference were asked to leave by ten o'clock and the next conference were told not to arrive before five; our wedding reception slotted neatly in between. The Boss said later it was the worst day of his life, but no one would ever have guessed. Two years later he wrote me another letter; it simply said, 'I can see how happy you are. I guess I was wrong about Tony, perhaps he just took a bit of getting to know.' He wasn't often wrong, but actually Tony was a loving, gentle husband and devoted father who made us all totally happy during the thirty years we had together.

Apart from his passion for cricket, Tony and I liked all the same things, so my childhood ambition to live in the country, keep chickens and have lots of children fitted his agenda perfectly. My mother, taking a leaf out of Grandpa's book, bought us a house for a wedding present, but unlike him she did not insist we lived close to home, so we settled just outside a Hertfordshire village near to the school where Tony had his first teaching post.

'The Good Lord knew' better than to match me with an A-level English teacher, but who could be more ideal than a husband who worked with children who had dyslexia and school phobia? He was brilliant at his job because he had a way of planting confidence in people who had been crushed by other teachers and then tenderly nurturing that confidence until his pupils discovered their own special abilities. His success with 'impossible cases' was widely recognised – and he did a pretty good job with my education too! He thought everything I did and said was wonderful, which built my self-esteem quite marvellously, and seeing I thought exactly the same about him we got on famously.

Gom came to Hertfordshire with us, too, leaving my mother in the capable hands of her latest secretary, Roberta, who was happy to add to her typewriting skills the role of housekeeper and caddy. Gom found a residential job cooking in a nearby care home and waited with happy expectation for us to produce a baby for her. I could never have coped with my six children, particularly during my wheelchair years, without her, but we could never have paid her for all she did. So she financed herself by part-time cooking jobs and sacrificial economy. However, she was often a hilarious liability! We had not been in the village for more than a week when I asked her to take two black sacks of rubbish to the council tip on her way home one evening. Gom, with her usual disregard for convention, merely threw them into the ditch that surrounded the immaculate village green. To our total horror the village bobby rode up to our house on his bike the following day. He had found a letter addressed to us in one of the sacks, and his comments about 'incomers' were so scathing that our hopes of being accepted by the local community were dashed. Once I began to look pregnant, however, we were definitely 'in'.

★ ★ ★

It must have rained sometimes during the next fourteen years or Tony would never have grown all his wonderful flowers and vegetables, but all my memories of that time are bathed in continuous golden sunlight.

Never for a moment did I miss life on the edge of my parents' limelight; I had found my niche as a housewife and mother, and I was content to stay in it for the rest of my life.

It was during those golden years, however, that my journey into God's heart all but ground to a halt. Happiness doesn't *need* to have that effect, but when the role, the possession or the person that brings you the happiness becomes more important to you than God himself he gets squeezed out; and when you achieve a heaven-on-earth existence, 'laying up treasures in heaven' seems slightly unnecessary (Matthew 6:19–20). My home, Tony and the babies who arrived with delightful regularity definitely took centre place in my world. As my brother so rightly said, when your need for God is paramount, that is when you really know him; so it follows that when you least need him, because other things are meeting your innermost needs, then your desire to know him fades. To be honest, I believe I idolised Tony throughout our marriage, to the point where I relied on him for everything. Sometimes God can sound very harsh and demanding because he insists that we put him first in our lives, but he does that because it is the only way to save us from the painful disappointment of putting all our trust in a human being. However much they may love us and however deeply committed they may be to caring for us, even the best human beings die or become ill – and in spite of all those romantic songs, human love doesn't always last for ever. It is easy to see all that in retrospect, but probably if someone had warned me at the time I would have taken no notice – few of us ever do!

We went to the sweet little church on the village green because that was all part of our 'pretty Christmas card' existence, but God himself had become a mere accessory – like a Sunday-best hat. The nice enjoyable things of life had buried the greater joy I had once known through intimacy with him. How terrifyingly easy it is to lose something so profoundly precious.

★ ★ ★

Every time I look at my watch and see that it says 6.45 in the morning I still shudder. That was the time when the phone rang one April morning in 1970. We had moved back to Kent by then, with our first two children, because Tony had been offered a promotion. The phone call was from Justyn, who with his wife Joy was working in a Christian conference centre in Canada. He told me that our father had just died of a heart attack in New York and asked me to go at once and break the news to Otty, our grandmother Lolo and the Hildenborough community.

'This will give Otty a heart attack too!' I thought desperately as I drove up to Shorehill Farm. Actually her vivid imagination had caused her to live through this awful moment hundreds of times already – whenever the Boss was late home. She had often prayed that when the dreaded moment actually arrived the Lord would help her to react in the right way. He certainly answered that prayer. She was sitting up in bed, with her dictating machine on her lap, happily working on her latest book when I burst in, but all she said was, '*The LORD gave and the LORD has taken away; blessed be the name of the LORD*' (Job 1:21, NKJV).

It was more difficult telling Lolo: the Boss had been a devoted son to her. By the time I'd seen the Old Contemptibles and everyone else at Hildenborough I felt like a mangled wreck. The only bright spot of that dreadful day was when I told Gom the news. She shook her head and muttered darkly, 'That's what 'appens if you go to New York!'

Poor Justyn had a far worse job than I did; he had to identify the body in a dismal New York morgue. The Boss had been on one of his American tours and had preached twice that day, then collapsed and died instantly on his way to see an old friend. That was exactly the kind of death he would most have wanted, because he always dreaded becoming too old to preach the gospel. However, his sudden departure plunged the rest of us into the middle of a crisis. What should we do about the massive 'Time for Truth' mission the Boss was about to run in London, and who would organise the summer programme of conferences at Hildenborough?

Being at the centre of this swirl of planning helped Otty through the first week, but she was vastly relieved to discover that the Boss, with characteristic efficiency, had already made all the necessary plans. He and Justyn had spent hours talking and praying together only a few months before. Their plan was that Justyn should add some experience to his degree in hotel management in various Canadian conference centres before eventually taking over the running of Hildenborough. The Boss's death merely accelerated the plan, and Justyn and Joy flew straight back to take over everything with quite remarkable success.

Once she had planned the memorial service Otty suddenly felt she had nothing more to do, and she began to drown in grief from which, tragically, she never recovered. She wrote just one more book, the Boss's biography (*His Name was Tom*, Hodder & Stoughton, 1971), but then all her creativity died. She never painted again and even golf was beyond her. Watching her enduring her last ten years was one of the hardest things Justyn and I have ever had to do. However much we tried, we never succeeded in making her happy, nor could we convince her that life was anything but weary and pointless.

For a while after the Boss died Tony and I lived up at Shorehill Farm to be with Otty and Lolo, and I was so busy I probably put my own grief on hold – but grief always hits you eventually. One morning I woke up knowing that God did not exist; it was as if someone had switched the light off inside my soul. When friends tried to comfort me by talking about heaven and the Boss waiting there for us until we joined him, I used to think, 'How ridiculous! All that stuff is just an invention to keep people from going off their heads with hopelessness!' My faith had never been rattled by doubts before, but because I had always so closely associated the Boss with God, the one seemed unable to exist without the other. Actually, because of my training as a bereavement counsellor, I now realise that shock can temporarily rob a Christian of faith, but no one told me that at the time. So for weeks I went plodding on through each bleak day, enclosing my children in such a rigid nursery routine that Nanny would have been proud of me; but inside I was dead.

Then one night I had a dream. I hardly ever remember my dreams but this one was so vivid I will never forget it; in fact I've often wondered if it was a dream at all. I was lying next to Tony in our double bed when the door suddenly opened and the Boss walked in and sat down on the bed beside me. He was wearing his favourite brown suit and tie and he looked well and happy.

'I've been sent to tell you something very important,' he said. 'You are finding it hard to believe that heaven exists so I've come to assure you that it definitely does! It's wonderful and I'm so enjoying it all, but the extent to which a person enjoys heaven depends on how they live on earth. Remember this: "Only one life, it will soon be past; only what's done for God will last."' Then he was gone.

In the morning I was too choked up to tell Tony anything about it, but all day that little phrase kept buzzing round and round in my head. 'Only one life, it will soon be past; only what's done for God will last.' I had never heard those words before but they were impossible to forget. That evening we were undressing for bed when Tony said, 'Do you ever get a tune stuck in your head, and it goes round and round all day until you could scream?'

I said that often happened to me, so he added, 'I haven't had a tune on the brain today but I keep hearing these words, "Only one life, it will soon be past; only what's done for God will last."' Of course I burst into tears of sheer astonishment because, to me, the fact that Tony had 'heard' the words, albeit subconsciously, seemed to indicate that they really had been 'sent from above' and had not merely been conjured up by my imagination.

Something even more curious happened the following day. Justyn rang me to say he had been sorting through the Boss's papers in his study when he had just discovered a letter addressed to 'Jennifer and Justyn, only to be opened after my death'. He had written it shortly after his own father had died, some years before. This is part of what Justyn read to me over the phone: 'When you are finally shot of me, remember this: "Only one life, it will soon be past; only what's done for God will last."'

The Boss did not leave us anything in his will because all he owned were his clothes and books; but those few words contained what he considered to be the most valuable inheritance any father would leave his children.

When I made my will recently I wrote the same message to my children, but with one small change: 'Only one life, it will soon be past; only *your love* for God will last.' To me that seems to emphasise the fact that our relationship with God is infinitely more important than anything we could do for him, and the tiny change in the wording reflects the enormous change in Christian culture during the last four decades.

★　★　★

If Otty had continued to live on their doorstep Justyn and Joy would never have been free to run Hildenborough in their own way, so Tony and I took her and Lolo off their hands by asking them both to come and live with us. That is not quite as horrific as it sounds, because we had found a very old house in the country near a village called Paddock Wood, where Tony was teaching in the primary school. It had originally been one long farmhouse but had later been divided into two. Otty moved into one end and we made a little ground floor flat for Lolo at the other end. We were somewhat squashed in the middle section, but it actually worked extremely well – or it would have done if the house had not been haunted!

While we were still revelling in the old beams and the inglenook fireplace, a neighbour from down the lane came to have coffee with us. 'Have you seen the ghost yet?' she asked casually.

'Don't say any more!' said Otty, quite aggressively. 'I'm not going to have fears like that planted in our minds.'

'Suit yourselves,' said the neighbour huffily – and she never returned our hospitality!

These days, when spiritual warfare is talked about freely, I would never dream of moving into a house without first praying in every room, not only asking for God's blessing but also his cleansing from any past contamination from contact with the occult. Sometimes there is nothing evil to oust, but previous owners might have left behind an atmosphere of sadness. When we moved into that gorgeous old house our side felt wonderfully happy to me, so when Sarah, our four-year-old, began talking about the 'grey people who live upstairs' I told myself she had inherited the vivid imagination that runs in the family.

As the weeks went by Otty became increasingly unwell, but the doctor merely said, 'She's grieving. Depression like this is quite normal for new widows.' So when she kept saying she heard footsteps walking round the house at night and someone knocking on her bedroom door, we just made soothing noises that must have infuriated her! Eventually we found her a companion/housekeeper, but the poor woman left after only two days, insisting that someone had tried to pull her out of bed in the night. Tony merely shrugged and said: 'She must have been nutty as a fruitcake.'

One cold winter afternoon I was out for a walk with the children when we met the man from whom we had bought the house a year before.

'How are you getting on?' he asked, rather nervously I thought.

'Mostly we're fine,' I replied, 'but my mother's been feeling a bit down.'

'Oh dear!' he said ominously. 'I was worried that might happen.'

'Whatever do you mean?' I demanded.

'Since the turn of the century everyone who has ever owned that end of the house has become mentally ill.'

'But *you've* been OK,' I protested.

'Yes, but the house was in my wife's name and she's been in hospital for some years now. Has your mother heard footsteps, and someone knocking on her door?'

I admitted that she had, and he then explained that the man

who had owned the house seventy years before had 'worshipped Satan and got mixed up in all kinds of funny things. Since then someone in every family has always gone mad.'

I hastened to assure him that my mother was far from mad, just a bit depressed after a bereavement, but he went off shaking his head and saying, 'You can believe it or not as you like, but at least I warned you.'

When I told the story to Tony he roared with laughter. He was always far too practical and down to earth to believe in the supernatural. 'Don't you dare tell your mother,' was his only comment.

Then the smell began. We thought it must be the drains and had an inspector out to take a look; nothing was wrong, but every evening at dusk the obnoxious stink, like rotting corpses, enveloped the whole property. Poor Otty used to sit by her television all evening with a hanky pressed to her nose and her fur coat wrapped round her head, even in high summer, because of the ice-cold draughts.

'You must remember to close your windows,' I would tell her crossly when she complained about yet another stiff neck.

'But I never open the windows because of the smell!' she would protest tearfully. I was sorry I had been so unsympathetic when I was watching the television with her one hot, airless evening. Without any warning her whole window, frame and glass, blew right out into the garden! If I had not seen it I would never have believed such a thing could happen. Unfortunately Tony did *not* see it, so he merely said, 'The frame must have been more rotten than it looked.'

The following week, when the replacement window met with the same eerie fate, I knew I had to take action so I asked the vicar to call round. I could see he agreed with Tony that the whole thing was a series of coincidences, but to keep me happy he began to pray in Otty's bedroom (she by this time had been admitted to a psychiatric nursing home for a month's rest). As the vicar began to pray the smell completely choked both of us and he positively ran out of the house, faster than I've ever seen a vicar move before.

'I'll ask the Bishop if he can recommend a "bell, book and candle" man,' he shouted over his shoulder as he raced for his car. He never managed to find anyone, however, and when Otty came home she began propping her large copy of Holman Hunt's picture *The Light of the World* outside her bedroom door every night. The picture shows Jesus holding a lamp as he knocks on a door, so whenever she heard the footsteps approaching Otty would shout, 'Go away, Jesus is looking after me!' Her strategy definitely protected her until we moved, which we did soon afterwards.

We had lots of rational reasons for leaving, such as Tony's new job and Otty's conviction that she would be happy if only she lived in a town, but I guess we were all reacting to the sinister happenings in the old house. How ridiculously ignorant we were! If only we had realised what enormous spiritual authority we had available through the name of Jesus, that house could have been entirely cleansed and tragedy could have been averted.

The first prospective buyers who arrived to view the house loved it so much they made an offer on the spot, but their enthusiasm faced me with a moral dilemma. I felt we ought to tell them about the ghosts, but before they arrived Tony had said, 'If you start talking about all that codswallop we'll never sell the house.'

'How can you possibly bear to move?' our prospective buyers asked incredulously; they were two brothers with their wives and children. 'We can have half the house each,' they added, 'and the granny flat will be perfect for our mother.'

'I think I should tell you something,' I began miserably, trying to avoid Tony's warning glare. 'We did have some trouble with ghosts.'

'Wonderful!' they said. 'We're spiritualists, so that makes the house all the more attractive.'

It was several years after we had moved that we discovered that the couple who bought Otty's end of the house had split up because the wife had become deeply depressed. Another couple had then rented that part of the building, but financial pressure caused so much stress that the husband killed himself in the back garden one evening. This news made me feel awful – particularly as the charismatic renewal had just 'opened my eyes' (2 Kings 6:16–17) to the existence of invisible forces of both kinds. Tony remained doggedly sceptical, but other Christians in the neighbourhood made sure the whole place was finally cleansed by someone with a special anointing for that kind of work, and no further trouble has been reported since.

I suppose the Devil has always liked it when people dismiss him as an old-fashioned superstition, leaving him free to get on with his work of misery-making unchallenged. Yet he is probably just as pleased now the pendulum has swung so far the other way that the secular world flocks for help to the occult, and some Christians give Satan more attention than they give to Jesus!

The renewal movement that began in the 1960s caused such a huge paradigm shift in Christian thinking, right across the denominations, that it is hard nowadays to realise that most ordinary churchgoers, like us, were blind to the existence of demons, angels, miracles, speaking in tongues – in fact, all the supernatural gifts of the Spirit. We thought 'all that stuff' was lost in a past dispensation and only felt comfortable with things we could see, hear, touch or explain scientifically. Our approach to God was cerebral, and huge emphasis was placed on academic Bible study while 'emotionalism' was frowned on in evangelical circles. We simply were not prepared to accept that knowing God means acknowledging that there are huge areas of his character and creation that we cannot possibly understand with our human minds. Nowadays, most of us are far more aware of the supernatural dimension that surrounds us.

Perhaps we sold that house in the country because we felt we'd had enough of old beams, cobwebs and spooks, but I still can't think why we went so far to the other extreme and bought a hideous modern house on a neat estate in Tunbridge Wells! You can't get much less 'haunted' than that!

★ ★ ★

'I'm not having disgusting books like that in the house! Go and put them all on the bonfire!' I had never seen Tony so angry as he was the day I came home with a bag full of books on the Baptism in the Holy Spirit. I had spent a whole week's housekeeping on them, but I was still living behind my sickly mask so I meekly set light to the lot.

The reason why I had splashed out and bought the offending paperbacks was because so many of our friends seemed to be 'coming alive' spiritually in a way that made me feel my own Christianity had become boring and lifeless. Tony loved the traditional evangelical Anglican church where we had settled in Tunbridge Wells, and had even been asked to serve on the PCC. However, by that time the issue of the Baptism in the Holy Spirit and speaking in tongues was splitting the congregation in half, along with thousands of other churches throughout the country. Tony was firmly ensconced on the traditional side of the fence, but to me the 'other side' seemed to be experiencing the same enjoyment of God that I had once seen in Mr Luff. I longed to join the fun but was not willing to cause conflict with Tony, so I rapidly became more miserable by the day.

'There's got to be more to life than this,' I used to think as I trudged along the neat dull roads on our estate. The rows of identical houses, peering across the road at each other through uniform lace curtains, made me feel I was back in Frinton with nowhere to hide. 'You're just feeling low because you're missing the country,' I told myself firmly, and when Granny sent me one of her delightfully large cheques for a birthday present I blew it all on a chicken house and twelve hens. Tony approved of them far more than the books on speaking in tongues, but the neighbours looked askance because you simply did not keep chickens in those neat back gardens. They should have been grateful I hadn't also bought a cock to wake them all at dawn!

The chickens failed to cheer me, so I decided my low spirits must be Otty's fault. She now lived in a nearby flat and was becoming increasingly impossible as she worked her way through a host of paid companions. They all left as rapidly as her secretaries had in the past – no longer to get married, but to save their sanity. Her constant demands were making me fear for my own! One day she wanted me to take her up to visit Granny in her little flat in Highgate. While they drank their way through numerous pots of China tea I took myself and my latest baby for a long walk in Kenwood, the park where, thirty years before, Gom had so often taken me to see the ducks. The previous evening I had been talking on the phone to my friend Trish, who told me she had just been filled with the Holy Spirit.

'Not you too!' I said caustically. 'What will your husband say when you start gobbling like a turkey and calling it prayer?'

Trish had simply replied, 'I'm so desperate for Jesus I wouldn't let anyone stop me from having more of him, not even John.'

Her words felt like a kick below the belt. Perhaps they reminded me of that half-forgotten covenant I had once made with God, sitting on the tree stump.

I had dutifully burnt those books because I didn't want to upset Tony, but was it right to let another human dictate the way you related to God? The curiosity that had led me to buy the books had lately become an urgent hunger.

As I pushed the baby buggy round the lake I knew God wanted me to decide if he was my Lord and my God – or was it Tony I worshipped? Finally I sat down on a seat and prayed rather a desperate prayer: 'O Lord, if there is such a thing as the Baptism in the Holy Spirit, please let me have it.' I am not sure what I thought would happen, but when nothing did I pottered dismally back to collect Otty and drove home to wash the endless buckets of terry towelling nappies. At least I'd tried.

Next morning, however, I woke to feel great waves of love

washing over me. Over the next weeks I drifted through life in a delightful daze. I read the Bible avidly, seeing things I could have sworn had never been there before, but sometimes I just sat still allowing my spirit to float effortlessly, luxuriating in that sea of love. At that stage of the renewal movement people honestly thought that if you could not speak in tongues the Holy Spirit was definitely not in your life. I could never go along with that theory, and was glad when it was eventually abandoned, but I will never get over the joy of being able to speak to the person I love best in a private language all of our own!

I never actually dared to tell Tony what was happening to me, but he must have realised because at church I was drawn irrevocably towards the people on the 'other side'. I guess we all felt we were 'spiritually superior' to the rest of the congregation who we saw as religious dinosaurs; to them, I guess, we must have seemed arrogant and smug. I am sure Tony would not have minded me going deeper into God so long as I respected his brand of spirituality. While it is never right to let someone 'hold you back' on your journey, it is just as wrong to look down on them as a second-class Christian because they relate to God in a slightly different way. Spiritual pride is such a subtle sin, and what fools we are to be taken in by it! If the Devil can't make us sceptical about spiritual gifts, he makes us proud because we have so many!

★ ★ ★

The renewal movement not only restored my desire for God but it also cured my shyness! One cold January afternoon I was standing at the school gate waiting for my second child, Justyn (called after his much loved uncle), to erupt from the reception class with all the other infants. I knew at once that something was wrong as he trailed across the playground towards me, his thick grey socks drooping dismally down his matchstick legs and his bag bumping along the ground behind him like a miserable puppy dog. Framed by the hood of his grey duffle coat his little white tear-stained face looked pathetically up at me.

'What went wrong?' I asked anxiously.

'*Everything*,' was the tragic reply. 'The teacher was cross, my sums wouldn't come right and nobody cared about me all day long.'

Six-year-old Sarah looked at him witheringly. 'You shouldn't have felt lonely,' she said. 'Jesus loves you and he's always with you, even in the toilet.'

'Yes, but,' said Justyn plaintively, 'Jesus doesn't have arms nowadays to cuddle sad people.' Those words were still haunting me when, that evening, Tony and I set out for house group, a new-fangled idea our church was trying out. It was the first time we had gone and we weren't looking forward to it – I was still horribly shy and Tony loathed turning out in the evenings; but with Gom always on hand to babysit we couldn't think up an excuse.

As we walked down the road between all those identical windows with their neatly drawn curtains, Tony said gloomily, 'How cosy they all look.' He probably wished he was safely at home himself.

Shyness may have prevented me from talking to my neighbours but I overheard enough gossip at the school gate to know that the lives behind the curtains were not always as cosy as they appeared. In number seven, for instance, they had such a severely disabled child that the mother could never go out. Next door, the teenage daughter had anorexia and weighed only five stone. I'd heard this mother couldn't go out, either, because the girl kept threatening suicide. As we passed I wondered vaguely how they did their shopping. Then, of course, there was the doctor who lived next to us. His wife was slowly dying from cancer. I had never met her but she hardly had any visitors from what I could see from my own lace-curtained windows. The Rowlands were opposite us. Everyone in the road knew about them. He was some kind of a civil servant, very neat and smart, but his wife was a huge woman who must have weighed well over twenty stone. Some nights he would knock her about until she ran screaming into the road in her nightie. Tony and I had always stayed firmly in bed, not wanting to get involved. At number twelve Robin had just walked out leaving no address or note, only a frantic wife and two tiny children. That evening I suddenly began to wonder how I could have lived so close to all these people and never made any attempt to get to know them.

'You're quiet tonight,' said Tony.

'They're not all as happy as they look,' I replied thoughtfully.

When we finally arrived we found twelve other people already there, drinking mugs of coffee. We sang some songs and listened to an excellent talk. It wasn't until the second round of coffee appeared and one of the 'other side' plonked herself down beside me and said, 'Are you still all right for Thursday morning?' that I remembered to my horror that she had bullied me into saying I'd go to an outreach coffee morning she was organising, and I mentally kicked myself for giving in to her. 'Don't forget to bring your fish,' she added brightly.

'Fish?' I said blankly. I thought I'd promised to bring biscuits.

'You know,' she laughed, 'an unconverted friend.' I had a terrible mental picture of lots of Christian women converging on this girl's house dragging behind them flapping fish on leads. I knew I would not be made to feel accepted unless I dug someone up from somewhere, but who could I take? I only knew the people at church because I could safely leave them behind at the end of Sunday; the thought of being sociable with anyone else in the week made me shudder.

'You look a little troubled this evening,' said the house group leader, taking the place of the 'fisherman' once she had whisked off to enthuse someone else. 'Did you enjoy the meeting?'

'Oh yes,' I assured him, 'but I've had this odd feeling today. Some of the people who live on the estate have such a hard time – it suddenly worried me.'

He looked vaguely at me over the rim of his mug. 'We don't

tend to know any of our non-Christian neighbours,' he said, 'we're really too busy doing the Lord's work,' and he also got up and hurried away.

What *was* 'the Lord's work', I thought miserably as we got into bed. Tony was already happily reading his paper with a 'better late than never' expression on his face, so I opened my Bible and found the bookmark in Matthew 25.

> *When the Son of Man comes . . . and all the angels with him . . . he will separate the people . . . as a shepherd separates the sheep from the goats. Then the King will say to those on his right, 'Come, you who are blessed by my Father; take your inheritance . . . For I was hungry and you gave me something to eat, I was thirsty and you gave me something to drink, I was a stranger and you invited me in, I needed clothes and you clothed me, I was sick and you looked after me, I was in prison and you came to visit me.' Then the righteous will answer . . . 'When did we see you hungry . . . thirsty . . . needing clothes . . . sick or in prison . . . ?' The King will reply, ' . . . whatever you did for one of the least of these brothers of mine, you did for me.'*
>
> Matthew 25:31–40

The previous week we had been riveted by a television documentary about Mother Teresa of Calcutta. One clip showed her washing the ulcerated body of a dying vagrant with such gentle tenderness that the interviewer had asked: 'What makes you able to treat a stranger with such love?'

'To me, this man is my Lord himself,' she replied simply. Mother Teresa knew God intimately and saw him in everyone she met; even the least attractive provided her with a tangible way of expressing her love for him.

Suddenly all the events of the day fitted into place like a jigsaw puzzle.

'You know, Tony,' I said to the back page of the *Daily Telegraph*, 'Jesus doesn't have arms nowadays to cuddle sad people.' The paper collapsed and he eyed me suspiciously as I added, 'But we are too busy enjoying our nice little spiritual ghetto to care!'

As I did the chores the following day I kept thinking of all the reasons why I couldn't possibly start getting involved with other people, but I knew the main reason was that old enemy, shyness. When it was time to go and fetch the children I noticed my gloves, lying limp and lifeless on the hall table, and it struck me how useless empty gloves really are; but when I put my hands inside them they took on a totally new life. The idea that God can speak to us directly and individually, not only through verses from the Bible, was still very new to me, but as I pulled on my gloves I felt, rather than heard, him say, 'I want you to begin showing your love to me by loving people. I'm not asking you to do that in your own strength: all I want is for you to be like those limp gloves and let my Spirit fill you as your hands fill the gloves when you put them on. I have no hands nowadays to care for people. I need to love them through your hands.'

The following Friday, when the milkman came for his money he was obviously full of news.

'Have you heard?' he asked as he handed me his bill. 'Mr Blake at number thirty-two? Died in the night, poor old chap. The undertakers are still there,' he added ghoulishly. The Blakes had no children and were so wrapped up in each other we never saw one without the other. Poor Mrs Blake, I thought, as I washed up the breakfast. Who would comfort her? As I turned on the vacuum cleaner I had an odd feeling that God hoped I would. The thought was horrendous; but perhaps I could just push a card through the door and then run away – fast. Somehow I felt that was not quite all he intended. Finally I set off, clutching a bunch of snowdrops and practising various comforting speeches in my head.

My heart felt as if it was kicking its way out of my rib cage by the time I reached her front gate, where I panicked and ran all the way back home, still clutching my flowers. The first things I saw when I opened the front door were my empty gloves, lying so reproachfully on the mat that I walked straight back up the road.

As I pressed the bell I felt quite as floppy as any empty glove, so I whispered, 'Quick, Lord, fill me with your love!' When Mrs Blake's crumpled old face finally appeared I just stood there holding her hand silently for a moment, before I fled back home, crying all the way.

It was a week after the funeral before I plucked up enough courage to ask Mrs Blake round for a cup of tea.

'You know the day I lost my husband,' she said shyly, 'and you came round with those snowdrops?' I mumbled something vague through my biscuit crumbs. 'Well,' she continued, 'you looked at me with such love I felt peaceful all over. I've never forgotten that look in your eyes. I felt God sent you that day.' Of course, God *had* sent me and it was *his* love that she saw in my eyes.

The lesson that I learnt from those gloves was life-changing for me. I had always loved the few people who were close to me very deeply but I had deliberately excluded the rest of the world behind high, thick walls. I called this barrier 'shyness' or 'busyness', but they were just nicer names for self-protection. Perhaps I was afraid to let people come close to me in case they saw how inadequate I really was. Once I had realised I only had to be the Holy Spirit's gloves, my inadequacy no longer mattered. My enemy still lurks in the shadows, especially when I have to walk on to a platform and speak to hundreds of strangers, but the memory of those gloves always defeats him.

★ ★ ★

Loving God by helping others in practical ways gave me such a buzz that our home was soon full of people Gom described as 'lame dogs having nervous breakdowns all over the place'. Life was enormous fun, perhaps because, like many inadequate people, I was discovering that doing things for others made me feel better about myself! However, I rapidly became so busy that there was no time left to be still in God's presence and I became increasingly aware of an inner tension, which I defined as the fight between

Mary and Martha. These two sisters were great friends of Jesus, and often had him to stay in their home in Bethany; Martha showed her love to him in practical ways, while Mary just wanted to sit close to him, hanging on his every word (Luke 10:36–42). The Holy Spirit had definitely reawakened the 'Mary' in me who desired intimacy, but he had also galvanised the 'Martha' side into action. The more time and energy I used up serving the Lord by loving his 'lame dogs', the less opportunity I had to be alone with him. St Theresa once said, 'Our Lord is best served by a blend of both sisters,' but my 'Mary and Martha' always seem to be fighting and the busy, practical Martha has often managed to crush the life out of poor Mary for long periods of my life. As the Christian writer Oswald Chambers so rightly says, 'The greatest competitor of devotion to Jesus is service for Jesus.'

Tony understood and related to my Martha side, and was far happier to see me dashing round doing things to help people than when I wanted to go off to charismatic prayer groups or extended worship sessions. He remained quite mystified by any form of spirituality that was not completely down to earth and practical until our fourth baby, Duncan, was born in 1975. I knew there was something badly wrong with the baby by the time he was five days old; he seemed to be in terrible pain and never stopped crying. After a few nightmare weeks the hospital diagnosed him with a rare disease of the digestive system and told us they could give us little hope for his survival.

The next fifteen months were ghastly. We had to feed Duncan with a synthetic substance from a bottle every three hours, day and night, and he was often in terrible pain. When he also developed breathing problems we forgot what a night's sleep felt like, and he soon looked more like a white shrivelled monkey than a baby. Tony found that time particularly trying because fixing everything that went wrong was so important to him; but there was nothing he could do to mend Duncan. The resulting sense of helplessness and not being in control rattled him badly.

When he actually consented to come with me to a large

charismatic gathering in our town I was astonished. He had never been to anything like that before. We trusted Duncan to Gom and went off together to hear the South American speaker Juan Carlos Ortiz. That night we were both deeply blessed. Typically Tony never managed to put into words what happened to him, but a few days later he suddenly said, 'I suppose the difference between giving your life to God and receiving the Baptism of the Holy Spirit is that when you give you can be proud that you gave so much, but when you receive you can only feel humbled at receiving such an enormous amount.' That is all he was prepared to say, but the gulf that had been growing between us had gone.

A few weeks later another job promotion for Tony gave us a good reason to leave our modern house in the tidy road and move back into the peace of the countryside. Duncan was due to go into hospital that same week for all kinds of major tests and investigations. At eighteen months he was still terribly frail but was just beginning to crawl, and while I was busy arranging my new kitchen he managed to find his way into the larder. There he discovered a box of groceries lying on the floor, and before I realised what he was doing he had eaten biscuits, sugar lumps and a cheese triangle (silver paper and all) and taken several bites out of an onion. Quite a meal, considering he had never had anything but fluids in his life! Even the smallest spoonful of food that the hospital had periodically tried out on him had caused a major allergic reaction, so I expected the very worst. No reaction ever came, and the doctors could offer no explanation for his sudden and complete recovery. He is now a six-foot-four rugby player and has not had a day's illness since!

* * *

'Lord, why don't you take her to heaven? Can't you see she's driving me mad?' I was pounding my kitchen walls with my clenched fists and I had not been so angry since the day I scratched Nanny's arms until she bled into the bath. It seems terrible to pray that your mother would die, but I knew that was the one thing she and I both wanted most.

When Otty had exhausted the supply of resident companions she systematically worked her way through the Tunbridge Wells hotels with similar rapidity, until her heart condition finally beat her and she needed major surgery. It was unsuccessful and left her confused and distressed. She constantly asked if she could come and live with us again, but by this time we had carved out such an idyllically happy life for ourselves in the beautiful Sussex village of Mayfield that I felt I could not take back that responsibility again.

We had five children of our own by then and one long-term foster daughter, and we all squashed contentedly into an elastic-sided, three-bedroomed semi surrounded by fields, woods and little winding country lanes. Tony's career was progressing well, and once the children were in bed at night I would climb up into the attic where I kept Otty's old typewriter. There I would pound out the stories that I had tried out on the children during the day, and with the help of Tony's famous red pen I had managed to get several more books published. Our large garden provided all our fruit and vegetables and the chickens were flourishing under the tyrannical rule of *two* cocks! We also kept ducks, but they fed the local foxes with disheartening frequency, and our other idea for producing protein, breeding rabbits, also backfired because we grew to love them too much to have them for dinner! On top of all this delightful activity I was still doing my 'God's gloves' thing and looking after people all round the village while Tony and I jointly ran the church youth group. There simply was no time in this delightful existence to take on the care of a frail, confused invalid.

To be honest, I think Otty's enormous gifts and glittering personality had always made me feel a failure, simply because I was ordinary. On our lounge wall hung the beautiful portrait of her in her early thirties which Grandpa had commissioned. The sight of it always took me back to an evening when, as an eight-year-old, I had sat on the floor of her bedroom playing with the silk folds of the evening dress she wears in the picture. She was brushing her long golden hair and coiling it up on top of her head because she and the Boss were going to dinner with the Duke and Duchess of Windsor – who wanted to meet this man who kept filling the Royal Albert Hall. 'I want to be like my mummy when I grow up,' I had told myself that night, but even when I *was* grown up I always felt eclipsed by her sparkling brilliance. With Tony's encouragement I had at last become a person in my own right and I did not want Otty to upset all that Tony had achieved.

Then, one Sunday morning when we were all crammed into one pew in our little church, Sarah, who was then twelve, began flipping through her Bible during the rather dull sermon. Suddenly I realised she was passing it, open, along the row towards me, pointing vigorously at some verses she had found in 1 Timothy. When I read them my cheeks turned scarlet.

But if a widow has children or grandchildren, they should learn first to carry out their religious duties towards their own family and in this way repay their parents and grandparents because that is what pleases God . . . But if anyone does not take care of his relatives . . . he has denied the faith and is worse than an unbeliever.

1 Timothy 5.4–9, GNB

'Look at that, Mum!' hissed Sarah in a hoarse whisper everyone in church could hear. 'We *ought* to have Otty to live with us.'

We went home and held a family council over Sunday lunch; all the children agreed with Sarah, and Tony was his usual easy self.

'I don't think I've got the time,' I said miserably, but inside I knew what the Lord wanted me to do. It is so much easier to be 'God's gloves' to other people than to care for someone in your own family, particularly when their personality constitutes a subconscious threat. I promised everyone I would pray about it, hoping to manipulate the Lord on to my side, but instead he simply showed me a picture as I prayed. It was of a brick wall and I was hurtling towards it at high speed.

'When I hit that wall I'm going to be smashed to bits. Is that what you want?' I demanded crossly. I think he just answered, 'Trust me.'

So we turned our lounge into a bed-sitting room for Otty, which left little room for the rest of us, and we soon felt like rats confined in an over-crowded cage. She was only sixty-seven and her mother was still alive and fit at ninety-three! I felt I had been given a life sentence.

When you are caring for someone with dementia freedom is definitely what you miss most. I dared not leave her alone, because if I popped out to the village shop or took the children to school I would come back to find her pattering up the lane looking for me, wearing no more than her petticoat. Or perhaps an unfortunate accident had occurred when she had not quite managed to reach her commode. Wherever I went in the house or garden she followed me, asking the same questions over and over again; and even at night there was no escape: every time I managed to get off to sleep she would ring her bell yet again, demanding breakfast. I began punching my kitchen walls the morning she upset her cup of tea all over her newly changed nightdress and bedding and then said, 'Mummy, I've wet my pants.' The realisation that the lady in the portrait, which now hung over her commode, had been reduced to calling me 'Mummy' was more than I could bear. So the wall took the brunt of my rage and despair.

'Lord, how could you let her suffer like this?' I prayed indignantly. 'Doesn't she deserve better after serving you all her life and helping thousands of people all over the world?'

There is a maddening verse in the Bible which people have often quoted at me when I have been in the middle of some major crisis: '*And we know that in all things God works for the good of those who love him*' (Romans 8:28). I have come very close to hitting several people who have trotted that one out at an inappropriate moment! The irritating thing is that it happens to be true. Now, years later, I can see all the good things God wanted to do for us through Otty's last months on earth, but at the time I could see none of them.

Later that day she had a stroke, and after the GP had examined her he said to me, 'I think for *your* sake it's time she went into a nursing home.' I knew he was right – I had run out of energy – yet Tony and I both knew that Otty's one great fear was to die alone, separated from us all.

'What shall we do, Lord?' I asked him desperately as I tried to get some sleep on a mattress beside Otty's bed. It was then that I saw the picture of the wall again and once more I was hurtling towards it; instinctively, I braced myself because I knew the impact was imminent, but just as I reached the wall it completely dissolved and I floated through to the other side.

'Trust me,' the Lord seemed to say again, and somehow I knew he would not let me be tested beyond my strength (1 Corinthians 10:13).

So we told the GP in the morning that we would try and carry on for a little longer. Two days later, Justyn called in to see Otty, and while he and I were sitting with her, each holding one of her hands, she died.

Feeling guilty is completely normal after bereavement but I did not know that then! So I suffered agonies as I remembered how frustrated I had so often felt as I coped with all her demands. I was also still feeling angry that the Lord had allowed her last ten years to be so difficult.

He had used a dream to help me after the Boss died and he did the same thing soon after Otty's funeral – although, this time, it felt more like a nightmare than a dream! I was washing Otty in her bed, as I had done every morning for so long, but suddenly I looked down at her and saw she was a skeleton. Only her eyes were alive, staring up at me, reproaching me for the way I felt about her. I knew I needed help, so next morning I went to see my friend Rhoda, who lived in a tiny cottage just round the corner from us.

'You don't have to be weighed down by all this guilt,' she told me bluntly. 'We'll confess it to the Lord and then claim his promise' (1 John 1:9). As Rhoda was standing behind my chair with her hands on my shoulders I suddenly saw that reproachful skeleton once again, but this time I was not dreaming. As Rhoda gently went on praying for healing I saw the skeleton falling away from me down into a dark ravine. Then above my head I saw a sunlit mountaintop, and there were my parents, smiling happily down at me. Otty was wearing the clothes she had worn every evening for all those meetings around the country during the Mission to Britain: her best blue coat with the fur collar and the feather hat she always loved. She and the Boss both looked young and full of life; they were holding hands as they waved reassuringly at me. Suddenly I knew their real life was just beginning, and it would go on being gloriously happy for ever. The Lord seemed to be telling me that, in the light of eternity, those last ten difficult years now felt utterly insignificant to Otty (2 Corinthians 4:17).

It was easy, after that, to confess all the resentment I had felt towards the Lord, and finally Rhoda said something that I have never forgotten:

'Love is not a feeling, it is an action word. You may not have felt loving towards your mum, but you acted out love to her by the way you looked after her. If you had pushed her away in some nursing home you would feel bad about that for the rest of your life, but, however you might have felt inside, you will always know you loved her right to the end.'

While I would never say that every family ought to look after their elderly relations in their own homes, I know it was right for us; God did not want my relationship with Otty to remain unresolved for the rest of my life. The lasting memory that I have of her during the time she lived with us is of her sitting with her Bible open on her lap. She could no longer read, but she spent hours just holding it while a stream of gobbledegook, that only the Almighty could understand, poured out of her mouth. Even though her body and mind were finished, her spirit had reached his heart and her lifelong desire had been fulfilled at last.

★ ★ ★

So we returned to the blissful existence which seemed to amble peacefully through the seasons: blackberry-picking, carol-singing under bright frosty stars, the WI pantomime, the first bluebells, the village carnival and the harvest supper. All those memories and many more made up the happiest years of my life.

For a month every summer we all went up to the new Hildenborough to help Justyn and Joy with the summer conferences. Tony and I ran games and activities for about fifty children so that their parents could attend the seminars. But as the years went on I became increasing concerned about my brother Justyn. He and Joy were enormously successful and the whole place positively hummed with life, yet every time I saw him he seemed to have retreated further into a private cell deep inside himself. One day he told me that he had been preaching on Easter Sunday morning and suddenly he found he did not believe one word he was saying. He did not feel ill, tired or depressed, but his faith had totally gone. For two years he went through the motions of running the centre while taking as much time as possible on lonely retreats searching for a God he felt no longer existed (*Honest Doubt – Real Faith*, Justyn Rees, Hodder & Stoughton, 1999). In the end he came to a decision, which I have always felt was made too hastily, and he handed Hildenborough over to our cousin Max Sinclair and emigrated to Canada. His faith rapidly returned and he now feels that his problem was due to the prolonged stress of taking on the vast responsibility of Hildenborough while he was still only in his early twenties. Justyn and I have always acknowledged what a privilege it was to have had two such wonderful parents, but perhaps we both found it hard walking through our lives in their shadow. Justyn has spent the years since leaving Hildenborough serving the Lord most successfully as an evangelist, writer and a pastor, so I guess once again it is a case of 'the Good Lord knows what 'e's a'doin' of'!

★ ★ ★

The other vitally important thing that happened to our family during the Mayfield years was the arrival of Sarah-Jane. One Christmas Eve, while we were still living in that excessively tidy estate in Tunbridge Wells, Tony and I were creeping round the house stuffing the stockings which hung from the bottom of the children's beds. In our desire not to be seen we were feeling our way in the dark when I fell over a chair and broke three ribs. I spent Christmas in hospital while poor Tony burnt the mince pies and served up raw turkey. In the next bed to me was another mum, called Freda, and because I had just been cured of my shyness we soon became friends. I used to love seeing her three-year-old, Sarah-Jane, running down the ward to find her mum at visiting time. Freda was in for tests, and after Boxing Day the consultant came to tell her the results. I was on bed-rest so I could not help hearing what he said through the flimsy curtains. Bluntly he explained that she had inoperable cancer and only a few months left to live. Later that day, again through the curtains, I heard the hospital chaplain leading her to Christ. We stayed closely in touch for the rest of her short life, and I can honestly say she became one of the most radiant Christians I have ever known. Her constant prayer was that her daughter would grow up to know the friend she had discovered in Jesus, and the last time I saw her she was lying on the sofa in her front room very close to death but praising the Lord with tears of joy pouring down her thin cheeks.

Soon after the funeral her husband, Roy, asked us to promise we would take care of little Sarah-Jane if anything ever happened to him. We promised happily, never expecting that it would; but three years later he died suddenly one night, of a heart attack. By this time we were in Mayfield and our youngest son Richard was only a few months old, but as soon as we heard the news early the following morning, Tony went straight into Tunbridge Wells to find out what was happening to Sarah-Jane. She was still only seven and we knew she had no one else in the world to look after her. By the time Tony arrived Social Services had officially taken her into care and firmly explained that the wishes Roy had expressed in his will made no difference; only registered foster parents could care for Sarah-Jane.

'Well, actually that's what we are,' smiled Tony. A year before we had begun the lengthy vetting process, even though we had no idea why it felt so important to put ourselves through all that complicated rigmarole when our family was already so large. We had only been officially recognised a couple of weeks before Roy's death; the God who understands the maddening slowness of red tape had worked everything out ahead of time.

When Tony first broke the news of her father's death she merely said, 'That's all right, I'll stay with you instead.' I was trying to raise a litter of orphaned kittens at the time, and they needed to be fed two-hourly by a dropper, so helping me rear them carried Sarah-Jane through the first few weeks, and she adored baby Richard. She appeared to settle down remarkably well – at first; but it is *not* easy bringing up someone else's child, particularly when they become a teenager!

As the years went by and our Utopian years in Mayfield were over, life with Sarah-Jane became nothing but a series of horrendous clashes of will, until she finally disappeared in London with her junkie boyfriend. I used to break my heart each year on her birthday because I couldn't even send her a card, and the thought of Freda and her earnest prayers for her little daughter made me curl at the edges with shame. One night I was lying in the bath, thinking of all the times when she had managed to needle me out of my candyfloss mask to shout at her. I began to worry about all the scars my words must have left on her soul.

'Forgive me, Lord,' I remember praying among the soap

bubbles. 'Heal all those scars and please *please* give me the chance to tell her how sorry I am.'

Late one night, some years later, the phone rang and a shaky little voice said, 'Mum?' She had become so desperate, late one night, she had knelt down by her bed and prayed, 'O God, if you love me, like Mum always said you do, then *show* me!' A few days later she had been approached in the street by a couple of Christian girls who asked if she would like to come to their church, and added, 'You know, God really loves you.' The church was soon Sarah-Jane's home and she was ringing to say she had just been baptised. Not long afterwards, at her new church, she met a super Christian guy who is now my delightful son-in-law. Freda's prayers, and mine in the bath, were answered in full measure!

7

The LORD says, 'The wise should not boast of their wisdom, nor the strong of their strength, nor the rich of their wealth. If anyone wants to boast he should boast that he knows and understands me.'
                                                          Jeremiah 9: 23–4, GNB

It is easy to look at people in the Bible who really knew God well, like Abraham or Daniel, and think God was always intervening in their lives or speaking to them direct from heaven. Actually those significant moments only happened occasionally; like the rest of us on this journey, they probably felt their rate of progress was boringly slow most of the time. Then quite unexpectedly God would intervene again, either directly or through circumstances, and their pace accelerated dramatically.

It was in August 1981 while we were on holiday in Devon that God began speeding my journey in that way. We always went back to the same spot each year, thanks to the incredible generosity of a lady called Marjorie Strain. She had been a good friend to my parents and always let them use her holiday house, Stillmeadow, whenever they needed peace in which to write a book. Tony and I could never have afforded holidays with so many children on just one teacher's salary unless Marjorie had extended her kindness to us as well. Because she, and her mother before her, had spent so

127

long praying in Stillmeadow, it has become what the Celts would call a 'thin place', a spot where the membrane between heaven and earth has become thin through all the prayer that has been offered there. I have always found it easier to hear God's voice in that house than anywhere else on earth.

During that holiday we enjoyed the usual happy round of rock-pooling, beach fires and walks along the cliff paths. Then, one morning, I was woken out of a deep sleep at five o'clock by a loud voice saying, 'Anna.' Tony was still sound asleep so I crept downstairs with 'Anna' still ringing in my ears, to sit in the room where, incidentally, I am writing this now. What did 'Anna' mean, I wondered, as I picked up my Bible. I knew there was someone called Anna the prophetess, and eventually I found her in Luke 2:36–8. For some reason I felt God was telling me to identify myself with this remarkable old lady who spent all her time in the temple, talking to people about God and talking to God about people. Because Anna was a prophetess I assumed he was anointing me to be a prophetess too, and for some unfathomable reason I thought that meant he wanted me to have the same kind of itinerant preaching ministry he had given my parents.

My reactions to that idea were decidedly mixed. On one hand I did not want to give up the country lifestyle I loved, but deep down I was beginning to wonder if it was right to be this comfortable and happy when there were so many people out there in the harsh cold world. They had to struggle through all kinds of horrible experiences without realising that Jesus loved them or was willing to help. The words from Romans 10 often haunted me:

For, "Everyone who calls on the name of the Lord will be saved."
How, then, can they call on the one they have not believed in? And
how can they believe in the one of whom they have not heard? And
how can they hear without someone preaching to them? And how can
they preach unless they are sent?

Romans 10:13–15

Richard would be starting school the following year and, like most of my friends, I was wondering what to do with all that glorious spare time!

My 'Mary' side was longing for more space to pray, and I would have been happy just to potter round the garden, visit a few old ladies and write children's books. However, my 'Martha' side was eager for action. I tried to push away this inner conflict by enjoying a glorious autumn back in Mayfield, but as I froze down the plums and picked blackberries I kept having the feeling that this happy life we had carved out for ourselves was only a preparation for the 'real thing' which was just about to begin.

* * *

It was a few months before I had a second God-encounter. I had decided to take a morning off while Richard was at playgroup, so I could go for a long walk alone in my favourite wood in order to ask the Lord a specific question.

To my surprise, I had begun to receive invitations to speak at Christian events simply because of who my parents had been. I needed to know whether I should say no or whether they marked the beginning of my ministry as an 'Anna'.

As I pulled on my Wellingtons I was savouring the thought of spending the morning in the beautiful place where we always took Gom for her birthday picnic in May. The previous year she had been following us into the woods, carrying her elaborately iced birthday cake, when she slipped and dropped it upside down in a muddy ditch. Unperturbed, she scooped up the mangled remains, declaring happily, 'A bit of good country dirt won't hurt us!'

In my mind Fir Toll Woods were perpetually full of the pungent scent of bluebells and the sun was always filtering down through the beech leaves to dapple the little stream with silver stars. But I had chosen a wet day in February for my walk, so it was ridiculous to feel so disappointed that there were no bluebells. The once green beech leaves now lay rotting in sodden black heaps on the ground, and it was dark and dismal as I splashed along under the bare branches. I did not feel remotely like praying, but suddenly God spoke to me instead.

'Your life has been full of light and colour, like this wood in the springtime; but if it became bleak, lifeless and wintry could you still praise me?'

'I don't know, Lord,' I replied out loud, feeling rather startled. 'I didn't manage too well while I was looking after Otty, did I?'

'In heaven,' he continued, 'your life will always be like the woods in May time.' That was *not* the kind of thing I wanted to hear. I had come out that day hoping for some great commissioning from him, but as I stood under the dripping trees I remembered a horrible dream I'd had the previous night. Something terrible had been about to happen to me, but to my relief I had woken before I could discover what it was. I suddenly felt very cold so I hurried home to make a nice cup of tea.

The following Saturday the telephone rang just as I was ready to dish up the lunch. Tony was at the farthest end of the garden, so I gave the saucepans an irritated shove to the back of the stove and picked up the receiver. It was Eunga, a Korean Christian friend of ours who was married to a local solicitor. She sounded upset.

'Jen, I just don't know whether I should have rung you or not,' she began nervously, 'but Charles and I have prayed about this and we feel that I should tell you.' I sensed she was crying but my mind was still with the Yorkshire puddings, which my watch told me would start to burn in exactly four minutes' time.

'What's up?' I asked, trying not to sound rushed.

'You know how God often shows me things in dreams? Well, last night I had a terrible dream that you were going to die soon.' I felt as if someone had kicked me very hard in the tummy and I sat down heavily on the bottom of the stairs. 'It probably doesn't mean anything,' she added quickly, 'but perhaps you ought to prepare yourself.'

A few minutes later we were all sitting round our huge kitchen table: three blonde girls down one side, the boys at the other, with Gom squashed in the middle to stop them squabbling. Tony smiled happily at me from the far end as I doled out the food. They were all laughing loudly at some joke he'd just made, blissfully unaware of the ice-cold fear that was beginning to attack me. That afternoon we were planning a long muddy walk together and then we would toast crumpets by the fire. It seemed outrageous that this safe, happy life we had so carefully constructed should suddenly be destroyed.

During the next few days I springcleaned the house, sorted out the cupboards and even attacked the attic – anything rather than have time to think. Tony was away all week at a maths conference, so I had to keep up my restless activity during most of the night as well! Finally I ground to a halt in the middle of a huge pile of mending and realised I had no choice but to face my fear.

But what was I frightened of? Death? No, I knew beyond any possibility of doubt that heaven existed and that Jesus had died to make it possible for me to go there. Perhaps it was the actual process of dying that felt so daunting. How was it going to happen? Would it be sudden or long and painful? I shuddered and wondered how Sarah-Jane would cope; she had only been with us a couple of years at that time and the loss of both parents was still so raw that she had become terrified of any kind of illness. I only had to sneeze for her to clutch my jumper with both hands and cling on tight for the rest of the day.

'You won't die, will you?' she would ask anxiously.

'Of course not!' I would reply, laughing at her fears. 'I'm as strong as a horse.' She would relax then, because she trusted me completely.

'O Lord, let me survive – if only for her sake!' I whispered as I knelt among the mending.

'You can trust me for yourself,' the Lord seemed to reply, 'but why can't you trust me for your children as well?'

Being a mother had made me feel completely indispensable, but suppose they all had to cope without me? Hastily I began to work through a mental list of my single friends, trying to decide which one Tony should marry in order to provide the children with a substitute mother. I was about to write him a letter pointing out the virtues of my choice when I thought, 'Suppose I don't die after all and Tony discovers the letter?' The thought amused me so much that I went off to bed laughing.

A couple of days later God intervened yet again. All the churches in Mayfield had combined to run a Lenten discussion group. I loved those Thursday evenings because Brother Tom was there. He was definitely one of the 'handful of people' my mother had told me about. He looked like Friar Tuck in his black habit and thick leather belt, which only just managed to meet round his remarkable girth. He was a Roman Catholic monk who cooked for a small monastic community in the village. He used to say he had once been a bad-tempered old man with a habit of swearing loudly, until a remarkable encounter with God in his cell one night had changed him into someone so full of joy that he reminded me of Mr Luff. He often tried to tell me exactly what it was that had happened that night but always broke down in helpless tears of gratitude before he could finish the story.

During a quiet period of prayer that particular Thursday evening, I was startled to hear Brother Tom speaking my name. I had told no one about my fears, except the Lord and the black book in which I wrote down the events that struck me as important. But suddenly Brother Tom said, 'Jen, the Lord is telling me to say that you are released from your fear!'

I was quite overcome with relief and joy! I wasn't going to die after all – those silly dreams and fancies had just been a test to see if I trusted God in death as well as in life. Looking back now, I realise that was not what Brother Tom told me. All he had said was that I was released from my *fear*, not from the threat of death itself, but I drove happily home, feeling I was sure to live to be as old as Anna the prophetess herself.

Later that evening, while I was making out my shopping list for the morning, I found myself writing words that just seemed to float effortlessly into my head. When I read through what I had written it all seemed a bit irrelevant, so I pushed the piece of paper into the kitchen drawer where it lay, forgotten, among the recipe books for more than two years. When I discovered it again I realised I could have saved myself so much doubt and misery if only I had stuck those words up on the door of my fridge! The Lord had obviously been gently preparing me for what was to come.

February 1982

I am training special people to be my companions throughout eternity, to be my heart's delight and joy. You will be able to praise and worship me so easily when you see me face to face, but I need you to learn how to do it now, down here. I do not want automatic praise, which costs nothing. I want you to learn to praise me when you are depressed, downtrodden, being tempted or not having your prayers answered. That is when your praise and worship mean most to me. Learn that now because it will matter in eternity. I did not promise you ease and comfort. Remember that the more difficulties you have now, the more real heaven will become to you. Here on earth I want to live in you so I can use your body, personality and circumstances to show my reality and power to other people.

Then, underneath, I had added the words of Habakkuk: I wanted to react to trouble as he had but I was far from sure that I would!

> *Although the fig tree does not blossom*
> *And there be no fruit on the vine,*
> *The produce of the olive fail,*
> *And the fields yield no corn . . .*
> *Yet will I rejoice in the Lord,*

And I will joy in the God of my salvation.
Based on words from Habakkuk 3:17–18

★ ★ ★

When May came we took Gom back to Fir Toll Woods again for her bluebell picnic – but this year Sarah insisted on carrying the birthday cake! I was not feeling well; for a few weeks I'd had a persistent headache, which now seemed to be spreading down my neck and spine. I had firmly ignored it because I always had a stupid guilt feeling about being ill; somehow it felt like failure to me. 'I ought to be one hundred per cent fit, with a lifestyle like mine,' I told myself, while I swallowed a couple of aspirins and forced myself on through each busy day, pretending nothing was wrong.

Fir Toll Woods could not have looked more beautiful as we laid out Gom's favourite cream éclairs and thick slices of new bread on a patch of grass by the stream. She sat on a fallen tree, beaming round at everyone, as the younger children threw off their school uniforms and headed for the clear water of the stream. I remember flopping on the ground and closing my eyes because the sunlight hurt so much.

'Come and paddle in the stream, Mum,' called Richard, who was four. 'We're turning over stones to find little wiggling things.'

'Mayfly larvae,' I mumbled, without opening my eyes. 'Go and see if you can find some more – *much* higher up the stream.' The sound of their voices seemed to grate on my ears too. All around me was the sweet, heady scent of the bluebells, but all I wanted to do was crawl into my bed in a dark room and sleep for days.

'Mummy, what *is* the matter?' asked Duncan who, even at six, had a great capacity for tuning into other people's feelings.

'I'm fine!' I said, forcing my eyes open, but that was the day I first realised I was *not*.

It is painful to picture those carefree children playing in the stream, knowing as I do in retrospect how much their lives were about to change. Only now that they are grown up can I see how God used the experiences that seemed so destructive at the time, even transforming them into definite assets (Romans 8:28). They all have an unusually deep love and understanding for people who are suffering and, far from resenting a God who had allowed their lives to be disrupted, they are all following him now, in their own different ways.

My instinct is to avoid the pain of reliving those eight years by leaving them out of this story, hurrying on to a happier part of my journey – after all, I've written about them before; but unless I give you a few little snapshots to cover those dark years the impact of events I have *never* written about will be lost.

★ ★ ★

One morning, a few days after Gom's birthday, I was trying to clean the bath, which looked as if a herd of hippos had been wallowing in it. By this time the pain in my head had become alarmingly severe and my neck was completely stiff. Suddenly I felt so giddy that my brain seemed to be swirling rapidly round inside my skull. I could not make my arm bend or my hand grip the sponge. Everything felt unreal, out of my control. Fortunately Rosemary, a neighbour from up the lane, discovered me and helped me into bed; but even then I refused to let her call the doctor. So she secretly arranged for him to call the following day.

That last evening at home stands out in my memory so vividly because life was never the same again for any of us. When the children came home from school I tried to get out of bed but my legs buckled up under me. I could hear the chaos going on all over the house, but for once I was not the hub of the wheel. Over the following months Sarah, who was then fourteen, stepped into the role of mother. This was tough on her because she was gifted academically, and the strain of carrying such a heavy load of responsibility as well as trying to keep up with homework resulted in her becoming ill herself and having to miss a lot of school the following year. Of course, I suffered agonies of guilt over that, but when she got a history first at Oxford and stayed on there to achieve a doctorate and then a lecturing post, I wondered why I had worried!

That last evening I could hear the two younger boys, Richard and Duncan, then four and six, giving Sarah a hard time as she tried to get them ready for bed while Tony watered the vegetable garden and collected the other girls from Brownies. Every time I opened my eyes Sarah-Jane's reproachful face would be peeping round my bedroom door – and this time I could not find any words to reassure her. At thirteen Justyn was fascinated by every detail of the Falklands War, which was at its height. When he switched on the TV news he turned the volume on full because he was sure I wouldn't want to miss it. Groaning, I pulled the duvet up over my head and stuck my fingers in my aching ears. Later I did do my best to tell the boys a story, even though my words sounded so jumbled and slurred anyone would have thought I'd been swigging whisky all day. The memory of Richard's warm little body snuggling up to me was something that meant a lot during the long months of separation that followed.

'Tony,' I whispered when he finally climbed into bed beside me, 'someone can't have encephalitis *twice*, can they?'

'Viruses can lie dormant in the body for years, and then just flare up again,' he replied gloomily. 'I've been watching you and all the symptoms are just the same as last time, aren't they?'

'No!' I sobbed. 'It can't happen again!'

★ ★ ★

As the ambulance drove away down the lane I felt completely detached from the woman lying in the back. I did not even mind that it was a stranger in uniform who sat beside me and not Tony – Richard needed him far more than I did. All I wanted to do was sleep. Vaguely I remembered the doctor's visit earlier that morning. He had only needed to make a brief examination before he hurried downstairs to ring the hospital. When we arrived in the Accident and Emergency Department of the Kent and Sussex I felt quite at home. I had spent many hours there in the past. Our children were always falling out of trees, burning themselves making camp fires or cutting their legs on barbed-wire. I was used to waiting for hours in long queues, but not this time! My trolley was swirled through the double doors at high speed and someone shouted: 'Ah! The encephalitis. Put it straight in there.'

People swarmed round me, but they were all upside down from my position – their mouths were where their eyes should be. I discovered that I could escape from them all simply by sliding under a soft, warm blanket of sleep. When Tony rang the hospital later they told him they thought I had encephalitis and that the lining of my heart was also inflamed. A further complication developed later when my nerve casing also became inflamed.

Encephalitis is an acute inflammation of the brain and the membranes that surround it, usually caused by a viral infection. In most cases it is a serious and life-threatening condition, and there is no known effective treatment. Depending on the cause and degree of severity, some patients die, some are left with brain damage and others make a slow recovery which can take up to two years. During that first week or two they could not give Tony much hope that I would survive, and even when they told him I was out of danger their gloomy forecasts of permanent damage did nothing to cheer him up. His goal was to maintain the children's security by keeping things at home as normal as possible, which was the right decision but it did mean the two of us were separated just when we needed each other most.

During the first week I was so ill that I remember very little, except for the chickens and ducks which I was convinced they kept piling on top of my bed! I told myself the only reason I could not move my legs was because a large goat was sitting on them. When the nurses put bars around my bed, in case I had convulsions, I just thought it was to prevent the goat from escaping!

They put me into a small room where I could be kept completely quiet and nursed in semi-darkness, but the virus which was causing the inflammation was gradually winning as one by one my body's systems went out of action. Tubes were pushed into all kinds of embarrassing places and my arms and legs wouldn't go where I wanted to put them.

I remember someone trying to help me sip tea through the plastic spout of a feeding cup and wondering vaguely why I could not remember how to swallow. I also kept forgetting to breathe and woke myself up gasping into my oxygen mask; it seemed most odd that people kept on shining a torch in my eyes and asking my name and what day it was. It seemed so strange to wake someone from a lovely sleep simply to ask something they must have known anyway!

The hospital chaplain, George Swannell, spent hours sitting beside my cot. He was another of my mother's 'handful'. He had been a friend of the family for years and I had always thought he lived closer to God than any other person I had ever met. Sometimes, when he sat holding my hand through the bars, I used to think it was Jesus himself, sitting there. At a different stage of my life he once said something, which I have always found profoundly helpful: 'The closer your relationship with God becomes, the more aware you are of your own sins and failures, and your need of his forgiveness. It is only the people who are still a long way away from his heart who think they have arrived.'

At first I was too ill to miss the children, but I ached for Tony. Gom was on holiday and had no idea I was in hospital, so Tony could only slip in to see me at odd moments; but I always seemed to be asleep when he did manage to come, and I thought he had abandoned me completely.

One day I kept hearing the words 'condition worsening', and there seemed to be a great increase in the activity around my bed. I suppose I was unconscious but I was still able to hear and a part of my brain was still totally aware of what was going on around me.

When I heard the voice of the ward domestic outside the door, saying to her colleague, 'Don't mop in there today, June, that one's dying,' I thought, 'No, I'm not ... or am I?' For the first time I remembered the dreams and forebodings and I began to panic. I wanted to flail my arms and kick, but all I could do was lie there and look as if I was asleep. I couldn't even scream for help. I wanted to tell the nurses, 'You can't let me die! I'm only thirty-nine! I've got six children!'

Then at last Tony was there. I could see his face quite clearly, spliced into two by the horizontal cot bars, and yet I could not reach out my hands to touch him. I wondered why he looked so ill in the gloomy half-light and why he just sat there, not saying anything at all. If I was dying then I needed to tell him all kinds of vitally important things, like 'Don't forget Sarah-Jane only likes peanut butter in her school lunch-box but Richard can't stand it.'

Suddenly I was angry; not with the illness or the doctors who could not cure it, but irrationally angry with Tony himself. In fact, I wanted to bite the hand that he pushed through the bars, and bite it hard! He ought to be able to do something to stop this powerful force that was wrenching us apart and ruining everything. He could mend the chicken house roof, unblock the drains and soothe a frightened child, so why couldn't he sort this crisis? I sensed he was angry, too, probably for exactly the same reason. The rage neither of us could express separated us more completely than the metal cot bars, and when I next opened my eyes he had gone. I will never forget the desolation of that moment; I had failed to tell him something vital – he must not feel bad about marrying again. I should have written that letter months ago!

During the evening Sister leant over me and whispered, 'Someone's here to see you – the minister of your church.' She looked as if she thought he had come to give me the Last Rites, but as Brian and his wife Penny crept in a great feeling of relief spread over me. They sat down by my cot while I managed to mumble something inane about going to heaven.

'We know,' said Brian. 'But we'll pray for you anyway, Jen.'

As I closed my eyes, the sound of his rich velvety voice began to fade away. Remembering to breathe was too much effort, and at the end of the bed I could see a gentle light beginning to glow. Gradually it grew brighter. 'That's curious,' I thought. Light of any kind had been painful for so long, yet here was a brightness that did not hurt my eyes at all. Gradually a cave was opening in the wall by the washbasin, leading up and out of the room. I found I was floating effortlessly away from the body that lay on the bed. Even my arms and legs moved about without pain and I could turn somersaults. It was rather like free-falling from an aircraft, except that I was going up and not down!

'So this is what dying feels like,' I thought. 'If I had known it was like this I wouldn't have worried. And at the far end of this tunnel I'm actually going to meet the Lord, at long last.' The thought was not frightening at all; I longed to see his face. But I never did and I have often wondered if Brian's prayers had anything to do with that! I knew I was standing on the threshold of somewhere infinitely beautiful, and behind and below me was the darkness and pain I had left behind. All around me was soft gentle light, and the thousands of exquisite shades were quite indescribably lovely.

I wanted to press on eagerly into that place which made my own familiar world at home seem like a poor counterfeit, but something seemed to be stopping me. I knew that down in the darkness below were Tony and the children; I pictured them huddled in a pathetic little group, and somehow I realised I was being given a choice. I could go back to them or move on into all the beauty and freedom which lay ahead. I felt most disconcerted, because I hate making choices.

'I'm too tired to decide,' I thought fretfully. But everything seemed to be waiting for me to do so. It was with a strange feeling of regret that I decided to go back to my family. Then I seemed to hear these words, 'From this moment you will recover and go back. It is going to be a struggle, but I will give you my strength.'

The pain was waiting to trap me as I felt the body on the bed closing round me once again. Brian was still praying but he finished rapidly as nurses bustled round the bed. I think I managed to mutter something about feeling better before he and Penny disappeared from view.

The night which followed was tough. The sense of anticlimax was devastating as I lay in the dark remembering all those glorious colours. My physical condition was definitely much improved, but that meant I could no longer escape into that drowsy world of unconsciousness. I was wide awake and starkly aware of my surroundings for the first time since I had left home.

It might just have been the hallucinations but I was also very conscious of the powers of evil that night, possibly more so than ever before in my life. They seemed to surround my cot – above me and below, angry, menacing, vengeful. I was shaking with terror when a white shape loomed over the cot bars. It seemed to have no head, but it spoke to me by name.

'Mrs Larcombe, are you afraid?'

'Yes, very,' I squeaked, 'but you can't hurt me, I belong to Jesus!'

'That's great, so do I!' and a large and very human hand gripped mine. The dim light from the porthole in the door revealed that the apparition was only a white coat worn by a very tall black man.

'My name is Mr Jones, and I am the Senior Nursing Officer,' he told me. 'I am in charge of this hospital tonight and I came to tell you I shall be taking special care of you. As I walk round the wards and corridors, I want you to remember that I shall be praying for you – all through the night.' Far from deserting me, God had sent one of his special servants to help and protect me.

A few days later, when my friend Rhoda came to see me again, she helped me to record the whole of that experience in detail while it was fresh in my mind. For a long time I actually thought my experience of 'dying' had been unique; it was not until I later published an account of the events of 2 June 1982 that I realised the 'near death experience', as it is called, is very common indeed, and much research has been done into the subject. People wrote to me describing their own 'near misses' and I was even asked by the BBC to take part in a programme on the subject. In the studio, Tony and I were introduced to a doctor who had spent years talking to newly resuscitated patients, and he had published a fat book on his findings.

'All that you describe is very common,' he said enthusiastically. 'In fact you are a textbook case.'

'Is "dying" always a good experience?' I asked him.

Glancing through the glass window at our producer he lowered his voice and said, 'I won't say this on the air for obvious reasons, but sometimes it can be very unpleasant indeed. The patient feels he is being pulled downwards into darkness and becomes extremely afraid. Fortunately,' he added with a stiff smile, 'people who have that kind of experience suppress the memory of it very quickly.'

★ ★ ★

I can never praise the National Health Service enough for the care and kindness shown to me during the following eight years. There was just one horrendous occasion when this was not the case, due to a staffing crisis, but although it was a terrible experience for me it actually marked a major milestone on my journey towards knowing God.

Soon after my 'near death' experience I was transferred to the neurological department of a large London teaching hospital. I dreaded the upheaval, and London seemed so far from my family. Tony managed to dash in to see me briefly before I left, and he gave me his extra-strong dark glasses to help my eyes cope with the light during the journey. They felt as precious as the cuff link he had once given me. The ward sister kindly packed my ears with cotton wool to cut out sound, and before I left in the ambulance she gave me a big shot of morphine so I have no memory of the ride. I remember all too well, however, the moment when I woke up. I was in a glass cubicle and piercing white light was attacking me from all four directions. The noise and clatter as people ran up and down in the corridor was indescribable, but worst of all I was ragingly thirsty. I sensed someone else was in the room so I asked if the curtains could be closed.

'No,' was the abrupt reply. 'I have a great many notes to make and I can't write in the dark.' I thanked God for Tony's dark glasses and tried to slide away from her into sleep.

'Come along now, Mrs Larcombe, open your eyes at once!' The rasping voice reminded me of Miss Mitchell and I began to shake uncontrollably. She was a young house physician, new to this department, and she had probably been on duty without sleep for far too many hours. Perhaps she had also had a row with her boyfriend, but after only a short time under the gunfire of her questions I was reduced to pulp. She bullied, shouted and banged the table in exasperation when I got muddled over dates.

'It's no wonder you can't hear me,' she shouted when she discovered Sister's cotton wool; pulling it from my ears she tossed it on to the floor. 'And I can't see if you're looking at me when you're wearing those ridiculous sunglasses.' When she snatched them away I felt she had severed me from Tony and my security was totally lost. Her 'bedside manner' may well have been a technique for rousing semi-comatose patients from their stupor, but when she tripped on my catheter bag she swore so loudly I was terrified.

'Please,' I begged timidly, 'could I have a drink of water?' My throat felt parched and raw after not being able to swallow for so many days. The saline drip had run out and no one had yet replaced it, so I was probably badly dehydrated, particularly as we were in the middle of a heat wave. The young doctor merely looked annoyed and glanced at my locker.

'They haven't been round with the water jugs yet,' she said. 'They're very short-staffed. You'll just have to wait.'

After she had gone I must have slept, but the thirst was horrendous when I finally woke. There, far above my head on top of the high locker, someone had placed a jug of water while I was asleep, but even if I could have reached that far I would never have been able to lift it. I thought it might help to suck my flannel, but then I noticed all my possessions had been left in a grey polythene bag on the far side of the room. Seeing them there, out of reach, accentuated the sense of being severed from everything safe and familiar. I could have rung for a nurse but the bell was hanging out of reach behind the back of the bed. I doubt if I would have dared to ring it anyway: the feet outside in the corridor sounded like frenzied lemmings scurrying to destruction.

On a level with my nose, just a few inches away, I saw a little Gideon New Testament slotted into a bracket on the side of my locker. With great difficulty I got it out and lay there with it open on my tummy. Of course I was quite incapable of reading it, but just knowing I was lying underneath all those wonderful promises was a great comfort.

When the house doctor suddenly pounced back at me through the door, she said, 'I'm just sending you down for an electro-encephalogram, then a brain scan and after that some X-rays.' Again I asked for some water, but before she could answer a wheelchair was pushed up to my bed. I had been lying completely flat and still for more than a week. As every nurse knows, even sitting up in a comfortable armchair for a few minutes would have been traumatic, and wheelchairs are notoriously difficult for patients with vertigo. As I was dumped into it, like a sack of potatoes, I heard someone murmur, 'Shouldn't she go on a trolley?'

'Trolleys take two porters,' snapped the doctor, 'and they're frantically busy today.' Bending to shout in my ear she added, 'This nurse will go with you, so you'll be all right.' The nurse was male and looked distinctly cross. When I asked him for a drink he merely replied, 'Can't keep the technicians waiting.' As we moved off down the busy corridor the steel back of the wheelchair bit into my painful spine, and there was nothing to support my head so it lolled about ridiculously as the world began to spin alarmingly.

All this sounds as if I am grumbling horribly, but right in the middle of that nightmare something very significant happened to me. As the wheelchair shot along at high speed, up ramps and round corners, the vertigo made it all feel like a speeded-up version of a fair ride. The pain in my head and spine was quite terrifying, while behind me the porter and nurse chatted away to each other amicably. Had they understood what vertigo is like they would have supported my flopping head or at least put a hand on my shoulder. I became aware of someone screaming like an animal in a trap and was deeply humiliated when I realised it was me! The two men behind me shared a joke with a passing porter, and at the time it felt as if they were all laughing at me. Then, suddenly, inside my tightly closed eyes I saw Jesus; he seemed far more real than anything else in that nightmare. He was hanging on the cross and I could see how his face was twisted with pain as the sweat stood out on his forehead.

I had never understood before what Paul really meant when he said he wanted to know Christ in the fellowship of his sufferings (Philippians 3:10). Although at that moment I was in no position to think out the theology behind that statement, I had never felt so completely identified with Jesus before. *He* had felt totally exposed, shamed and humiliated, just as I was. *He* was mocked by uncaring professionals and hurt by their utter indifference (Mark 15:24). People he had counted on for support just were not there for him (Mark 14:50), and he too felt lonely and abandoned.

Most of all, I realised that thirst must have been one of the worst ingredients in his suffering. He had drunk nothing since the previous evening and the burning sunlight, salty taste of blood and the gasping effort to breathe when his hands and feet were nailed to the cross must have caused serious dehydration. I had never been thirsty enough before to realise how terrible that must have made him feel. Life faces most of us with various horrid experiences, but we can almost always discover that Jesus, or God the Father, endured a similar scenario. You know and understand someone on a far deeper level when you glimpse how they feel from personal experience.

Behind me I could still hear the porter whistling as he shot the chair over some bumps and swerved violently to avoid a passing trolley. Perhaps my encounter with Jesus lasted only a second or two but it was so intense that it felt like an electrical shock shooting through my body. I guess that God finds it so desperately hard to watch us suffering that just now and again he breaks through the windows of heaven and comes right down to comfort us. That has only happened to me very occasionally, but the sheer thrill you feel when you meet him unexpectedly in the darkest places cannot possibly be forgotten.

I knew I was going to faint, but just before I slumped forward and fell out of the wheelchair I prayed, 'Please don't let me lose Tony's sunglasses.'

'A patient in this condition should never have been in a wheelchair; fetch a trolley at once,' boomed a voice of authority far away in the swirling blackness, but I was past caring.

The next day could not have been more different. Sister was back from her holiday and the ward was restored to a state of purring efficiency. The scowling lemmings of yesterday turned out to be human after all, and the Whistling Porter padded into my room with Tony's sunglasses. 'Found them under the radiator,' he said, and actually smiled.

★   ★   ★

Life at home, during the months that I was away, was extremely tough for the family. Holding down a highly responsible job as well as organising six children was exhausting for Tony. It became a little easier for him to visit me when I was eventually returned to the hospital in Tunbridge Wells, but his face always looked grey and expressionless with fatigue. He reminded me of someone who had just had a massive haemorrhage – all his vitality and strength seemed to have drained away. His maxim when facing any kind of crisis was the same as the Horse in George Orwell's book *Animal Farm*, 'I will work harder,' but the unrelenting round of chores was definitely taking its toll. Sarah did her best to feed everyone and Gom came over each evening after work, but she was older now, and often tired after a long day cooking in a care home.

Tony always told me everything was 'fine', but other visitors were more explicit. Apparently Sarah-Jane spent most of her time locked in her bedroom refusing to speak to Tony, while Duncan had apparently changed overnight from being an engaging six-year-old into a monster who was totally out of control at school. One evening he was so naughty that Gom said indignantly, 'I'm not surprised your mummy's so ill, having to put up with a naughty boy like you!' Sarah heard this tactless remark and hoped profoundly that Duncan had not. He appeared to take no notice, but seven years later he told me that he thought Gom had meant my illness was his fault entirely, and I believe it was guilt which made him so naughty. He could not concentrate at school and became terribly disruptive and aggressive. When kind friends asked him to tea after school he refused to eat anything and promptly ran away. While they searched the village for him he would be hiding in our garden, watching for Tony to come home from work.

I yearned to see him, but when Tony finally 'risked' a visit he looked unnaturally clean and tidy and he had grown so much thinner and taller that he did not seem *mine* any more. He stopped beside my bed and stared at me balefully and then backed himself into a corner. I thought if I talked to him soothingly he might settle down, but because I was agitated the words came out in a tangled, unintelligible rush. When I reached out to him with a hand that shook alarmingly, something inside him seemed to explode and he sent everything on my locker crashing to the floor and then began to scream. Tony hurriedly removed him, kicking and squirming. I could hear him bellowing all the way to the car park, but I could do nothing whatever to comfort him.

I used to lie looking at the family photo on my locker, watching the clock throughout the day, picturing what they would all be doing as the long days ticked slowly by. Then one afternoon a ray of hope arrived when two people in short white tunics bounded up to my bed and announced they were physiotherapists.

'We'll soon have you back home,' they said cheerfully. 'We've had patients far worse than you running round the corridors. But you won't like the things we make you do.'

They were right there. Shaking my head like a dog after a swim and rolling my eyeballs round in circles were the very last things I wanted to do!

'It makes me feel so giddy,' I explained as I clutched the vomit bowl.

'But we *want* to make you giddy,' they explained kindly. 'The brain has to be trained to find new nerve pathways when the old ones are damaged.' When they stood me up by my bed the floor had a nasty way of coming up and hitting me, but they made their daily visits such fun and also gave me a feeling that I was doing something to help myself at long last.

'You're going downstairs to Physio today,' said a porter one afternoon as he pushed a wheelchair up to my bed. This was a real promotion. The vertigo was just as unpleasant, but it was no longer terrifying because I'd had plenty of time to get used to sitting up. Still, just to be sure, I hastily secured Tony's dark glasses to my head with sticky tape.

The lift was full of people from the outside world. They all looked so well: nice, ordinary people who might easily have lived in our village. I had a sudden yearning to talk about absorbing things like vegetable marrows and the church fête, so I smiled up at them encouragingly as the lift descended. They all hastily looked the other way. Was I invisible, just because I was in a wheelchair? It was a long time since I had looked at myself in a mirror but I was conscious that my face twitched and winked in an unpredictable manner, and the patch which the physios had put over one eye to stimulate the muscles of the other must have made me look very odd. I even began to regret the sticky-taped glasses. Concentrating on not allowing my hands to shake, I smiled once again. Surely these people must realise that inside I was still a perfectly normal housewife?

'It's a bit hot today,' I said to the woman carrying a bunch of roses. Well, that is what I *meant* to say: actually it sounded more like, 'Icha bitcha ot tomorrow.' She looked embarrassed and hastily turned round to talk to her husband. Mortified, I wanted to shout, 'There's nothing wrong with my speech usually, I just get a bit muddled when I'm nervous.'

'Does she like grapes?' asked another woman, addressing the porter as if I did not exist. 'My sister's too ill to eat these.'

I was not going to risk speech again so I nodded vigorously and held out my wobbling hand to her, but she gave the grapes to the porter, who hung the bag out of reach on the handle of the chair.

'There you go,' he said as the doors slid open, and before I could make those people realise I was not an imbecile he whisked me away out of sight. Perhaps the hardest part about being disabled is the moment when you first realise that you are.

The memory of the faces in the lift haunted me and I began to wonder how Tony would feel if I stayed like this permanently. Would he go on loving a disabled wife who wet herself, sounded like a turkey and shook like a geriatric? How was I going to bring up so many children from a wheelchair; and would we be able to go on living in our country paradise if I could no longer drive the car? Every night I had a recurring nightmare in which I was desperately searching for something I had lost. When I woke up, sweating and crying, I would realise it was my body and strength

I had lost; it takes a long time to work through that kind of a bereavement.

★ ★ ★

It was a hot August afternoon when we began to be a family again. I had imagined this moment so many times in hospital and I had always been sure that once I was safely home again I would easily manage all the chores. How naive can you be! As it was still the school holidays Tony was at home, but so were all the children – and I had forgotten just how much noise they made.

'What shall I cook for supper?' I asked Tony brightly as I tottered about the kitchen making 'busy noises' to indicate I was back in control. I was not totally dependent on a wheelchair until a couple of years later, but I needed two walking sticks to stabilise myself and I had no idea where I was putting my feet because I still could not feel them. When I fell over the rug on the kitchen floor my dignity took a heavier knock than my nose!

'Just sit down and let us get on,' said Tony crossly.

'I can do it if you'll just give me time,' I protested, but I soon had to leave Tony and Sarah to clear the chaos I had created. Over the next few weeks I was to discover that something had gone wrong with my ability to think, and I could not even remember the way to cook fish fingers. When I reached for the frying pan my hands were too weak to lift it, and the tomatoes I tried to slice slithered away from me, leaving me to chop my fingers instead. Fortunately they did not hurt because I had little feeling in my limbs, but the downside meant if I picked up a dish I did not realise it was hot until I noticed my fingers were blistered.

When the food was finally dished up, that first day, and the whole family gathered round the kitchen table, it was anything but the idyllic experience I had anticipated so often in hospital. Sound was still a problem, and when everyone talked at once their voices were just a distorted roar. When I tried to say something I muddled words like 'his' and 'hers', 'down' and 'up', and I forgot vital words in the middle of sentences. So my frantic efforts to communicate with the children were met with baffled stares. When I told Richard to 'hurry up and sit on his pudding' it was Justyn who saved the day by beginning to laugh. During that first meal I realised that by allowing my oddities to become a family joke I would prevent the children from realising how much they worried me.

As the day progressed, however, it became increasingly hard to keep cheerful. The house and garden all seemed in such a mess that I found it hard to relax, so I staggered round picking things up and putting them down again in a vague attempt at tidying. After an hour of my getting in everyone's way Sarah was looking thunderous and Sarah-Jane was in tears, while Justyn soothingly suggested, 'Mum, why don't you just sit down and I'll make you a nice cup of tea.'

'We managed fine while you were away,' muttered Sarah. 'Dad relied on me for everything and we all knew exactly what we were supposed to do. Now you're home you're just upsetting everything!' She was only expressing her own pain; while she had been mothering everyone else, including Tony, she had yearned for a mother to cosset her sometimes. Now I had finally come home, looking more like a frail old granny than a mum, she must have felt she had been landed with yet another burden.

As I was trying to drink Justyn's cup of tea Duncan came running in from the garden, his nose streaming with blood. Once he would have come to me for comfort but he ran straight past me to Sarah. I felt redundant and almost like an intruder in my own home.

When Tony finally climbed into bed beside me, he was so tired he was asleep within seconds. That first day must have been as hard for him as it was for me, but I will always be grateful that his anxiety never made him wrap me in cotton wool. Although I operated at the pace of an elderly tortoise he let me do as much as I could to help, which must have been maddening for him at times. During the following eight years onlookers might have thought he was unfeeling, but actually his detached approach helped as much as Justyn's laughter to maintain my self-confidence.

*   *   *

When the school term began I insisted on going with Tony to take Richard to school for his first day. Handing your five-year-old over to a reception class teacher is a symbolic moment in a mother's life, but it was also the first day I had appeared in the village since coming out of hospital. Normally I would have bounced into the centre of the group of mums standing round the school gate, demanding to know everyone's news, but as I walked slowly across the car park clutching Tony's arm and a walking stick I was conscious of eyes staring at me from all directions. It must have been a bit of a shock for them, I suppose, because I weighed at least four stone less than when they had last seen me and I still had the patch over one eye. Some people smiled, but I saw pity in their eyes, while others turned hurriedly away and pretended they had not seen us at all. I am sure they were just embarrassed, or perhaps afraid of saying the wrong thing, but the fact that they said nothing made me feel excluded. That night at supper Duncan capped it all when he said, 'Mum, don't come up to school again, will you? I don't like my friends staring at you.'

So I stayed home, where boredom soon became my biggest problem. I was still too weak to do anything much in the house or garden so two of Otty's sisters kindly paid for daily help; but I missed the usual round of chores and village activities, and without Richard the house felt like a silent tomb. In the distance, across the fields, I could see the village nestling round the church on the hill; I knew it would be humming with all the usual autumn events. 'I don't fit in with them any more,' I thought, 'but where *do* I fit?'

Of course, this loneliness was my own fault. Plenty of people trekked down the lane to visit me, but when I heard the doorbell I hid. I told myself I couldn't concentrate long enough to hold a conversation, but actually my old enemy shyness was slinking up behind me. The memory of those limp gloves did not help me this time because being on the receiving end of other people's help and kindness is not nearly as comfortable as being used as God's gloves yourself! I had lost all the roles and responsibilities that gave my life a purpose and I was reverting to those old destructive thinking patterns that had imprisoned me as a teenager. They told me I was a worthless wreck and a burden on my family and community – so I'd better keep out of the way.

I used to laugh bitterly sometimes as I wondered why I had wasted all that time, earlier in the year, asking God what he wanted to do with my life after Richard started school. The 'Martha' in me had been put out of action – but so had my 'Mary' because I couldn't concentrate to pray or focus my eyes sufficiently to read the Bible. I concluded that I had got it wrong when I thought God was calling me to be a prophetess. Instead of addressing the Almighty directly I wrote him rude notes in my journal.

25 September
All I ever wanted to do was know you and serve you but you've chucked my life away on the scrap heap.

Life in our house was not pleasant that winter. Between them the six children managed to produce enough insecure behaviour to provide material for a whole textbook on disturbed children! We were faced with nightmares, bed-wetting, truancy, aggression, shoplifting, hyperactivity, eating problems and many other horrors! It was all quite overwhelming, coming as it did when Tony and I were also struggling with our own emotional reactions to my illness.

'We never seem to laugh at mealtimes any more these days,' commented Sarah one evening as we sat round the kitchen table; and it was then that it began to dawn on me that I was depressed.

Now, through my job, I often meet people who have recently gone through a serious illness or life-changing loss, and I always tell them that reactive depression is quite normal. However, in 1982 I honestly thought Christians should never be depressed. In the evangelical circles in which I grew up, depression was seen as a sign of weakness or the result of some buried sin. So I was far too embarrassed to tell anyone about the terrible grey cloud of misery that had descended on me – not even Tony. When you have taught your face to wear a habitual smile you can fool the world quite successfully.

Depression is the worst experience a Christian can ever go through. In other forms of illness, loss or distress you have God's presence to comfort you, but depression robs you of the ability to feel God's love.

The morning I found Otty's sleeping pills I had written in my journal:

29 October
I am lost. Life is quite hopeless. Why didn't I die on 2 June when I had the chance? Tony and the children would all be happier without me. I am just a useless zombie. Perhaps I should destroy myself before I damage them any further.

The sleeping pills were tucked in among some of Otty's things that I had pushed into the bottom drawer of an old chest. I stood for a long time looking down at them, thinking, 'If I took all these pills I could be out of this pain and misery for good.'

One of the causes of my depression would have been a chemical imbalance after such a serious viral illness, but looking back I can see that I was not helping myself by wallowing in so many dismal, negative thoughts. It is not what happens to us in life that affects our feelings, but *what we think* about what has happened to us. Constant negative thoughts were killing my hope and making me feel gloomy and dismal. I was probably also very angry but struggling hard to hide the fact from everyone, including myself.

God had allowed my carefully constructed world to be so utterly destroyed, but at that time I would never have admitted I was angry with him.

There is nothing more harmful than anger towards God when you have set your sights on knowing him. I don't mean the kind of quick, indignant explosions that are a healthy part of any close relationship, but the chronic, smouldering resentment you hold on to silently for months and don't even let yourself realise is there. This kind of frozen rage makes you turn your back on him and walk away in the other direction. I know he is big enough to take all our anger, which is utterly normal when we are badly hurt; but he had, after all, explained his reasons for allowing these things to hit me three months before I became ill (see p. 133). He could hardly have done more than that, but the bit of paper was still lost in my kitchen drawer! Being constantly misunderstood by his friends must hurt him so badly.

* * *

The day I stood gazing down at Otty's sleeping pills I realised at long last that I needed help, so I asked Tony to take me to see George, the hospital chaplain.

'I think I'm depressed,' I admitted wretchedly, waiting for him to start digging up my sins and failings, but he was far too wise for that. He simply asked the Lord to take the depression away. It did not disappear instantly, but from that day it gradually began to lift. I guess George went on praying for me, because a few weeks after I visited him something else happened which definitely speeded my recovery.

For a special treat Tony took me to a concert in Eastbourne; it was the first time I had been out in public so the noisy crowds thronging to the foyer fazed me slightly. 'They all look so happy,' I thought and inwardly prayed, 'Lord, I've totally lost my joy.' Distinctly I heard him reply, 'Then take mine instead.' The following day I was reading the Beatitudes in Matthew 5: *Blessed are they that mourn: for they shall be comforted*' (v. 4, KJV), and I suddenly realised that the comfort is optional – we have to choose to be comforted by the Lord. I had been refusing his comfort (and his joy) because I had been too angry to receive it. Over the following months I tried fighting the dismal thoughts by deliberately choosing 'his joy', and by the time the bluebells were back in the woods life began to feel worth living again.

★ ★ ★

Although the physical problems were still there, I was definitely feeling stronger, and the pain, although it remained constant, had now subsided to a more manageable level. There were also other reasons why I felt so much better. Gom had finally retired and was now spending most of her time with us. Her company was lovely and her physical help invaluable, but she was getting old and the Lord must have realised her energy was limited because he sent extra help – but from a very unlikely source!

It began the evening I finally felt well enough to go back to our church house group and discovered that Brother Tom had defied his Superior by becoming a regular member. That evening he told us about a wonderful dream he'd had several nights in a row. He was cooking in the monastery kitchen, he told us, when the Lord himself had knocked on the door.

'I wanted to make him the best meal I've ever cooked,' Brother Tom told us ecstatically. In his dream he finally placed before his master grilled fish covered in cheese sauce with fluffy white potatoes and green peas. 'But,' finished Tom sadly, 'I always wake up before I see him enjoying it.'

The following week he told us, with many tears, the sequel to his story.

'Last Friday I had just taken my brothers their meal into the refectory, leaving my own in the oven. When I came back to fetch it, I heard a knock on the back door and outside in the rain stood a very smelly tramp, who asked for a meal. Communities like ours are obliged by our rule to give hospitality but there was no food left except my own plate in the oven. So, rather crossly, I served him with it at the kitchen table, but as I stood watching him eat I realised that it was grilled fish in cheese sauce with potatoes and peas. I was so overwhelmed I had to start washing the saucepans to hide my tears' (Matthew 25:40).

It so happened that John, the tramp, had recently been converted and baptised by a missionary who worked with the local 'travelling' community, and we soon found John could praise the Lord even louder than Brother Tom when he began coming to church. He supported himself by doing odd gardening jobs round the village but continued to sleep in barns or haystacks. One Sunday during a cold winter, as he sat stinking in the pew in front of us, Sarah whispered, 'Mum, let's ask him back for lunch.' We did, and he stayed with us for the rest of the day while everyone breathed through their mouths and not through their noses! When it was late and we began to make 'final noises' in John's direction Sarah, who had obviously been deeply impacted by Brother Tom's dream, drew me into the kitchen.

'Mum,' she said, 'it's snowing. You can't let us sleep in warm beds while John sleeps under a hedge.' We had no room in the house so we let him sleep in the shed at the bottom of the garden, which Tony had fitted out as a study when Otty had lived with us.

'You're welcome to stay here tonight, John,' we said, but he was still there two years later! He hacked the garden back into shape, mended the drive, cleaned the car, and then quietly took over the housework too, spending his days vacuuming, peeling potatoes and scrubbing the floors. All we could give him for those hours of devoted service was his food, the shed and Tony's cast-off clothes – but how we loved him and I think he genuinely loved us in return. Whenever he saw me looking tired he would say, 'You sit down, Mrs Woman, while I make you a nice cuppa tea.'

Unfortunately John did not stick to tea himself: all the money the state gave him each Thursday went on alcohol. He tried so hard to kick his life-long addiction but, in spite of Brother Tom's earnest prayer, he never quite managed it. He and Gom were about the same age and soon developed a hilarious relationship; they both loved talking and did so continuously, but neither of them ever listened to a word the other one said. As they were both deaf and spoke very loudly, the noise was quite indescribable. The only thing they ever agreed about was their devotion to our family. What a lot those two unusual people taught us about love!

One summer day when Sarah and I were sitting in the garden, under the apple tree, she suddenly said, 'Mum, why don't you write a proper novel, for people of my age?'

'I don't think I'm quite well enough yet to sit at a table and type,' I said doubtfully.

Tony, who with John's help was weeding the nearby potato patch, joined the conversation by saying, 'You could write if your head and arms were properly supported in a comfortable armchair. I could make you a special table to fit over your knees.' Throwing down his spade, he hurried away, and loud sawing and hammering noises could soon be heard coming from his workshop.

The following morning, feeling rather a fool, I typed 'Chaptor wun' at the top of a piece of paper, and the hours the children spent at school never seemed to drag after that. By the end of October the story of *The Broken Stone* was finished, but because Tony was really too busy to correct the spellings we sent it to someone who advertised 'help with typing' in the local paper. She told me brightly that spelling was her strong point, but six weeks later she rang to say she had just been put on tranquillisers!

'You've made me lose my nerve,' she complained. 'I'm even having to look up words like "was" in the dictionary now.' All the same she did a grand job, and when Naomi had wrapped the manuscript up in brown paper, Sarah took it up to the post office in the village addressed to a publisher.

But just when we all thought life was fun again we were plunged back down into misery.

* * *

It was November when we all went down with flu. The children were back at school a few days later, but the effect the virus had on me was catastrophic because it triggered a return of the previous inflammation. When the walls of that London hospital closed round me yet again I was in despair. After a whole range of electrical tests the neurologist told us that he thought I now had more than one problem. First there was the permanent damage left by the encephalitis. This showed up quite clearly in the tests as damage to the central nervous system. Scarring on the casing of the nerves was the reason why I couldn't always make my arms and legs do what they were told and why my skin couldn't feel things properly. It also accounted for my bladder and balance problems and my occasional 'bumpy' speech.

'Your brain is taking longer to get messages through to the rest of your body,' the consultant explained, 'and we can't expect any more improvement at this stage, I'm afraid.' He also thought that some of my symptoms, particularly the constant pain and muscular fatigue, were because the inflammation of the brain and spinal cord had now become chronic, and he labelled this as myalgic encephalomyelitis. 'We'll do everything we possibly can to make you comfortable,' he promised, 'but you're just going to have to make the most of a rather limited life.'

Tony and I were both stunned. We had been so sure that I was gradually getting better and would soon be my old healthy self once again. Perhaps we would have been even more shattered if we had realised what the next six years were going to be like. Any kind of infection would trigger another acute episode of serious, life-threatening illness, sending me back into Intensive Care followed by many more weeks recovering in hospital. The other day I found a cassette tape of a sermon Tony preached towards the end of those six years, in which he describes our lives as 'a constant struggle to climb up from a deep coal mine, inch by inch, then, just before reaching the top, falling all the way back down to the bottom again'.

★ ★ ★

A few days after we had talked to the consultant, Tony dropped his bombshell.

'I can't cope any longer,' he said in a dull flat voice, quite unlike his own. 'We simply can't go on living out here in the country if you aren't going to get better. Ferrying the children around, keeping such a big garden going … it's all too much. We're going to have to move back to Tunbridge Wells so the children can take themselves to Brownies, music lessons and football. And I know Social Services would give us loads more help if we were living in town.'

All I could think of was how I could live without the sound of a fox barking across the fields in the moonlight or the sun setting behind the old windmill.

During the months that it took to sell our lovely home in the country and exchange it for a terraced house near the station in the centre of a busy town, I worked extremely hard to convince God that if only he would heal me he could spare me from such a ghastly fate! By February, however, I was beginning to realise he had no intention of doing so, and I wrote in my journal:

25 February
Why are you letting all this be taken away from me? Don't you realise all this loveliness that I can see all around me here is you to me, not just your creation, but a see-able, feel-able YOU? I won't be able to worship you without it.

Brother Tom, who visited us often to give Sarah Latin lessons, had no sympathy for me whatsoever.

'I'd live in a sewer if Our Lord asked me to,' he said shortly.

'But I'll lose all my friends,' I protested.

'You won't lose Jesus.'

I felt like slapping his beaming red face, but as usual I merely smiled politely to hide my resentment.

That winter was just as difficult as the proceeding one when I had been so depressed. By now I was holding back so much anger behind a wall of silence that it drove Tony into an equally stony fortress. He bought his first computer that winter and began spending every spare moment gazing lovingly into its face – but he never looked into mine! As the months went by he became so withdrawn I persuaded him to come with me to see some Christian marriage counsellors who I secretly hoped would make him see that I simply could not survive in a town. I was somewhat dashed when they said, 'Jen, you don't need woods and fields, you only need Jesus.'

They were right, of course, but I did not want to hear that just then! 'Your illness is making life very difficult for Tony; you must try and ease things for him.' When we finally drove home my face was positively aching with the effort of holding in place the smile that covered my rage.

All our Christian friends seemed to know *exactly* why God was not healing me. By the early 1980s healing had become the major issue in British churches. The charismatic movement had reminded us of the miracle dimension which Protestants had ignored for so long; now suddenly we were aware of this dimension which exists beyond the skill of doctors, drugs and surgical techniques. Discovering the glorious fact that God still heals people led to the conclusion that it must be his will for every Christian to be perfectly fit and healthy. If they did not recover when they were prayed for, then it was because they lacked faith or were holding on to some secret sin. Fortunately most people have moved on from that extreme attitude these days, perhaps because so many charismatic leaders have become ill – in spite of their faith and the prayers of other Christians. While most of us still believe God can heal people physically, we have to concede that he does not always do so in this life. *Of course* it is his will for us all to be perfectly fit and well, but for a reason which remains a mystery, he sometimes waits to heal us until we step into heaven.

When I failed to recover, all the books that our friends were reading at the time led them to believe I must be 'blocking' my healing. Their many and widely differing suggestions for removing the block seemed to come at me like gunfire from all directions.

'You aren't trying hard enough.'

'You're trying too hard, just "let go and let God".'

'Just look to Jesus and start praising him.'

'It's Tony's sceptical attitude that's holding you back.'

'You've put yourself in Satan's power through some unconfessed sin.'

'It's a generational thing; your parents must have sinned.'

'You need deliverance from a spirit of infirmity and doubt.'

I was so keen to get well and avoid having to live in a town that I took all these statements very seriously, even if that meant going through long deliverance sessions, a week of fasting and repentance and all kinds of other investigations and humiliations. When all their efforts failed I felt I had disappointed everyone, and that hurt more than anything else because I still had the crazy desire to please everyone. So I let them cart me off to different healing services around the country, and I had so much 'laying on of hands' it was a wonder I did not go bald! Finally we 'called the elders' of our church for anointing with oil (James 5:14) but still nothing changed. Perhaps I had to learn the hard way that healing cannot be earned by faith or good behaviour.

Finally, one Saturday morning just before we moved from the country, God intervened in a most remarkable way. The day started badly. Tony made a bright remark about how much easier life was going to be for us all in town – and my candyfloss mask flew right off! The steam iron was standing on the ironing board just behind where he sat peacefully reading his paper. Furiously I lunged at the iron, hoping to send it flying in his direction, but my arm did not have enough strength so the iron just fell to the floor, broke apart, and died with an indignant hiss of steam.

'It'll cost fifteen pounds to buy another,' said Tony mildly, without looking up from the sports page. He had also been brought up to hold in his anger!

As I looked round at all the packing cases I wanted to scream – but was afraid of upsetting the children. So I shuffled out into the garden on my elbow crutches and stood looking across the fields and woods I loved so much. It was one of those days in late March when everything seems just about to burst into life – but this year I would not be there to see the bluebells. I tried to fix every detail into my mind as I had done the evening when I was twelve sitting, for the last time, beside the lake at Hildenborough.

At the end of the garden a row of weeping willow trees hung over the fence from the field beyond. The cows loved to shelter under those trees and, being cows, they did all that cows have to do. After rain a small pond of slurry would seep through the fence into our garden; it stank but John loved spreading it on the rhubarb patch. It was there that I lost my balance and keeled over, flat on my face, in thick brown muck. Frantically I tried to stand up but I simply did not have the strength in my legs, and suddenly I felt angrier than I ever had in my life. As it dawned on me at last that it was God himself I blamed for everything, I used words that would have made Granny turn in her grave! Writhing about like a demented warthog in disgusting muck that seemed to suck me down and drown me, I thought, 'This is like my life!'

'You've turned it all to nothing but shit!' I told God loudly. The more I struggled to get out, the deeper I sank, and it seemed to be the same with my problems.

'This is all your fault!' I added furiously. 'You could change everything if only you'd heal me! Why tell me you want me to be your prophetess and then leave me like this? I'm fed up with being trapped inside this body that hurts all the time, my marriage is in ruins, the children are vile and you don't take a blind bit of notice!'

As I lay there, beside myself with rage and frustration, God actually came to me. I didn't 'see' him but the sense of his love all around me was so intense it made me gasp. I always think of that moment when I sing the song 'Overwhelmed by Love', because I literally was! I did not hear an audible voice but I felt he wanted me to know that he cared about the awful mess I was in, and he *minded*. Yet instead of taking it away he wanted me to let him into the middle of it, right into the core of the pain and bewilderment. I only had to ask, and he would come.

For a long time I lay still, with the mud oozing around me, trying to absorb what he had said. *Had* I been pushing him away? For months I had been convinced that he had moved away from me because I had unwittingly offended him in some way that he was not prepared to divulge. Was he saying that it was *me* who had pushed *him* away, excluding him from the centre of my life?

We all have a place in the very middle of our being which God wants to fill. Yet, even when we are Christians, we do not always allow him to stay in that central place; he gets pushed out on to the sidelines of our lives by all kinds of things. That day I realised anger had been taking up so much room inside me that it had pushed him off-centre and usurped his place at the controls of everything I thought, said and did.

As I've already said, knowing God is about opening ourselves up to him so he can fill every part of us. I wonder why I have so often excluded him from the private cupboards where I hide my resentments, disappointments and fears.

It was a long time before anyone in the house realised I was missing and came out to look for me, so I just lay there, asking his forgiveness for all that buried rage. Then, carefully and deliberately, I asked him back into that middle space while the intensity of his love became practically unbearable. When I think of that moment it reminds me of a phrase from one of Christina Rossetti's prayers: 'Give us grace in loving penitence to cast ourselves down into the depth of thy compassion.' That experience was so important to me that I have shared it almost every time I have ever spoken anywhere in the world. How could I ever get tired of talking about love like that?

★   ★   ★

It would be nice to say that once all that buried anger was released I was physically healed and we all lived happily ever after! Actually my body had to wait another six years for that miraculous healing, until 13 June 1990, but I still think that what happened the day I fell in that cow dung was a far greater miracle than my eventual recovery. It seems almost simplistic to say we lived in the light of that miracle for the following six years, but I cannot think of a better way of explaining the difference my walk to the end of the garden made to our family. Once my heart was no longer dominated by resentment and the Lord was back in his place, I changed. An inexplicable sense of well-being characterised those years, and we christened this feeling 'peace-joy' because it was an inseparable blend of the two words. Tony found living in town so much less stressful that he soon reverted to his old self, and the children loved the independence of getting themselves to school. The boys gained massive 'street cred' by their prowess on skateboards and the proximity to the shops delighted the girls; universally they preferred vegetables from the supermarket because they came ready scrubbed and slug-free! We even found a church we all liked and the following six years were extremely happy for us all.

Yes, even for me! A few weeks after we moved an entry in my journal reads:

25 May
I am actually happy! I never thought that could be possible again.

My father's irritating quote, 'The Good Lord knows what 'e's a'doin' of', was proved correct yet again! God knew I could never survive a life surrounded by pavements, shops and traffic, so he provided me with the park. Our house was at the end of the terrace so I had a choice of two views from my window. If I looked in one direction I could see shops and the busy road leading to the station, but in the other direction I could see a wide swathe of green, dotted with mature trees. When my brother

Justyn next came over from Canada, he decided that I needed an electric wheelchair so I could go out round the park on my own. They were extremely expensive in those days and he could not possibly afford one – but a small thing like that never stopped my brother! I christened the chair 'The Bug' and spent hours cruising about the three beautiful parks that were in easy reach. Otty's youngest sister Geraldine gave me a little white dog called Minty who used to ride along on my lap when she was not walking to 'wheel' behind me.

John came with us, of course, and for a while slept in the cellar, but when it flooded he managed to find accommodation in a housing association complex where he ended his days very happily, loving us all to the end. Gom was given a snug little pensioner's flat next to our church, and when she was not with us she used to sit by her TV watching tennis, cricket or golf while wearing a floppy sun hat 'to put herself in the right mood'. I earnestly hope that when I am in my eighties I will be as contented and easily pleased as John and Gom! Their help was replaced by the DHSS once I was officially placed on the Disabled Persons' Register and awarded invalidity and mobility benefits at the highest rate. They sent us a lovely carer called Lyn who came each morning to wash and dress me; and she kept the housework under control too, by doing far more hours than she was ever paid to do. Michelle came in to cook the evening meal and pack next day's school lunches. So life was organised again and we ticked over uneventfully, in spite of the long stretches I spent away in hospital.

★　★　★

One afternoon Tony was taking the boys to watch a football match near Rochester, so he suggested dropping me, and the Bug, in the cathedral.

'It would give you an afternoon out,' he said, but initially the idea did not appeal; I would have preferred the shops if it hadn't been pelting with rain. I suppose cathedrals were designed to demonstrate the lofty grandeur of God, and as the Bug glided silently over the polished floors the great pillars and arches rose protectively around me like the beech trees in Fir Toll Woods. The choir was practising a rendering of Psalm 27 and the presence of God filled the vastness of the building. I parked myself in a side aisle and sat still, letting the music waft around me.

After a while, as I sat there with my eyes closed, I became increasingly aware of an unpleasant smell, which distinctly reminded me of John when he was a 'Gentleman of the Road'. Opening my eyes I saw 'Anna the prophetess' herself (Luke 2:36– 8)! Well, the old woman sitting in the row in front of me *reminded* me of Anna as she sat with her gnarled hands folded over the handle of a stout stick. She had obviously been living rough in the open air for years, because her wrinkled skin was brown as a walnut and all her worldly possessions were stuffed into the two polythene bags on the seat beside her. She seemed to be enjoying the music as much as I was, and I guessed she must have been a regular visitor to the cathedral by the way the sextons smiled and nodded as they walked by. Perhaps, like the real Anna, she enjoyed spending her time in God's house surrounded by his presence. The words that the choir was singing at that moment added to that idea:

One thing I ask of the LORD, this is what I seek: that I may dwell in the house of the LORD all the days of my life, to gaze upon the beauty of the LORD and to seek him in his temple.

Psalm 27:4

The sense that God wanted me to identify with Anna the prophetess, when I woke up so suddenly that morning in Devon, had been so strong at the time, but obviously I was never going to be a jet-setting evangelist now! As I sat watching the old lady gently tapping her grubby shoe in time with the organ, I realised that the real Anna would have sat just like that, perhaps listening to the same psalm being sung. In fact, sitting in God's presence was all she did most of the time.

It was then that I realised I had totally misunderstood what being a prophetess would have meant to her. She hadn't gone off round the world in search of people who needed help. When her husband died, seven years after their marriage, she had spent all her time in the temple. She loved worshipping so much that for eighty-four years she had attended every single temple service and call to prayer. If there were no official services at night then she spent long hours in prayer by herself (Psalm 134:1). Far from preaching to great crowds, the only time we are told that she ever addressed a large group of people was the day when she recognised a peasant's baby as the Messiah. At the time when she met Mary and Joseph, people would have been flocking into the temple for the afternoon call to prayer, and Anna was just so excited she could not help telling them that all their hope for the future was wrapped up in that tiny bundle in Mary's arms. Because she would probably have been married at the age of 14 she could have been at least 105 before she became a mass evangelist!

But that did not mean that she lived like a contemplative hermit; in order to earn the title 'prophetess' she must have spent those years helping the people who came to the temple to know God in a deeper way themselves. She obviously spent a lot of time praying for them, too, while denying herself the things others took for granted (Luke 2:37). In fact, she had her 'Martha' side and her 'Mary' side in perfect balance.

When the old girl in the row in front of me suddenly heaved herself to her feet and shuffled away, clutching her bulging bags and muttering to herself, I wondered how I could have thought she was like Anna. Far from being a ragged old vagrant, Anna must have been a well-known and highly respected figure because no one else, male or female, had been officially recognised as a prophet in Israel for the last four hundred years. So I guessed that people must have realised that Anna had a special ability to hear God and explain to others what he was saying. My imagination began to picture the mothers and young girls, who came to the temple for the various feasts throughout the year, sidling up to sit next to Anna. I could 'see' them sharing their worries and desires with her, knowing that she would pray for them in the coming weeks; she probably also gave them a message of guidance or comfort direct from the Lord himself.

Evensong was just beginning by the time it dawned on me that although Anna might have occasionally talked to people about the God she loved so much, the main reason for her existence was to worship him and spend time in his company.

'What a *fool* I've been,' I muttered. 'If that's what he was calling me to do, then I can do it just as easily from a wheelchair!'

It would have been impossible for me to sit in a church all day, as Anna had done, but I had enough sense to realise that I could 'live perpetually in God's presence' in my own home. It was just a matter of realising he was there with me.

To be honest, the idea of 'praying without ceasing' (1 Thessalonians 5:17) had always seemed utterly ludicrous for someone with so many children! In fact, I would often come to the end of the day and realise that I had hardly thought about God once since I finished my prayer time in the early morning. Intimacy with God only seemed possible in pre-planned time slots, rather as I had once had my time with my father in his study each day between 1.30 and 2.00; but I longed to share *all* my life with the Lord, not just a daily appointment.

Soon after that afternoon in the cathedral I discovered something which helped me with that problem. It was a tiny little book that had belonged to Otty, and it had been tucked away behind the many much weightier volumes I had inherited from my parents. It was called *The Practice of the Presence of God* and had been written in the 1600s by Brother Lawrence, a monk who was probably very like Brother Tom. He had also cooked in a monastery kitchen, but at first he would much rather have been allowed to spend his time worshipping in the chapel. He was barred from doing that because he was only a lay brother, and the Abbot thought he was nothing but a 'great clodhopping fool' and banished him to the kitchen. For a long time this really upset Lawrence, until he realised that God was just as much with him in the busy rush of preparing meals as he was in the stillness of the choir stalls. So he began training himself to be aware of God whatever he happened to be doing, whether it was turning the joints on the spit or sweeping the floor. Even in the middle of conversations with the other kitchen hands he was in perpetual communion with God, and sometimes the joy of this companionship was so great he wept tears into the soup he was stirring! He claimed that being aware of God's presence with you constantly throughout the day was merely a habit which, like any other, could be practised until it became automatic.

'If Brother Lawrence is right,' I told myself when I had finished his book, 'I want to train myself to do the same.' Ever since then, I've been working hard to acquire this skill, with varying degrees of success!

Naturally I did not start talking to God all the time under my breath or I would soon have been certified; but when you know a person really well you can enjoy being in their company without needing to talk. Eventually thinking in God's presence can become a most comfortable form of prayer.

During the first six years after we moved to Tunbridge Wells, because there was little else I could do all day except sit still in a chair, I used to spend hours watching the people hurrying past our window. The early morning joggers on their way to the park, commuters taking a short cut to the station, children dragging their school bags, harassed young mums and old ladies with shopping trolleys – the stream was never-ending. I looked out for my favourites and developed the habit of praying for them as they went by each day. Two of these 'window people' quite unconsciously gave me a very clear picture of the depth of intimacy with God for which I have always craved.

The house that stood in the terrace opposite our own was divided into flats, and every evening around five I used to see a small face appear at the first-floor window. It belonged to a five-year-old whose nose was regularly squashed against the glass as she gazed down the road, watching for her father returning from work. The moment he turned the corner from the station she would hurtle out of the front door and rush down the pavement towards him. He was an enormous plumber with a bushy red beard; as soon as he caught sight of her in the distance he would throw down his bag of tools and crouch down, his arms open wide, ignoring all the other commuters hurrying home from the London train. I used to love the way she flung herself into those arms; he would make one of his legs into a little seat for her while she snuggled up as close to him as she possibly could. All the time she was busy telling him about the caterpillars she had found or the cakes she had made for his tea she would sit gazing up into his face while she gently stroked his beard.

I was listening to a teaching tape, about that time, which said that the Hebrew phrase 'seek the Lord's face' or 'enquire of the Lord' can just as easily be translated as 'to stroke the Lord's beard'; and the word 'worship' could also mean 'to move towards someone in order to kiss'. Whenever I think of the word 'intimacy' I always think of that plumber and his little daughter. It was not just the child's delight that I remember, but the way the father's face lit up with joy as he caught sight of her running towards him through the crowds and the absorbing interest with which he listened to the tiny details of her day. Their pleasure in one another was mutually satisfying.

It would be terrible if I gave the impression that, from that time on, I lived in a heavenly bubble floating above the rest of the world, entranced by the Lord's company. Knowing God just isn't like that! We might go through patches when he feels deliciously close; but then, for no reason we can understand, he seems to hide. All desire for him goes, we don't seem to 'get through' when we pray, church and Bible reading feel dry and boring. He is not being mean or capricious when he hides; he just wants to keep our relationship with him as fresh as a new love affair. If he allowed those times of *felt* intimacy to become a permanent way of life, we would soon take them for granted and lose that tingle of delight when we *feel* his company. Otty often used to say: 'The Lord promised we would have his presence with us always [Hebrews 13:5] but he never promised that we would always feel it.'

* * *

One morning I had a letter that caused me to shriek so loudly the family came running to my bedroom from all over the house to find out what was the matter. It was from the publisher to whom I had sent my teenage novel the previous year.

'They want to publish it!' I shouted, waving the letter about like a banner. '*And* they want to give me a contract for a couple of sequels!' Life was such fun after that as I lay in a reclining chair, clicking away happily on my typewriter.

About the same time I also wrote an article which caused quite a stir when it was published in a leading Christian magazine. Tony and I both felt desperately sorry for the thousands of other chronically sick and disabled Christians, and their families, who were still being put under pressure because they did not get better the moment someone prayed for them. We heard tragic stories about people who, instead of finding support and comfort in their churches, were treated as second-class Christians or even forced to leave their fellowships altogether. Perhaps I might have wanted to forget about the whole healing controversy if my friend Rhoda had not been diagnosed with liver cancer. The day after the news broke a group of friends took me with them when they went to the hospital to pray for her. As we were heading for her ward I suggested we might go into the chapel first to ask the Lord *how* he wanted us to pray.

'Why?' they said looking at me blankly. 'Surely the Lord wants us to pray for her healing.'

'He probably does,' I replied awkwardly, 'but don't you think we should ask him first?'

After we had done so I definitely felt that he wanted us to pray for peace and not healing, but the others felt I had a negative attitude and implied that if I had more faith I would be well myself. So I kept quiet while they prayed round Rhoda's bed so earnestly that a fly on the ceiling would have got the impression that the worst thing that could ever happen to a Christian was to go to heaven – instead of the very best.

A few days later Rhoda secretly confessed to me that she loved the Lord so much that her greatest desire was to go and be with him. She had no children and her husband had left her long ago, so although she enjoyed her life as a nurse, she shared St Paul's feeling that '*to live is Christ but to die is gain*' (Philippians 1:21). Over the next few weeks she had to endure enormous pressure from friends who were sure God would heal her when she would rather have been allowed to anticipate the joy of heaven. In the end she went to stay with her sister, who lived too far for most of her friends to visit, and she wrote to tell me she felt that at last she could die in peace. About a month later, I finally managed to find a way of visiting her; she was propped up in bed, not far from the end of her journey into God's heart, but looking more radiant than I had ever seen her before.

'I'm sitting here, looking right into heaven,' she told me, 'like I was looking through the window.'

'If you are offered the chance to come back to earth,' I told her ruefully, 'don't take it, will you?' She smiled, remembering how she had helped record my own 'death' experience.

'No way!' she murmured ecstatically. 'I can see all those colours you talked about.'

'Give my love to Jesus,' I said wistfully.

'He's coming for me,' she smiled, and a few hours later he had safely carried her home. Many of Rhoda's friends felt it was a failure of faith that had taken her there, but to me it was a *triumph* of faith.

It was my indignation on behalf of people like Rhoda that led me to write that article. A few weeks after it was published I received a letter from the senior editor of Hodder & Stoughton. It was short but life-changing: 'I've just read your article and wonder if we could discuss the possibility of expanding it into a book, based on your experiences of the healing dilemma.' They wanted some sample chapters but I was so full of ideas and strong feelings that writing them was easy.

I finished just before we left for our summer holiday, so I decided to take them with me to read to Tony while we were away. The older children had reached the stage when they wanted to be more adventurous so that year we exchanged our holiday at Stillmeadow in Devon for the horrendous discomfort of a youth hostel in North Yorkshire. I should never have gone too, but I did so hate being left out of family activities! How I longed to hike over the moors and climb the limestone crags. My 'peace-joy' was definitely strained to the limit, and so was Tony's as he tried to get so many children, plus a wheelchair and a dog, into the back of the car. He never had time to listen to those chapters, but I had plenty of time to think about them. And I panicked as I realised that writing this book would mean exposing ourselves, and all we had gone through, to public scrutiny. What about all the criticism we would get because we claimed that it isn't always God's will to heal us in this life? Perhaps I should just climb down off my hobbyhorse and leave time to bring the whole issue to a logical conclusion.

One glorious evening everyone decided to walk to a tarn they had seen on the Ordnance Survey map, so they left me in the car on a rough moorland road. I was sitting there, feeling very much alone but trying hard to pray about the book, when I heard the same distinct voice that had roused me from sleep on a previous holiday, but this time it did not say 'Anna' – it said, 'Abraham.' At first I thought God was trying to dispel my loneliness by telling me I was his friend, just as Abraham had been. I was settling down to enjoy this aspect of knowing God when I thought I had better not fall into the same trap as I had done last time and assume I knew what he was saying without stopping to ask him.

'Why did you say "Abraham", Lord?' I queried. At once I sensed he wanted me to read about this character so I scuffled in my bag to find my Bible. Genesis 12 seemed like a good place to start, but as I opened the page a single phrase stood out in bold black letters: *'I will bless you and make your name famous, so that you will be a blessing'* (Genesis 12:2, GNB). I underlined the verse and wrote beside it, 'August 1984 Ayton, my answer over the book.' From that moment to this I have never once doubted that God directed me to those words. The exposure entailed in writing *was* costly – and still is – but he certainly kept his promise of blessing. In his book *Telling Secrets*, Frederick Buechner states that nothing is more important 'than that we keep track, you and I, of who we are and where we have come from and the people we have met along the way because it is precisely through these stories in all their particularity that God makes himself known most powerfully and personally'.

With a lot of help from my cousin Tanya and long delays while I spent months in yet another London hospital, the manuscript was finished; we were delighted when it was accepted but amazed when it became a Christian bestseller. Soon the postman was jokingly telling us to get a bigger letterbox as he tried to push hundreds of letters from all over the world through our front door. To my relief we only had a very few critical ones; most were from people who said they were so pleased to find someone who had voiced their concerns at long last. As Oswald Chambers once wrote: 'The author who benefits you is not the one who tells you something you did not know before, but the one who gives expression to the truth that has been struggling for utterance in you.'

Somehow we had filled a gap that badly needed to be filled, and books can get into places where a 'jet-setting prophetess' would never be invited. When Tony was running a maths conference for teachers in the north of England, he was in the bar one evening with a teacher who had no interest in Christian things but seemed curious to know how Tony managed to cope with six children and a disabled wife. Before they said goodnight, Tony gave him a copy of the book, which he 'just happened' to have in his case. The book probably lay in the man's house, gathering dust, for some years, but one day he and his wife were chatting to their neighbour, Betty, who admitted she was terribly depressed and couldn't find anything to help.

'I'm sure I've got a book somewhere indoors,' said the teacher. 'It was written by a woman who got over depression – her husband gave it to me. You can have it, it's too religious for me.' Betty had no interest in Christianity either, but she needed something to occupy her mind so she began reading *Beyond Healing* at once. Late that same night she reached the part where I talk about the difference it made to a friend of mine when she asked Jesus into her life.

'I'm going to do that!' Betty told herself, and sitting all alone she did so – then and there! Soon after that Betty's husband changed his job and told her they would be moving to Tunbridge Wells.

'That's where the woman lives who wrote that book!' said Betty, and as soon as they moved in she looked up 'Larcombe' in the phone book. As we were the only ones listed she was soon dialling our number and the following day she came round for coffee.

'As soon as I'd asked Jesus in, my depression lifted, just like that!' she told me happily.

'Who was praying for you?' I asked her curiously.

'No one,' she replied, 'I don't know any Christians.' I was puzzled because I'd never heard of anyone finding Christ unless someone, somewhere, was praying for them.

Betty soon knew lots of Christians because her home was right by our church! Her husband Malcolm, a long-distance lorry driver, did not object to her coming with us but certainly did not wish to come too; so Betty and I made a pact to pray for him every day. A few months later, sitting alone in the cab of his lorry, he too asked Jesus into his heart.

That summer Malcolm and Betty went to Cornwall for their holiday because she had been evacuated there during the war. 'I'd love to go to the town where I lived,' she said. 'I had such a happy time because the people were so kind.' She even managed to find the house!

'I wonder if the present owner would let me have a peep inside,' she told Malcolm wistfully. When an old man finally answered her knock, she began, 'Would you mind if . . .' but the moment he heard her voice he shouted to his wife, 'Come quickly! It's our little Betty come home to us at last!'

Over scones and Cornish cream they told Betty they had prayed for her every day for the last forty-five years; Betty, who had never gone near a church, was reached by a book!

★   ★   ★

We often have the idea that some of us serve the Lord like busy Marthas while others are called to the more private, contemplative relationship which Mary enjoyed. I do not think we have to choose to be either one sister or the other; it is from the depth of our 'Mary' experiences that we move out to serve as Marthas. Once I had happily laid down the thought of serving the Lord in any kind of active or public way and learnt to enjoy being his 'Mary', he promptly allowed me to serve him again! Other books followed *Beyond Healing* and I soon had a regular page in various magazines; I was even invited to do some things on TV and radio. Occasionally I went to speak at outreach events, but it was always extremely difficult in a wheelchair and going out anywhere exhausted me for days afterwards. I was hardly the globetrotting evangelist I had expected to become, but I did meet people from all over the world through the letters that continued to pour in. Keeping in touch with them, however, took such a lot of my time that one of the children remarked one day, 'Mum, you need a secretary.'

'No, she doesn't,' said Tony, 'she needs a computer.' The

following day he confiscated my typewriter and, despite my loud protests, rigged up a computer in its place. 'Try it for a week,' he said, 'and if you still don't like it then, I'll give you the typewriter back.' Needless to say, once I discovered the spell check, I never used a typewriter again!

So life moved into one of those peaceful, uneventful stages. Tony and I enjoyed watching our children grow up and the older ones began to move out into the world; his work with slow learners was now recognised nationally and I had my writing to interest me, Lyn and Gom to look after me, and John to make me laugh. We might all have lived happily ever after had not the Lord suddenly set in motion another series of gentle interventions which led up to our lives being turned upside down yet again.

8

For my determined purpose is that I may know Him, that I may progressively become more deeply and intimately acquainted with Him, perceiving and recognizing and understanding the wonders of His Person more strongly and more clearly. And that I may in that same way come to know the power outflowing from His resurrection.

Philippians 3:10, AMP

Mother Julian, who lived in Norwich five hundred years ago, always maintained that when God wants to do something he first gives us a burden to pray that he'll do it. We think we are trying to persuade God into making our ideas work while actually the opposite is the case! It was the summer of 1989; and while I had totally accepted that God was not going to heal me physically, I began to yearn for him to use me, just as I was, in a much more powerful way. People were beginning to come to talk over their problems and ask for prayer, rather as temple visitors must have come to consult Anna. I longed for supernatural wisdom and a gift of healing with which to bless these visitors.

This new anointing for ministry felt so important to me that I wanted to wait for the right moment before asking for it; and the location of our holiday that summer provided me with the perfect setting. We went to Keswick in the Lake District, and while the more adventurous members of the family climbed Helvelyn and Skiddaw I glided happily round the shores of Derwentwater in the Bug. God had spoken to so many people in Keswick during a century of great Bible conventions that I sensed it was a very 'thin' place indeed. The spot that eventually seemed 'right' for my special request was a little beach near Friar's Crag. Apparently it got its name because in the days of the Celts a hermit lived on the little island just off the shore. Occasionally he would row across to this beach in order to pray for people who had a special request to make to the Lord. I wanted an anointing like his.

I saved my special prayer time up to the very last day of the holiday, but unfortunately, when I looked out of the window that morning, it was pouring with rain – as it so often does in the Lakes! Nothing was going to stop me, however, so in spite of a chorus of discouragement from the family, I put on the huge macintosh that covered not only me but also the Bug and set off for my special appointment with God. I am still not sure what I thought was going to happen that day at Friar's Crag, but the weather was so frightful I certainly had no witnesses.

At the time I had never heard of a man called Jabez who once prayed: '*Oh, that You would bless me indeed and enlarge my territory*' (1 Chronicles 4:10, NKJV), but as soon as I discovered him I knew that I had been yearning for a similar kind of blessing and spiritual expansion in all departments of my life. After I had prayed I waited a long time, watching the raindrops making perfect circles in the still, grey water – but God was silent and I had the distinct impression that he was hesitating, almost reluctant to give me something which I might not be able to handle wisely. Of course, he knew just how that anointing would change not only my life but also the entire family – and perhaps many others besides.

As we drove away from Keswick the following day I decided that his silence must have meant that he wanted to see just how persistent I was prepared to be in prayer, so I decided I would ask again in another 'thin' place to which we were headed for the second week of our holiday.

That place was Stillmeadow, in Devon. Again I waited until the last day of the holiday, and while the family were swimming I sat in the Bug, watching them from the cliffs overlooking the beach while I repeated my request. This time the answer came instantly. There is a red rock which rises out of the sea just off the beach; I can see it now as I look out of the windows of Stillmeadow where I am writing all this. Suddenly I knew Jesus was standing on that rock. I did not see his face but I was aware of an outline of someone far larger than a human being. In answer to my request he said: 'All you need is *me*.'

I've been working my way down into the depth of that statement ever since. It is so starkly simple but so profoundly true! At the time I thought it was just a gentle way of refusing my request; now I can see that he was trying to urge me to keep him as my focus and source of satisfaction in the new life which he could see lay just round the corner for me. The afternoon when he first spoke those words I actually had plenty of other things in my life besides him. I may have been a wheelchair-dependent cripple but I had a husband who took care of every detail of my life with great tenderness and children who were still at home or close by. Today they are all scattered around the world and I live alone, struggling to exist without them. Faced by so many gaps in my life, it is often hard to hold on to the fact that when I have Jesus I really do have everything I need. One thing *is* certain: while the pain of loss is often intense, I have definitely moved deeper into his heart since that sunny day in 1989.

★   ★   ★

'Why did I bother to ask for an anointing?' I asked myself as I watched the morphine dripping steadily from the bag suspended over my head. Far from being given some wonderful new ministry, that winter I became dangerously ill once again and we all plummeted back to the bottom of Tony's coal mine.

I might have given up all hope if a strange thing had not

happened to me one morning when I was back home again, struggling to recover. A man called Clem rang our doorbell very early one morning. He was elderly, retired and a semi-invalid who lived out in a village some miles from Tunbridge Wells.

'In the night, the Lord woke me,' he explained when he was shown into my bedroom. 'He told me to come round and tell you he *had* anointed you; he wants you to do a very special job for him in the future.' I had told *no one*, except my journal, about the request I had made the previous summer; only the Lord could have sent Clem with a message like that, but it must have taken a lot of courage to say such a thing to a woman who was almost too weak to move! He was the kind of person the world would have written off as 'past his sell-by date' but he was definitely one of my mother's 'handful'. He was so intimately acquainted with God that he knew instinctively what God was thinking, so he was often sent out with very surprising messages for other people (Acts 9:10–18).

By March I was beginning to feel a little stronger and Tony decided I needed a few days' break in Alfriston, a little Sussex village nestling in the Downs not far from Eastbourne. He was not free to come with me, but we knew of a place where they were able to give me the help I needed and he left me there with my computer set up by the bed.

'Get writing,' he told me. 'Nothing does you more good.'

This latest bout of illness had interrupted an attempt to write my first adult novel, *Leaning on a Spider's Web*. It was set in our road in Tunbridge Wells and all my characters were drawn from the people I watched from our windows. The Lockerbie air disaster had recently shocked the world, and in the last chapter of the book I planned to have a similar disaster wipe out most of my neighbours. The problem that faced me in Alfriston that day was, which of them should I allow to survive?

After a good night's sleep the ideas were beginning to flow nicely and, as Otty would have said, I was in 'orbit'. Suddenly, without any warning, I heard the voice I was getting to know quite well by that time (John 10:4): 'I want to heal you.'

The words were a complete shock to me. At the time I wasn't praying, reading the Bible or even thinking about healing; I was wondering if I should spare the life of Clare, the hairdresser, or bury her under the rubble of her salon.

'It's just my imagination,' I told myself firmly. 'It's hyperactive today!' And I turned back to my keyboard. But I had completely lost the 'orbit'; instead, those unexpected words kept going round and round inside my head.

If they had just been a vague premonition I might well have been more able to dismiss them as a figment of my own subconscious desires; but when the Lord speaks, his voice is always clear and specific. Perhaps I was just afraid; his words were facing me with the biggest faith challenge of my life.

Abraham had many faults and failings, but when God spoke he always believed him (Genesis 15:6), and his faith gave God such pleasure that he forgot all his other failings. I longed to be God's friend, as Abraham had been, but I also realised that real friendship depends on trust. My heart wanted to trust God too, but my mind was telling me that healing was impossible after eight years of disability. The medical profession did not expect me to recover after so long; the last DSS doctor who had examined me for my benefits had told me they would not need to assess me again as no further improvement was likely.

But the words 'I want to heal you' kept repeating themselves like an old-fashioned gramophone when the needle gets stuck. I could not help thinking about the massive changes that healing, after so many years, would entail. Our life in Tunbridge Wells was peaceful now; the DSS paid for my carers and had provided me with all kinds of gadgets and equipment, and had installed rails and ramps, a lift that took me and my wheelchair upstairs and an intercom by my bed so I could open the front door to visitors. Healing would remove the cosy security of that life just as surely as the illness had destroyed the 'Good Life' we had enjoyed in

Mayfield. Supposing I got ill again after I had given all those benefits and appliances back?

It sounds pathetic to admit that my biggest worry was how we would manage financially without all my weekly benefits. My mind just did not seem able to grasp the fact that if I was well I could earn my own living and do my own housework, so we would not need to pay for the help we depended on now.

As the day wore on I also began worrying about all my disabled friends, right across the world. Because of the books I had written I had become a kind of champion for those who had *not* been healed, so how would they all feel if God suddenly singled me out for the miracle they all wanted so much? Knowing how many of them deserved one so much more than I did made the whole thing seem thoroughly unfair!

It is most embarrassing having to write about all this but I must be honest and admit how I felt, even thought it shows I wasn't trusting the Lord to look after what was surely his own business! It is odd how quickly the things we do for the Lord become *our* ministry – rather than *his*. Knowing God must result in the handing over of every detail of our lives into his control, and every time we think we have done that he changes all our circumstances so we have to do it all over again!

All that day I wrestled with all these questions, and when I finally put out the light that night I was still not prepared to believe I had heard the Lord's voice.

'Please,' I whispered, 'I need to know for sure if I'm imagining all this! Please give me a sign.'

When I woke, early the following morning, I knew instantly what the sign would be, and I wrote it down inside the front cover of my Bible.

13 March 1990

I must wait patiently for someone to come out of the blue who will confirm this, pray and lay hands on me and I will be well. Thank you, Lord. I want that . . . I thought you could best use me . . . from a wheelchair. I give you permission to use my life any way you want. It's yours.

Eight years earlier, he had offered me the choice of stepping into heaven or going back to my family. That day in March he was facing me with another choice. I could have opted to stay ill and remain sheltered and safe, but as I wrote those words in my Bible I was choosing to step into a very different life indeed. Had I known how much that life would cost I doubt if I would have chosen it.

Before I left Alfriston I felt the Lord wanted me to write a few more words under that prayer of response: '*I must wait quietly.*' He seemed to be saying I was not to try and '*do*' anything to make all this happen. I was not even to tell Tony about it, so that when this mysterious person arrived I would know that it could only be God who had prompted them. Perhaps I was also afraid that Tony would tell me not to be stupid enough to let my hopes be raised all over again!

★ ★ ★

Three months later I was still waiting, and my faith and hope were beginning to droop. It was just so difficult keeping the whole thing to myself that I had actually confided in one other person, and I am sure God guided me to do that. Diana Priest was an elder of our church who was also a health visitor and a trained counsellor; telling a level-headed professional such an unlikely story was a huge risk but, bless her, in spite of all her medical training she actually believed me!

'You're going to need every bit as much help adjusting to recovery as you needed to accept your illness,' she said wisely, and began coming to see me every week so we could talk through all my feelings, hopes and misgivings. Together we faced the practical changes that healing would make, rather as a long-term prisoner needs to be prepared for his approaching release.

By nature I am extremely impatient and I found those three months of waiting very trying! Every time the doorbell or the phone rang I used to think, 'This might be the person who has been sent to tell me I'm going to be healed.' For some reason I always imagined this mysterious individual would be a man – either a particularly holy clergyman or one of the 'Big Names' in the healing ministry. However, it was a female voice on the phone which eventually sent my hopes rocketing one day in early June. She was part of our church's ministry team and I knew she had been given such a particular burden to pray for my healing that she fasted every Tuesday. When she rang to say there was something special she wanted to tell me, I asked her over at once, quite convinced I knew what she was going to say! My disappointment was vast when all she wanted to do was discuss a family problem.

'If you ever felt God was giving you a special message for me, you would tell me, wouldn't you?' I said, biting back my desire to tell her the whole story.

'Oh yes,' she smiled, 'I promise.'

Abraham had no problem in believing God had promised him a son, but he got into terrible difficulties when he tried to help God out by finding himself a surrogate mother (Genesis 16:1–3). That kind of thing is always a temptation when we have received a promise from God, and I soon succumbed by going off to healing services and trying to build up my strength by forcing myself through an exercise routine which was way past my capabilities. As usual, this resulted in a nasty relapse as well as a serious attack of doubt, and I told myself off roundly for being such a fool as to imagine I could ever be healed.

★ ★ ★

There was a certain date looming in my calendar which I was dreading: '13 June: All Day Ladies' Conference, Haslemere'. I had never attempted anything like this before; even in a good patch my stamina gave out after giving just one talk. In Haslemere I would have to keep going all day and the relapse was making me feel ghastly.

The conference was being organised by a group of ladies from one of the churches in the town, but they were opening it up to anyone in the area. Worse still, their chosen subject was 'Why does God allow suffering?' and in my present state of mind that seemed the very last thing I wanted to talk about! In the end I rang them up and explained I just did not feel up to coming.

'I'm so sorry,' I added, 'but I honestly don't feel I've got anything to say.' They were very sympathetic but gently pointed out that they had invited a great many people who were hurting for all kinds of reasons. Surely if we were all praying for strength the Lord wouldn't allow them to be disappointed? So, reluctantly, I agreed to let them pray for me and tried hard to prepare my talk; but by the day before the conference I still hadn't the slightest idea what to say!

During that night the spasms in my legs were so bad that I decided to leave Tony to sleep in peace. Taking myself, and my wheelchair, down in the lift, I settled in the corner of our lounge which I called my prayer corner. It was about four o'clock and just beginning to get light.

'If I can't work out what I'm going to say,' I told myself nervously, 'I'll have to sit in front of all those women dumb as a post!' The embarrassing thought added urgency to my prayers. Just as I was murmuring, 'Lord, I'm desperate, you really *must* help me,' I began to see one of those moving pictures that feel like a video playing inside my head. I was standing in front of God's throne, still praying hard, and holding out towards him a little wooden begging bowl. I couldn't see him, because the entire throne was enveloped in a towering column of brilliant white light. Behind me I was conscious of many other people – row upon row of them. Somehow I knew they were the women I would meet in Haslemere later that day, but when I looked more closely they were more like an advert for Oxfam than women from Surrey's prosperous commuter-belt. Their emaciated faces were twisted with suffering and stress and, like me, they were all holding out begging bowls in silent appeal.

'Please ...' I began, turning back to the throne, but I stopped abruptly. Someone was kneeling beside me, praying at the foot of the throne, and I sensed he was interceding for the women from Haslemere. I could not hear the words plainly but I knew he mentioned each one by name and seemed to know all their most intimate and private needs. His voice sounded so full of tenderness that it was obvious that he cared about them intensely – in fact, he was crying as he prayed. Although I could not see his face because his head was bent, I knew it was Jesus himself (Hebrews 7:25).

I am embarrassed to admit that I was still wondering about what I was going to say when he suddenly stood up and walked back towards the waiting women. Slowly he moved along the rows, stopping beside each one in turn and gently cupping their faces in his hands. I could see his own face, too, and how I wish I had inherited Otty's artistic gifts so I could have painted a portrait of how he looked early that morning. Words are totally inadequate, but I will never forget the laughter lines around his eyes and the compassion with which he looked down at each person in that crowd.

Whenever I see one of those dismal works of art that show Jesus looking like a depressed anorexic I almost laugh, because I know he doesn't look like that at all. Of course, he suffered all kinds of different agonies during his thirty-three years of life, but he was a man of joy as well as a man of sorrows. Working men like Peter would never have followed a gloomy aesthetic; it was his humour, enthusiasm and zest for life that drew the crowds, as well as his passion for people and his power to set them free.

As he moved past each of those women he seemed to be putting something different in each of their bowls; I had no idea what it was, I just knew it was exactly what they needed at that time. Sadly, some threw their bowls down on the ground and turned away. I longed for him to come and fill my empty bowl, too, but before he reached me the scene gradually began to fade away and I was back, sitting beside the marble mantelpiece in Sutherland Road, Tunbridge Wells.

For a long time I sat motionless as I realised there was nothing I needed to do or say that day. It was all going to be done by someone who was infinitely better at the job than I could ever be. Since that day I have ministered healing prayer to thousands of people all over the world, and I'm sure that has only been possible because of the 'video' I saw that morning. It showed me so clearly that it is Jesus who places his hands on the people who ask for prayer and it is *Jesus* they encounter; I'm just his gloves!

Getting me ready to go out anywhere was always a major hassle; and that morning it all had to be done before 7.30, when Penny, the wife of our minister in Mayfield, was coming to pick me up. Tony checked the wheelchair and fixed the headrest in place while Naomi found my surgical collar. I rummaged in my bag to make sure I had the necessary nappies and spare underclothes and Lyn popped in to see I had the usual arsenal of pills.

'Here's your dark glasses,' said Duncan, who had borrowed them to watch a school cricket match, and Richard blew me a sleepy kiss from behind the packet of cornflakes.

'You don't really look fit to go,' muttered Tony doubtfully, as he helped me into Penny's car. In the back sat Jo and her guitar, ready to lead the worship that day, and with all the family waving us off we pulled out into the traffic.

'Don't worry,' I whispered to the organisers when all my paraphernalia had finally been carried into the church at the other end of the long tiring journey. 'Everything is going to be all right today!' But my confidence wavered a little when Jo began to sing and I had the chance to look across the sea of faces that filled the church. Had I just been imagining things that morning? These women didn't look gaunt and miserable; they were all beautifully made up with immaculate hairstyles and expensive clothes. I suddenly felt ill with that clammy, breathless feeling that comes just before you faint. So I tried to breathe deeply and concentrated hard on the worship. When I was finally pushed up to the microphone, I began very badly, stumbling over words and forgetting what to say next, but suddenly something strange happened. I felt as if warm treacle was being poured all over me and the words I was speaking began to penetrate those carefully contrived masks. Jesus himself was moving among those women, meeting their needs just as I had seen him doing that morning. 'This is the anointing I asked him for in Keswick,' I thought reverently, as the masks seemed to melt away and tears washed the mascara down their faces.

Just as we were nearing the end of the morning session the still, attentive silence in the room was shattered when someone interrupted what I was saying by asking a question. Feeling slightly startled I hurriedly answered her and was moving on again when I realised she was standing up, right in the front row, looking terribly embarrassed.

'Nothing like this has ever happened to me before,' she mumbled. 'I've only been coming to church for a few months and I only just got baptised; but I feel God is telling me to tell you that he is going to heal you.'

It had happened. I had no doubt whatsoever about that. Here was the person I had been expecting. A shiver of hostility shot around the room as people wondered how anyone could be so publicly tactless. I caught Penny's startled expression and the organisers moved uncomfortably in their seats.

'Would you mind saying that again?' I asked. 'You see I've waited three months to hear someone tell me that.' As she nervously repeated herself I burst into tears of sheer relief. Jo reached for her guitar and everyone sang extra loudly to hide their embarrassment; but I didn't sing, I was far too busy thinking, 'That girl has to pray and lay hands on me, that's part of the promise.' So, as everyone began to surge in the direction of the buffet lunch, I tried to push myself in her direction but lost sight of her completely in the crush. I had no time to ask someone to find her for me because people who had been moved by the Holy Spirit were flocking to the front from all over the church. There were so many that we were kept busy praying with them throughout the entire lunch hour.

Then as the hands of the clock crept towards half past one I began to think, 'Suppose that girl doesn't come back for the afternoon session?' But she was there, right in the front row once again. The moment we had finished the last prayer I thrust my wheelchair forward in her direction.

'Please,' I said breathlessly, 'would you mind praying for me?' She gazed at me in dismay, so I continued. 'I'm sure if you laid hands on me, I would be healed.'

'Didn't I make it clear?' she said looking down helplessly at me. 'I'm new to this kind of thing. I've only just become a Christian and I've never read any books on healing. I couldn't pray for you, I wouldn't do it properly.'

'Please . . .' I said urgently, but just at that moment someone came up carrying a tray full of teacups and by the time I looked back I caught sight of the young woman disappearing out of the back door of the church.

'Wendy's got a new baby,' explained the lady with the tea tray. 'She's probably gone to feed him.' But Wendy had gone to the minister's office to persuade him to come and pray for me.

'No,' he said pleasantly, 'you are the one who has been given this conviction, you must pray.'

Poor Wendy, this was a major faith hurdle for her, too. Before she had found the Lord she had lived a very promiscuous life, which had resulted in a trail of broken relationships and five abortions. In Johannesburg, where she was living, abortions were illegal, and in order to pay for them she had sold her body many times over. Although she now knew the Lord had forgiven her, she felt he would always see her as second class and the idea that he might ever use her was right out of the question.

'You know I'm not the right kind of person to pray for this woman,' she pleaded, but her wise minister firmly sent her back to find me. Many people had already gone home by this time, but quite a crowd still lingered over their tea and they gathered round us in a circle. Someone told Wendy to put her hands on my head, and she was so terrified I could feel her hands shaking violently.

'Lord Jesus, Jen's been ill for eight years. Please will you make her well – now.' That was all she said! There were no 'thees' and 'thous' and she quite forgot the 'Amen'. The prayer could not have been more simple – but I knew I was healed. When I opened my eyes no one was gazing at me to see if I would stand up, because no one expected that I would – except Wendy – but she had gone to see to her baby.

'Well,' I said to Penny, 'I'm not going out of here in a wheel-chair.' The moment I moved I knew something was different. Whenever I had been sitting upright for a time my muscles used to stiffen until they locked me rigidly into a fixed position. Before I could attempt to stand, it took a long time and a great deal of effort to get my knees and hips to straighten themselves out. That day I simply stood up.

Privacy was the first thing I wanted – so I could feel myself all over and discover exactly what had happened. So I walked away from everyone and locked myself in the ladies' loo; it was probably the first time anyone had ever hidden there in order to waggle their limbs about, jog on the spot and see if they could squeeze the toilet roll flat!

We were very quiet in the car as we drove home from Haslemere. Probably we were just too dazed to speak! Tony was ready at the front door to 'deal' with me – the routine was always the same after I had been out to speak. I would be too exhausted to get myself to bed so someone always had to get me into the lift, undress me and leave me alone in the dark to sleep it off. I will never forget the expression on his poor face as I jumped out of the car, lifted my wheelchair out of the boot and bumped it up the front steps towards him.

If I were making this story up I would describe how I floated euphorically round the house all the evening smiling angelically at my delighted family. It was not like that at all – I was abominably bad-tempered. I think there were too many emotions spinning inside me to be handled all at once; I just did not know how to tell them what had happened. So, without a word of explanation to Tony, I marched straight into the kitchen and proceeded to tell the boys off roundly for leaving their school bags and blazers in a heap on the floor. Gom, who had been looking after the dog all day, was now cooking the supper, and for some obscure reason I crossly told her she was doing the chicken all wrong. Too stunned to retaliate she sat down heavily on a kitchen chair and said, 'Well, I'll be blowed!' Tony, looking completely baffled, disappeared to his allotment without eating the offending chicken and stayed there until it was too dark to dig.

I was actually quite glad to have him out of the way, because all I wanted to do was bake a birthday cake! My youngest daughter Naomi had a birthday the following day, and for eight years we had been making do with shop cakes to celebrate important occasions. So I set to work as soon as Gom had gone home on the bus, still declaring she was 'blowed'. After a positive frenzy of activity I had to admit that I was distinctly out of practice when it came to cooking, and the cake finally came out of the oven humiliatingly flat.

'Never mind,' I told Duncan, who was watching with the kind of speculative interest that was to turn him into a highly successful journalist, 'I'll cover it with icing,' but I put in far too much cochineal and the result was revolting.

'No one will eat a cake that colour,' said Duncan, but that did not stop him from licking out the bowl.

'Who cares?' I snapped. 'Help me blow up some balloons.'

'Help?' he replied scornfully. 'I'll have to do them all, because you know you can't blow.'

'Just watch me!' I replied. When I climbed on the dining-room table to tie them to the light he stood gazing at me like someone who has woken from a dream to find it is real after all.

'If God can do that kind of thing,' he said, rocking precariously on the back legs of the kitchen chair, 'he can do anything!'

I finished the evening by doing three large baskets of ironing!

Early the following morning I groped towards the chest by my bed for the plastic container of pills Lyn always left ready for me. By five o'clock painkillers were always vital necessities. Sleepily I scooped them out of the pot and lifted the glass of water. Then I stopped. What was I doing this for? I wasn't in pain and my muscles were not stiff at all. Beyond the curtains the sun was already shining but it would be at least two hours before the birthday breakfast. For the second morning running I slid out of bed carefully so I wouldn't wake Tony – but this time I did not go downstairs in my lift!

Grasping my two walking sticks I made for the front door, and then stopped again. Why take the sticks? I wasn't dizzy and my legs no longer felt like wobbly jelly. But the sticks and the wheelchair had been extensions of my body for so many years that going out without them was the first of many psychological barriers I had to push through during the next few weeks.

Somehow I felt too embarrassed to go into our own little park, in case my neighbours would see me through their lace curtains. So I hurried across the road to Calverley Gardens – I felt less conspicuous there because it was a much larger park. The rose bushes looked magnificent in the neatly weeded flowerbeds and their scent was intoxicating. 'I can *smell* them!' I thought ecstatically; I had not realised until that moment how much I'd missed my sense of smell during the last eight years. The dew looked like scattered diamonds on the sloping lawns and I began running about leaving crazy footpath patterns wherever I went. Minty, my little dog, trailed behind me, looking distinctly cross. She was getting old now and had enjoyed riding sedately on my lap in the Bug. Her patience snapped completely when I climbed on to a low wall and ran along the top, simply for the thrill of feeling my body move through the air. She yapped indignantly, leaping up to snap at my heels.

Suddenly the joy of it seemed to erupt inside me as I realised that even if I could collect up all the most beautiful things I had ever seen and give them to the Lord as a 'thank you' present, they would still be an inadequate offering. So I began to sing at the top of my voice:

> Were the whole realm of nature mine,
> That were an offering far too small,
> Love so amazing, so divine,
> Demands my soul, my life, my all.

Time after time, during those eight years of illness, I had gone back to what Paul said about knowing God in Philippians 3:10. Being ill had definitely helped me to know Jesus in a far deeper way as I had identified with him in his sufferings; but now I understood the first part of what Paul was saying: '*I want to know Christ in the power of his resurrection . . .*' Awed by the magnificence of that power I shouted, '*Yes!*' at the top of my voice, and encountered startled glances from two early morning joggers.

When I finally arrived home I came down to earth with a thud.

'Where have you been?' they all demanded. People receiving the severe disability allowance at the highest possible rate simply do not disappear for long solitary walks. They had been about to ring the police. Tony was very quiet throughout the birthday breakfast but Justyn, who was home on study leave from London where he was doing his degree, was wildly excited and Duncan looked as if some great burden of guilt had finally been lifted from him. Richard's initial reaction was more restrained. He had only been four when he had last seen me running about the house, and he said he felt as if he had lost the mum he had always known and wasn't sure he liked this 'high-powered' replacement.

That was definitely my fault because one day, when they were all at school during that first week, I decided to spring-clean their bedrooms. My lift had not been able to take me up to the top floor where they slept and the mess I discovered when I went up to have a look was quite indescribable. So I took the vacuum cleaner, a roll of black polythene sacks and a bucket of disinfectant and had a glorious day; but when they came home they were furious!

'It might have looked a mess to you, Mum,' they said, 'but we knew where everything was and now we'll never find a thing!'

Poor Tony was so bewildered by it all that he went into one of his silent shells. He had not had the three months of mental adjustment I had been given – or the counselling help from Diana. He said later that he was afraid to let himself believe it in case it suddenly stopped, pushing us all back down that 'coal mine' of despair. So for ten rather tense days, he reserved judgment.

A few days after the Haslemere conference I went to our GP; he seemed as surprised as everyone else, but after he had given me a thorough physical examination he was obviously delighted. He is a Christian and had prayed so faithfully for our family all through our difficult years.

'All I can say is that I thank God with you,' he said, but with professional caution he added, 'We'll have to wait and see how things go over the next few months.' A physiotherapist friend of mine had no such scruples when I had coffee with her later that week. She insisted on poking and pressing my arms and legs and then she squatted back on her heels.

'This makes me feel nervous,' she muttered. 'It would have taken me months to work up muscle tone like this.'

It was not long before Sarah came back from Oxford, where she was doing her PhD, to see what all the excitement was about.

'I hope you aren't going to be cross, too,' I said anxiously. 'I don't know what's the matter with the rest of them.'

'I don't think any of us can cope with the change in you,' she said thoughtfully. 'Everything about you is different – your whole face has changed, and the colour of your skin. We've forgotten how to relate to a mum who doesn't need to be helped all the time, or who wants to be in charge of the kitchen and never sits still for a moment!'

Naturally, over the years various routines and arrangements had been developed to keep everything running smoothly. Now suddenly every one of those structures was upset, roles were changed and responsibilities altered. They were so used to helping me up out of a chair they went on doing it automatically, in spite of my protests. No one, including the dog, knew what they were expected to do next.

'I guess we all feel a bit upset with God, too,' added Sarah thoughtfully. 'If he can heal you like this now, why didn't he do it years ago when we all needed a mum so much more?'

While the tension inside our house continued to be oppressive, I only had to step out of the front door and my joy bubbled back to the surface. I was passing the baker's shop, round the corner, when one of the ladies who served behind the counter left the queue of customers and dashed out to catch me up. 'Excuse me,' she gasped, 'have you got a sister in a wheelchair?'

People who had once looked the other way when they saw me in my chair now smiled and said, 'Good morning', and others stopped to ask me what had happened. 'Someone prayed for me,' I would reply simply.

It always surprises me that people who are not churchgoers often respond so much more positively to my extraordinary story than do Christians. They'll say, 'Well, it just shows there's someone up there after all.' Christian people, on the other hand, seem to find the whole healing thing so much more complicated. Traditional evangelicals had felt I was their spokesperson in the fight against the extremes of the charismatic movement, and many of them turned on me after I was healed, in some cases quite viciously. The charismatics wanted to dissect the whole experience to discover how I had finally 'cracked' the mystery of healing so they could add it to their theology. I have had to spend the last fifteen years running about in the crossfire between the two extremes, trying to persuade one side that God actually does still intervene miraculously and the other that there is no way you can *make* him do so!

Ten days after I went to Haslemere I finally persuaded Tony to come for a walk with me in the country. The route I chose led us through fields full of buttercups, and I raced Minty down the hill, swung myself over the five-bar gate at the bottom and then climbed the hill on the far side at a cracking pace. When Tony came puffing up behind me I suddenly realised a light had been switched on inside his head. 'We really do have a future together, don't we?' he said huskily.

He had seen me carried off to Intensive Care so often that he had decided it was easier to 'let me go' emotionally rather than suffer the pain of repeated goodbyes, and so he had built thick, protective walls around himself. During that walk he finally dared to demolish them. For the rest of the afternoon we strolled along, at a kinder pace, and discussed a whole range of delightful options.

'We could go back and live in the country,' he suggested.

'Run a bed and breakfast?' I added.

'Get some more chickens.'

'And let's have a goat this time!'

That evening Richard asked, 'Why are you two laughing so much today?'

'Perhaps we're only reminding ourselves how to,' said Tony.

From that evening the whole family seemed to take their cue from him and all the doubts, fears and negative reactions were dispersed by what I can only describe as a blast of joy. Tony and I seemed to fall in love all over again. Perhaps we had to, because after all we had both gone through we had each become very different people since our wedding. We wandered round Tunbridge Wells holding hands like an engaged couple, talking non-stop. It felt wonderful after all those years when conversation on a walk had been impossible because he was always behind the wheelchair!

One day the doorbell rang and there on the step was the biggest bunch of flowers I have ever seen in my life. They were from Sir Harry Secombe. I had done a TV programme with him not that long before, and he had been so delighted to hear that I was better that he said, in the letter which accompanied the flowers, 'I cannot tell you how absolutely delighted I was to hear that you are marauding all over Tunbridge Wells on your own two feet ...'

All kinds of little ordinary things had become a huge delight, like putting on my own tights in the morning, and taking Richard to the cinema and sitting in an ordinary seat! Previously we could only go if we rang the management first so they could remove a seat to make room for my chair! A trip to the swimming baths or a ride on the top of a double-decker bus made me as excited as a small child. When I discovered that sound no longer hurt my ears I turned the stereo up so loud that I damaged the speakers – much to Duncan's wrath!

The following month I wrote in my journal:

23 July
Bought myself a new pair of climbing boots and a rucksack for the holiday.

We were going back to Stillmeadow again – but this time I did not sit on the cliffs watching the others swim. I was down in the sea with them.

13 August
Two months to the day since Haslemere and what a way to celebrate! Walked twenty-two miles along South Devon coastal path. High cliffs, blue sea – and the views!

I had to do that walk on my own. Richard and Duncan firmly refused to come with me. 'Mum,' they said witheringly, 'you walk too far and too fast for us these days.' Minty wouldn't come either; she used to lie on her back with her legs in the air whenever she saw me putting on those new walking boots. One morning her annoyance got the better of her when she saw me doing my aerobic exercises, and she bit me!

My brother Justyn and his family came over from Canada at

the end of August and treated us to two further weeks' holiday in Scotland 'for old times' sake'. Kirkland, the farmhouse on Grandpa's estate where I had lived as a small child in 1944, now belongs to my uncle, who inherited Glenluffin. So we rented Kirkland from him and had such fun showing all our many offspring the places that had always been so special to us as children. We played golf, too, and I was so pleased when I found I could still send a ball down the middle of the fairway. On the eighteenth green one day, when I had just beaten my brother hollow, he stood with his hands on his hips and said with a sigh, 'There ought to be a special handicap for people who've had a miracle.'

★   ★   ★

It was so wonderful to be well that it began to bother me to see our house still full of all the paraphernalia of illness. Wherever I looked there were wheelchairs, commodes and piles of incontinence pads. Drawers were full of plastic sheets, spare catheters, bottles of pills and feeding utensils. The lift seemed to take up so much room in the lounge and bedroom and I kept falling over the Bug parked in the corner of the dining room.

'I want to get rid of all this,' I said.

'You mustn't do that,' said my friends in horror. 'Suppose you get ill again?'

'I refuse to "suppose" anything of the kind,' I replied, 'and that's exactly why it's all got to go!'

Even the orange badge in the car caused arguments: the family wanted me to go on using it when we couldn't find a parking place! So I gave the Bug to a friend who has MS and then piled a supermarket trolley high with everything from a ripple bed to elbow crutches and pushed it up the hill to the doctor's surgery, where I left them, with a note of thanks, for the health visitor. When I put all my benefit books and my orange badge down on the doctor's desk beside a vast array of pills, he laughed out loud!

'Well, this has never happened to me before in all my professional life!' he told me.

It actually proved more difficult to get rid of those pensions than it had been to get them in the first place because we were going against the tide of red tape!

11 September
Went to the doctor to be signed off at last. He says I can drive the car again now, if the licensing people at Swansea agree.

My licence had been withdrawn when I was officially registered as disabled.

3 October
Drove solo!

To attempt a 200-mile round trip after not having driven for years was probably rather stupid, but one of the girls was starting her university life in Southampton that day and I just could not resist taking her myself. I soon discovered that roads had changed considerably in eight years, and as I drove along the M25 for the first time I was so scared the police stopped me for going too slowly!

Remembering the day that the lift was removed still makes us laugh. I was out dog-walking when Gom opened the door to a small, gloomy-looking man wearing a black tie.

'I've come for the lift,' he murmured, sounding more like an undertaker arriving to remove a body. As Gom made him a cup of tea he added, 'When did . . . the . . . er . . . decease occur?'

'Eh?' said Gom, startled. The little man looked startled himself when I walked in from the park at that moment. He explained that his job was a difficult one because lifts were usually only removed after their user had died.

One of the most delightful events of that summer was the arrival of a black Labrador puppy called Brodie. She had been born blind and no one else seemed willing to offer a disabled dog a home, but we had learnt from experience that being disabled does not make you worthless. At six weeks old she was already twice the size of Minty, but having someone else to boss and bully gave the little dog a new lease of life and provided the rest of us with endless enjoyment (*The Gospel According to Brodie*, Zondervan, 1995).

★ ★ ★

In a comparatively small town like Tunbridge Wells the sudden change in me was bound to cause quite a stir. For some years I had been seen in the parks, shops and streets in the Bug with Minty on my knee, but suddenly I was bounding around, full of energy. For a while after I was healed, whenever we went out we were aware of people pointing us out to one another and whispering. It was not long before a reporter from the local paper arrived on the scene. She was such a nice girl that I found it all too easy to chat away to her without realising the implications. When her photographer arrived he noticed my manual wheelchair, waiting in the hall to be collected by Social Services.

'Don't suppose you can lift that, can you?' he said rather sceptically.

'Of course I can lift it,' I said, falling naively for his bait; once I had hoisted it up above my head he took the photo of me which, when it was printed on the front page of the paper, made me too embarrassed to go out for several days! When the national papers and TV news wanted interviews too we refused, feeling our privacy was being invaded. We felt even more threatened the following day when we found a woman squatting outside our front door, looking through the letterbox. She explained to Duncan, 'I just wanted to see if your mum *really* can walk.'

That weekend Tony and I were invited to a wedding in Mayfield. Social functions had never been much fun in a wheelchair, but that day I could drift about talking to people, eye to eye, like a real human being, *and* choose my own food from the buffet! Finally, I sat down next to a stranger who was soon telling me about his fascinating life as an international journalist.

'But I'm having to give all that up,' he finished sadly. 'I've developed a lot of arthritis so they want to put me out to grass. I suppose you don't happen to believe in divine healing, do you?' He did not wait for me to reply before adding, 'There was something in the papers last week, about a housewife who was healed after eight years in a wheelchair, just through prayer. Do you believe that kind of thing actually happens?'

When I told him that I definitely believed the story because I was the housewife he turned on me angrily: 'Why did you sit there talking to me for two hours without telling me something as important as that?'

'Well, I feel a bit exposed,' I replied awkwardly.

'But don't you realise what a story like that does for people like me? It gives us hope! I've spent my life reporting bad news – isn't it about time people had some good news for a change?'

Tony and I talked late into the night about the journalist's reaction; were we so busy enjoying the gift of health the Lord had given to our family that we were forgetting to give God the glory? When Tony finally quoted one of his favourite bits from the Bible, *'This is a day of good news and we are keeping it to ourselves'* (2 Kings 7:9) we decided that, although we would not court publicity, neither would we continue to hide from it.

It was not long before the national press and TV came down on us like vultures, and I remember one particular reporter being especially obnoxious and insisting on lurking about outside our house. Brodie was at the stage of loving everyone and expressing her affection by jumping all over them, so on the way to the park she leapt rapturously at the journalist and her sharp puppy claws ripped the woman's flimsy Indian cotton skirt to shreds.

'I can't go back to London on the train like this!' she exclaimed indignantly. I gave her enough to buy a new skirt from our housekeeping purse and that was the last we saw of her!

★ ★ ★

Why did Jesus ask people who had been disabled for a long time if they really *wanted* to be healed (John 5:6), and why doesn't he heal people suddenly and dramatically more often nowadays? I had so often asked myself those questions, but during those first few months the answers gradually began to dawn on me. While I never lost the exhilaration of being well, adjusting to any sudden, dramatic change is extremely difficult – even if it's a change for the better! Had my recovery been gradual it would not have been so traumatic, but all at once every single department of my life was altered: the way I related to people, how they felt about me, what I did each day, the way I looked, felt and moved about. Change also involves a certain amount of loss and many of the perks of illness were suddenly gone – I no longer had a good excuse if I did not want to do something! I missed Lyn's company, and many of the friends who had been 'God's gloves' to us in practical ways suddenly withdrew, perhaps a little hurt by being unwanted.

Perhaps what the people who were close to me found most difficult was the new poise and confidence (which really amounted to a complete personality change) that came with my healing. For forty-eight years I had been so timid I certainly could not have said 'boo' to a goose, and for the last eight I had been totally dependent on other people to do everything for me. Overnight I had turned into someone they could hardly recognise. I still have not been able to fathom whether the Lord actually healed me psychologically as well as physically or if this new assurance and boldness was part of the anointing I had asked for in Keswick. Without it I certainly would not have been able to serve the Lord as I have in recent years, but the people who

204

preferred me wrapped in candyfloss found the change difficult to handle.

The counselling I had from Diana, our church elder, definitely had a lot to do with this change, and she continued to spend a lot of time with me during the first weeks after my healing. One day she kindly said she would drive me to the speaking engagement that had been in my diary for months. We arrived early at the church hall where the outreach coffee morning was to take place, but the organisers were obviously already inside, setting up the tables. As we walked up the path a huge poster confronted us; it showed a picture of me in my wheelchair with the headline: 'Come and hear disabled mother of six.'

'Horrors,' I said to Diana, 'people are going to be a bit disappointed when they arrive to find I'm well!'

'Sorry! You can't come in yet,' snapped a large woman in an apron who was barring the door. 'We aren't ready.'

'But I'm your speaker,' I told her. She looked me up and down sceptically.

'We booked a woman in a wheelchair,' she said shortly.

'I'm terribly sorry,' I said apologetically. 'But I'm afraid I've been healed since you sent the invitation.'

'That'll ruin the talk!' she said gloomily. 'Still, I suppose now you're here you might as well stay.'

When I finally stood at the microphone I apologised again for not being in a wheelchair and explained as simply as possible what had happened to me. As I did so I felt the atmosphere in the hall take off with the power of a jet plane. At least half of those who were there were not yet Christians but had been brought along by praying friends, and I had never had an audience who listened with deeper interest. When I went on to talk about how Jesus can heal us on the inside just as easily as he had healed me outwardly and can set us free from our sins and failures just as he had set me free from a disabled body – they positively drank it all in (Luke 5:17–26). As the Holy Spirit's power moved through the room, something very important suddenly became clear to me.

For the last six years I had been speaking and writing about my strong belief that physical cure was not half as important as healing of the spirit through salvation. I was telling these people exactly the same thing, but today they were listening with infinitely more attention simply because I had been physically healed. Jesus knew that forgiving people's sins was far more important than healing bodies which, however thoroughly healed, were bound to be dead and buried a few years later. Yet it was the physical healings that brought the crowds to hear his message of salvation. Did God want to use my healing as a 'carrot' too, I wondered.

This question felt so important that I decided to get up early the following morning and go for a prayer walk. It was a perfect summer day and I walked through the park at Penshurst crying with the joy of being able to walk alone through such beauty. As the dogs scampered around me, sniffing for rabbits, I asked the Lord, 'Please will you show me what you want me to do with this anointing I asked you for last summer?'

In the distance, scattered all over the vast expanse of green grass, a large flock of sheep were peacefully grazing. Suddenly, as if by some secret signal, they all stopped chewing and began to run eagerly towards me, until they were packed in a tight circle round the place where I had stopped in amazement. In all my years of living in the country I had never seen sheep do that before, particularly as I had dogs with me. Then I heard that familiar voice say, 'I am going to send people to flock around you, hungrily, just like these sheep.'

The ghost of shyness inside me was not too happy about that, so later that week I decided to test those words by going back to the same spot at exactly the same time of day. Perhaps the sheep might have mistaken me for the farmer, arriving with their breakfast. The dogs and I hung around for a long time on the same spot, and this time not one single sheep took the slightest notice; but I heard the Lord speaking again, 'People will flock to you, but only for a season. Afterwards you must be just as happy for them to ignore you.'

The Christian world is actually very small, so our news spread rapidly all over the country, probably because I was already quite well known. The fact that my parents had been major spiritual superstars in their generation had made people read my books simply because I was the daughter of Tom and Jean Rees. During the previous six years I had not only written popular books but contributed regularly to most Christian papers and magazines. So I was not some unknown woman claiming to have been healed. The inevitable consequence was a flood of invitations asking me to speak at all kinds of different Christian events. At first I did not answer any of them but stuffed them in a file and took them away on holiday with us.

★ ★ ★

'So what do you think that odd business with the sheep actually means?' I asked Tony. It was our wedding anniversary and we were staying in Devon at Stillmeadow. We had decided to fast that day and ask the Lord together what he wanted to do with our lives. I had saved up my 'sheep story' because I wanted to tell Tony about it on that special day.

'Well, the Lord's obviously telling us we've got a brief time in the public eye as an opportunity to reach people for him,' said Tony. 'In other words he wants us to go for it – flat out – while we've got the chance.' Then he dropped another of his bombshells. 'I've been feeling I want to leave education and serve the Lord full time.'

'You can't do that!' I said, quite horrified. 'You love your work!'

'Yes, but what's happened to you is so amazing I want to give the Lord everything I've got as a way of saying "thank you".'

I did not feel happy about him giving up his involvement in education, either then or later, but he seemed so wildly enthusiastic I agreed we should pray for a definite sign. He had always been such a cautious, reliable man, a bit of a stick-in-the-mud some-times, and he was now earning a very good salary. Without it, how could we provide for the children – particularly as I had just given up all the state benefits I had been raking in each week?

From the window of the room where we sat I could see the rock where Jesus had told me, 'All you need is me.' I wanted to trust him to provide for us, but it is often difficult to tell the difference between faith and human enthusiasm, particularly after such an amazing change in our lives. Tony's spirituality had always been more conservative than mine, but for once it was my feet that were dragging!

At the end of the day, when Tony opened his Bible to read the passage assigned for that day it was from Matthew 10, where Jesus sends out his disciples in twos to preach and heal.

'They'd all just thrown up their jobs,' Tony pointed out. 'And Jesus was asking them to live by faith from one day to the next. "Freely you have received," he told them, "so freely give" ' (Matthew 10:8). Tony was so sure that Jesus was saying the same thing to us, but I have often wondered since if he made the right decision.

So I answered the letters in that file with a 'yes' but I also agreed to a different kind of invitation. Because I had written about the issue of *not* being healed, my publisher was keen that I should 'set the record straight' by writing an account of how God had eventually healed me.

'You need to do it soon, while it's all still fresh in your mind,' commented Edward England, my literary agent. So I spent much of that winter writing *Unexpected Healing* and finished the last chapter in Alfriston exactly one year after that extraordinary day when he had told me he wanted to heal me. What an eventful year it had been!

Tony and I then began to take every possible opportunity to tell people what Jesus had done for us. Our spiritual pockets were positively bulging with all the 'treasures of darkness' (Isaiah 45:3) we had discovered in Tony's 'coal mines', and we longed to share it all with others who were still trapped down there.

We did not only feel called to a ministry of physical healing but we also wanted to see others experience the kind of inner healing miracle I had experienced the day I fell in the cow dung. We knew from bitter experience how vital the Lord's 'peace-joy' is to people struggling to come to terms with loss, disability and terminal illness (2 Corinthians 1:3–4). Finding financial support for this kind of work might have been difficult if it had not been for the Hildenborough Trust. Soon after my brother had gone to Canada, Hildenborough Hall had been sold and the money was now used to support several people in various forms of evangelism. After a lot of discussion and prayer the trustees agreed to take us on.

Then, just as life felt good, we hit one of the most painful experiences of them all! Our GP had given me hours of help while I was writing *Unexpected Healing*. He insisted on going through the manuscript with a fine toothcomb because he said, 'A patient's perception of her illness can be very different from a doctor's, so it is vital that we get the medical details accurate or God will not have the glory.'

In spite of all his hard work, when the book was published in November 1991 it caused an enormous amount of controversy. It shot instantly to the top of the religious bestsellers' list and generated more invitations than ever, both in this country and abroad, but the scathing comments it received in the more conservative Christian press hurt like mad. The reviews triggered a head-on clash between Christians who say God no longer intervenes supernaturally today and those who are convinced that he does. What had happened to me challenged traditional evangelical doctrine, so people on that side of the controversy were forced to dismiss as untrue what I had described in the book. While my family, church, doctor and friends were in no doubt about what had happened to me, people who had never met me when I was ill were so outspoken in their attacks on my integrity that their comments were even reported on the front page of the *Daily Telegraph*, as well as on TV and radio.

Our GP was furious, and the letters he wrote defending me

were also published. When one reviewer suggested that I had
been wrongly diagnosed he felt so insulted he considered taking
legal action, then let it drop because the writer was a fellow
Christian (1 Corinthians 6:1).

Others said the whole illness must have been psychosomatic
and demanded to see all my medical records. I was more than
happy for that, and so was my doctor, because we knew they
contained test results showing permanent damage to the central
nervous system left by the encephalitis. For some reason our
accusers ignored these completely, and when they could not find
any record that I had ever been referred to a psychiatrist they
suggested that my hospital records must have been muddled with
those of another patient.

Another person voiced the suggestion that I had staged the
whole thing to sell my books, just as Agatha Christie had come to
fame by faking suicide. That one didn't hurt so much because it
was so ridiculous. What an exceptional gift of acting they must
have thought I had, to deceive so many doctors, not to mention
friends and family – and how did I manage to forge the results of
so many medical tests?

Being accused of dishonesty in such a public way felt awful,
particularly for someone with such a strong desire to be *seen* to be
'very very good'. Our personal reputation can so easily become
more important to us than God himself, so perhaps we ought to
be glad when it takes a battering!

Perhaps the most painful part of that storm for me and Tony
was the frustration we felt when we told people about the
wonderful things God had done, only to have our story coldly
rejected as something 'God doesn't do nowadays'. Sadly, miracles
never convince anyone – unless they want to be convinced.
Accepting that God has done something that can't be explained
scientifically leaves you with a choice: either you have to believe
that God is bigger than science and, as sovereign, has the right to
do unpredictable things whenever he chooses; or you have to
find some other explanation for what has occurred. For a while,

everyone we met seemed to be on one side or the other; some treated us like the latest 'flavour of the month' while the others eyed us with suspicion and sat through our talks as if they were judge and jury in a court case.

'If this is what working for you is like,' I told the Lord one day, 'I would prefer to be back in my wheelchair!' But, of course, walking in his shadow means going through the experiences that hit him too. It really comforted me to realise he understood what it felt like to share things that were infinitely precious to him, only to have them dismissed with icy disbelief. He had to admit that even if someone were to rise from the dead in front of people's eyes they would not believe unless they wanted to (Luke 16:31).

One day, after a 250-mile drive all on my own, I arrived to speak at a ladies' outreach event to be met with the chilling news that most of the organising committee were refusing to talk to me. Apparently the previous week they had been to a seminar given by a medic who was one of my most outspoken critics. He had used me as an example of the dishonest lengths to which the charismatic movement will go in order to manipulate people into believing their phoney doctrines. I was told the committee bitterly regretted having asked a patent liar to speak at their event but, seeing it was now too late to stop me coming, they had agreed that if I mentioned the word 'healing' during my talk they would all be obliged to stand up and publicly expose me.

I dashed out to ring Tony from the nearest call box, pleading with him tearfully to let me come straight home.

'No,' he said calmly, 'stand up and talk about all the other things we've seen Jesus do. After all, your healing certainly wasn't the most important!'

In spite of his encouragement, few things have ever been more difficult!

When the whole furore was beginning to rattle my confidence badly Tony encouraged me to go off by myself to seek the Lord about the whole experience. Sarah and her husband Paul were on holiday, so I stayed in their little house in Oxford for ten days and fasted on nothing but water. (It was coffee I missed more than anything else!) It was about the time when I was learning so much about forgiveness through Miss Mitchell, and during those bleak days in Oxford the Lord made it abundantly clear that I would never be free of my tormentors until I forgave them – utterly. I know now, for sure, that when I get to heaven and find myself sitting next to that particular medic who hurt me so much at the time, I'll have to thank him for pushing me further into Jesus than any of the preachers I've heard or authors I've read! Over the years I've gathered a little list of people, which I keep in my journal so I can pray every day for God's blessing on them. They are all people who have caused me major damage and pain – fortunately for me the list is short! I've discovered that forgiveness is not something you do once: you have to go on and on choosing to forgive that person every time you think about them. Every day Satanists will stick pins in a model they have made of someone who has hurt them, cursing them as they do so. Jesus makes it plain that he wants us to do the exact opposite: we are to pray for the people who hurt us and bless them (Luke 6:27). I have to confess that I don't enjoy that part of my daily prayer time very much, but after hearing a talk by Graham Cooke I now call the people on that list my 'Grace Growers', because I have had to draw on so much supernatural grace in order to handle my feelings towards them.

Because forgiveness is so important to Jesus (Matthew 6:14–15) he doesn't only want us to forgive major wounds but all the little pinpricks as well. Just recently he reminded me of this in rather a curious way. I had done my best to forget that outreach event and the disapproving faces of its organisers, but for years even seeing the name of their town on a map made me shudder and I promised myself never to go there again. Then one day, a couple of years ago, I was driving along the by-pass that skirts that town on my way to speak somewhere else when the exhaust fell off the bottom of my car. I knew I would have to find a garage to fit a new one very quickly if I was to reach my destination in time for the meeting. So I had no alternative but to drive into my 'no-go' area – but the very idea revolted me!

While I sat in a dingy garage, waiting for my car, I had time to relive all the memories of that last visit, and I realised I had not actually forgiven the ladies of that committee. It was not that I had refused; it was simply that I had never thought of doing so because I had been so busy trying to forgive the man who had upset them through his seminar. So I used that hour to good advantage, but I did feel slightly embarrassed to realise, when I came to pay the garage bill, to what lengths the Lord had to go to make me realise how important forgiveness is to him!

★ ★ ★

Looking back now, with the benefit of hindsight, I am more than ever convinced that what happened to me at 3.15 on the afternoon of 13 June 1990 was a miracle. It would not be classed as one by the Medical Board of Lourdes because, in order to pass their criteria, a recovery must be totally impossible medically or by any natural means – such as the restoration of an amputated leg. Although doctors could offer no cure for my condition, it could have improved by itself just as such things as cancer suddenly disappear for no apparent reason. Yet the fact that the illness disappeared at the time Wendy prayed is just too big a coincidence for me to swallow. Since then I have defined a miracle like this: 'God doing something for a human being which they could not do for themselves and no other human being could do for them.'

I still have no idea *why* he did it. It certainly was not because of my faith; I can think of a whole string of people who deserve a miracle far more than I did, but they still remain ill or disabled. Perhaps we just have to accept that healing will always remain a mystery, and knowing God is not about understanding him intellectually; our human brains are just too limited. Fortunately you don't have to understand him to know him; all that is required of us is our trust.

The arguments and criticism rumbled on in the background for years but soon ceased to bother us; we felt like the blind man in John 9 who said, when he was caught in similar crossfire, 'Once I was blind but now I can see!' (John 9:25). Whatever anyone said, the fact remained that I was gloriously fit and full of energy after years of well-documented illness. Everyone has a right to their own opinions about what triggered the change.

9

The people that do know their God shall be strong, and do exploits.

Daniel 11:32, KJV

A mixture of awe, fun and exhaustion! That is how I would describe the six years that Tony and I worked together in ministry. We travelled all over this country and abroad, spoke to many thousands of people and felt as if we had slept in as many different beds! Every time I stood up to speak I felt utterly amazed by the way God just gave me what to say. (It is a very good thing he did, because if he had not done so I would merely have stood there squeaking like a terrified mouse!) Whenever I sat next to someone at the end of a meeting while they asked the Lord into their hearts for the first time, I felt the same exultant joy that had made my father want to leap eight feet off the ground!

Richard and Duncan were still at home doing O and A levels, so Tony and I would never have been able to work together if it had not been for Julia. She joined our family because she needed a home after her marriage broke up, and in return for board and lodging she kept house for the boys when we were away. They loved the arrangement and thought she was more fun than Gom and *much* more attractive than John!

All the adverse publicity the book had received never seemed to diminish the crowds who wanted to come and 'hear us tell our story', but strangely we never got tired of telling it. I'm sure that was because before we spoke we always asked the Lord to make the story as fresh as if it was the first time we had ever told it.

At the end of most meetings people would come up asking for prayer, and the first time this happened I was not sure quite what to do! It was at the end of that very first coffee morning, when I was advertised as 'a mum in a wheelchair'. Kathy had come to hear me that day because she was also a mum confined to a chair, but she had rheumatoid arthritis. When someone pushed her to the front I stood looking down at her, not knowing how to pray. Then I remembered Wendy's apparently inadequate prayer at Haslemere a few weeks previously. Her *words* had actually been irrelevant; it was the surge of supernatural power that had brought healing. Wendy had merely put a hand on my head connecting me to heaven's resources – like a pipe that conveys water through a desert. So, as I prayed silently for Kathy, I pictured myself as a pipe with God's healing waters flowing through me. Nothing seemed to have changed as Kathy was pushed away, but not long afterwards I heard she had been totally healed. This definitely gave me the confidence to pray 'as a water pipe' for other people; all I had to do was make sure that, like a water pipe, I was open at both ends: to Jesus (by faith) at one end and to the person in need at the other.

Praying for people in that silent, effortless way soon became the thing I loved doing most in life – and it still is. Sometimes I am completely melted by the intensity of his compassion for people whose hearts have been broken by suffering. I feel more aware of his presence and compassion when I am praying for other people than at any other time. There is just nothing as beautiful as watching their faces change as they also become aware of his love surrounding them.

Tony and I both enjoyed spending time with individuals, far more than speaking to huge crowds, not only praying for physical healing but also helping them to handle the nasty experiences we had grappled with ourselves. We began taking small groups away for short breaks, either in this country or abroad, to give them the chance to talk, space to think and the chance to find God in the situations they faced. These breaks were so popular we had to run more and more each year in order to keep pace with the demand for places. Tony was brilliant at the job; he had the gift of making people feel safe and infinitely special, which of course was a huge asset when so many of our guests were newly bereaved or terminally ill.

Of course, we had some hair-raising adventures; one summer there were sixteen people in wheelchairs in our party when the hotel fire alarms went off in the middle of the night. Lifts must not be used if there is a fire, so we had to carry them all down two flights of stairs – only to find it was a false alarm. No sooner was everyone settled back in bed, with hot drinks to soothe ruffled nerves, than the alarm went off again. We obviously had to carry them all down once more, and one lady, who suffered from angina, was so upset she felt an attack coming on. She was even more distressed when she realised she had left her pills upstairs! Her chest pain stopped completely, however, after one of our care team prayed for her, and she has never had another attack in all the years since. Once again, all our frenzied activity had been caused by a fault in the system. 'Won't happen again,' promised the management, but those loud bells woke us all yet again just when we had fallen into a deep sleep. As we took our places in the garden for the third time we could only thank God it wasn't raining!

We both hated it when I had to go off alone, but there was one occasion when Tony was delighted he hadn't come with me. I had to stay with an extremely hardy family in the north of England during a bitterly cold spell in January. There was no heating anywhere in the huge, draughty house except for the kitchen Aga, so the family all wore woolly pompom hats, even in bed, and at least three pairs of socks. I had not come similarly prepared, but they told me if I was cold I could always have a bath. 'There's plenty of hot water,' they assured me brightly – but there was no door on the bathroom! I decided shivering was a less embarrassing option!

There was another occasion when it was me who was glad Tony wasn't there. My hostess took me aside as soon as I walked through her front door and whispered, 'When you use the loo, only look to the right.' Of course the first thing I did, after locking the door, was to look *left!* The man of the house was not yet a Christian and obviously felt he needed to counterbalance all the texts and Christian posters his wife had put up on the right-hand wall of the toilet. I had better not describe his portrait gallery of well-endowed, scantily dressed ladies!

After a couple of years Brodie, our blind Labrador, had mellowed considerably and had become a definite asset to our ministry. If someone came to see us who was feeling sad or fragile Brodie seemed to know instinctively and she would come and sit very quietly next to them. After I had written a little book about our hilarious attempts to train a blind puppy we were often asked to take her into primary schools. She adored the children but also provided us with a perfect way of demonstrating to the children that individuals with a disability are just as valuable as anyone else.

Constantly moving round the country certainly makes you very conscious of those 'thin places' I've mentioned before – places where many years of prayer have cleared away the spiritual clouds between earth and heaven and the Lord's presence hangs over the place like a lovely fragrance (2 Corinthians 2:14). Speaking there is so easy because, as the Boss used to say, 'you feel the wind is behind you'. However, there are also places where the Holy Spirit has been unwelcome for so long that a whole area of the country feels spiritually dark. I never feel that 'warm treacle' anointing when I speak in those places; my words just seem to hit a granite wall.

I was asked to run a Quiet Day in a parish church in Cornwall one time, and as soon as I arrived in that corner of the county I felt oppressed by a dark atmosphere. The group who had invited me gloomily explained how difficult it was to organise Christian events in their area; churches were either apathetic or discouraged by repeated disasters.

'Don't be surprised if not many turn up tomorrow,' explained my hostess when I arrived at her charming old farmhouse. She was a delightful lady who adored dogs so she let Brodie sleep in my bedroom rather than in her usual bed in the car. I was very glad of Brodie's company because there was a vaguely sinister feeling in the wing of the old house where the guest rooms were situated, but I was so tired after the journey I soon drifted off to sleep, comforted by her snores. We'd both been asleep for some hours when I woke with a start: someone was standing over my bed. Brodie, who was usually a useless guard dog because she adored everyone she ever met, leapt out of her basket, growling ferociously. Before I could find the light switch I felt, rather than heard, a menacing voice say, 'Go away! You should never have come! You're not wanted round here!'

The sense of evil was almost overwhelming, but I had come a long way since the days when we had let Otty be bullied by evil spirits so I told whatever it was to leave in the name of Jesus and hastily put on a cassette of praise music. My friend Barbara, who had come with me on the trip and was sleeping in the next room, told me next morning that she had also been woken in the night by 'something' she felt was trying to strangle her.

When we mentioned our 'visitor' to the owners of the house they were as dismissive as Tony and I had once been about the supernatural, but later, at the Quiet Day, we met a girl who had once rented that wing of the farmhouse. She asked, tentatively, if we had been 'troubled by anything' while staying there, and then went on to share similar experiences. I did some serious cleansing prayers before we went to bed that second night, and after we had spent some time singing praises and worshipping the Lord, Barbara and I both slept perfectly – and so did Brodie.

Not long after this I was asked to speak in South Wales and was surprised when I was told that the area had been blighted for

years by the same spiritual oppression until a group of local
Christians had taken action. They spent a week fasting and prayer-
walking the whole area, singing songs of praise and claiming the
land back from the Enemy before they opened a Christian healing
centre there. We really do not have to fear the powers of darkness
when Jesus has given us all the authority of heaven!

Brodie continued to be a very good barometer for the supernatural. Although she could not see anything in the physical world
I sometimes saw her sightless eyes follow something invisible
moving about the room. I took it to be an angel because her tail
would wag a welcome (Numbers 22:23–34).

Boredom certainly is not a job hazard when no two days are
alike. One day we might be invited by a group of inner-city
single mums who met in a dismal backstreet Scout hut, while the
following evening we would be the after-dinner speakers in a
five-star hotel. One day we found ourselves driving up to a stately
home through a wide expanse of parkland. We had been told that
half the titled people in the country had been invited to hear our
talk, and I was distinctly nervous as Tony pulled the front door
bell. When we heard it ring, miles away in some distant servants'
hall, we expected the shuffling footsteps of an ancient butler, but
it was the Marchioness herself who flung open the door. As I
moved forward to take her hand I tripped on the top step and fell
flat on my face at her feet. My nose had only just stopped bleeding
when we were ushered into the crowded drawing room, and by
the end of the talk my left eye was an aristocratic shade of blue!

Perhaps the most embarrassing moment I ever had was the day
when I arrived at St Andrew's Church, Chorleywood, where I
had been invited to lead a Ladies' Day. I was slightly mystified
when Bishop David Pytches met me in the lobby and, instead of
taking me into some cosy side room to meet a small group of
friendly ladies, marched me to the front of a crowded church
packed out with men wearing their collars back to front. During
the first hymn I looked surreptitiously at my invitation and
discovered to my horror that my old enemy, dyslexia, had got me

again. I had misread 'Ladies' Day': it was a 'Leaders' Day' I had been asked to lead! My Brethren forebears would have died of shame at a woman addressing so many men, particularly as she was totally unprepared and wasn't even wearing a hat!

The funniest moment must have been when the boys and Tony came with me while I did some speaking engagements in Scotland during a spring half-term holiday. The three of them happily played golf all day, but on the last night they decided to come and support me at a very prestigious gathering in a wealthy suburb of Glasgow. The venue was sumptuous and the specially invited guests looked as if they were off to a royal garden party. I had to speak with my back to a huge wall of plate glass that overlooked a public park, and just when I was in mid-flow an extremely drunk man appeared at the window behind me. He urged me on with vigorous clapping and hand-waving, drank to my health from his whisky bottle and danced around like a performing bear. The organisers tried desperately to find a way into the park to remove him but failed, so I had to carry on regardless. The faces of the smart Glaswegians showed no emotion whatsoever, but Richard, Duncan and Tony, who were sitting in the front row, were totally helpless with laughter. I tried hard not to look at them as they shook, cried and stuffed hankies in their mouths, but I was soon equally afflicted and the meeting ended more rapidly than expected.

When you spend your life travelling you certainly appreciate the quieter patches when you can be at home; but like both my parents before me I often used them to write a book, my only excuse being that I always find writing more relaxing than just relaxing! When I finished *Turning Point*, a book about hope for broken lives, my publisher sent two photographers to take a picture for the cover.

'We want you to look wise and calm, like a counsellor,' the publishers told me, but that was *not* as easy as it sounds. The only time the photographers could come was an hour before Tony and I were due to leave for a tour of Northern Ireland. While they were filling our dining room with lights, screens and huge white umbrellas, Tony was lifting our cases into the car, when he damaged his back.

'You'll have to do this trip without me,' he groaned as he lay on the floor in agony. So I had to try and gaze into the camera, looking calm and wise while mentally I rang the airport and the organisers in Ireland, not to mention the doctor! As the camera was just about to flash, the phone rang. Tony couldn't move so I apologetically picked up the receiver in time to hear a hysterical voice sobbing, 'I've just taken all my sleeping pills, antidepressants and a whole bottle of painkillers!' It was a very close friend who had just lost her husband. By the time I had rung for an ambulance and arranged for someone to sit with her until it arrived, the photographers were looking restive, but no sooner had I pinned the smile back on my face but the doorbell rang. It was the police. Someone had reported seeing Richard throw a petrol bomb on to a busy road from a footbridge. The despairing photographers took the photo between my phone call to cancel our flight and my departure with Richard to the police station! (Fortunately it soon turned out to be a case of mistaken identity.)

The other day I was standing beside someone in a bookshop; as she looked at that picture on the back of *Turning Point*, she said, 'You look so wonderfully peaceful,' and then asked me why I was laughing!

Quite the worst moment in all those six years was at four o'clock one morning when my mobile phone rang loudly on the table by my bed. I was staying in Bristol, doing a number of outreach events for ladies in the West Country. There was no easy way for Tony to break the news that Gom had died earlier in the night. It felt like a very long drive home to Kent, thinking about all the years of self-giving love she had lavished on us all. She was a perfect example of the ravens Jesus talked about in Luke 12:24. She never worried about anything or saved for her future; in fact she gave away anything she ever earned. She happily trusted the Lord to take care of her and he most definitely did! She never quite grew up, and even at eighty-seven she savoured all the simple little things of life just like a five-year-old. That quality of childlike trust characterises each of my mother's special 'handful'.

★ ★ ★

In May 1994 I went to Canada to speak at two conferences in Ontario; as they were for ladies poor old Tony was not invited! I kept being told shocking stories about the 'disgraceful goings on' at a church near Toronto airport.

'They've all gone mad!' was the general opinion among the respectable Anglican ladies who were organising my tour. By the time I arrived home the following month the same rumours had reached Britain, and when I heard that someone who had just come back from this Toronto hot-spot was giving a talk in St Paul's, Onslow Square, on what she had seen, I said to Tony and Richard, 'Let's have a night out in London and see what's going on.'

Crowds packed the building that night, and when the speaker said, 'Come, Holy Spirit!' I will never forget the pungent stillness that descended. Tony described what happened next as 'all hell breaking loose'. People began to bounce up and down like rubber balls, high into the air; others writhed on the floor, sobbing like children or making weird animal noises; but it was the laughter that flooded my spirit with joy. Wave after wave swept round the building – glorious, child-like, refreshing laughter. I spent the rest of our 'night out' lying on the stone floor, but Tony remained quite unmoved, standing like a lone pine tree after the rest of the forest had been flattened by a hurricane. 'Mass hysteria' was his mild comment as Richard and I giggled all the way home on the train.

Tony and I used to run several holiday conferences each year, which we called 'Handle with Care'. They were designed for people who were physically challenged and their carers. A month after our extraordinary evening in London we set off to lead one

223

of these special weeks in Torquay. By that time the Toronto Blessing was spreading all round the country and I kept thinking about the book on revivals that Otty had never managed to write that summer in Scotland. Perhaps it was a revival we were experiencing now.

On the second night of the conference I was closing with prayer after giving a brief talk when I simply asked the Holy Spirit to come. There was no emotion, hype or manipulation, but the result was glorious! The laughter lasted for several hours: people slid out of their wheelchairs and lay giggling happily on the floor, while their carers rocked with mirth beside them; even the guide dogs, accompanying our blind visitors, lay on their backs kicking their legs in the air. People were healed, set free from long-standing bondages, and one widow, who had been trapped in her grief, was able to cry for the first time in a year; she found the evening a wonderful release. Tony, and a few other people who were as upset by it all as he was, walked out and left us all to party on, late into the night.

Most people agree now that the blessing that came from Toronto was not a revival, just a brief time of spiritual refreshment, but it stands out in my memory like a delightful summer holiday in the middle of years of hard work. I believe it marked the end of our absorption with the Holy Spirit and his gifts and power and helped us to fall in love with Jesus himself: not as the 'Man of Sorrows' but the one who invented fun and laughter in the first place. Above all else, it made intimacy with him fashionable once again.

At the end of that week in Torquay we were praying with our team of helpers and with Marilyn Baker, the blind singer who had been leading the worship. (Perhaps it would be more honest to say the prayer was mostly drowned by fresh waves of laughter!) I was lying on the floor enjoying myself enormously when I saw a picture of a country garden in which was a courtyard full of tubs of flowers; in the middle was a fountain. Beyond the courtyard a door led into a room, and I could see people coming from all directions to go in through that door because they wanted healing prayer for all kinds of different needs.

Fortunately we were leaving that day for our summer holiday in Stillmeadow, so I had plenty of time to ask the Lord what the picture meant and to share it with Tony. Although he was still not happy about 'all this crazy laughing', he was deeply interested in the picture.

'Now you are well again there's absolutely no reason why we shouldn't move back to the country,' he said. 'Perhaps that's what the picture means.'

'It would be wonderful to have a place that was easier for people to come and see us,' I added. A constant stream of folk visited our home in Tunbridge Wells; some wanted advice while others just needed to talk, but I always spent time allowing the Lord to use me as his silent 'water pipe'. Parking in our busy corner of town was a nightmare, and our lounge had now become an office. We had to talk to these fragile visitors in the kitchen, which could be tricky with two hungry teenage boys in the house!

'It would be wonderful to have a room that was separate from the family where we could see people in private,' I said. 'Like the room beyond the courtyard in my picture.'

'And a lovely garden where they could relax after a long journey,' put in Tony, and his eyes gleamed as he added, 'I could have a greenhouse again!'

'And I could have a bluebell wood for dog-walking!' I sighed happily.

So after our holiday we began looking at country properties that were reasonably near to the school where the boys were happily settled. The last thing I ever wanted to do was to run a residential centre – I had seen how that occupation had aged my father. We preferred to run our conferences and breaks in other people's centres, so if the cook walked out or the roof fell in it was no concern of ours! Our vision was for a tranquil place where people could come, just for the day, to receive ministry.

Finally we found a three-bedroomed bungalow set among Kentish apple orchards and hop gardens. It had a huge greenhouse and was near *several* bluebell woods; best of all it was within walking distance of my childhood home, the first Hildenborough Hall. We loved the bungalow the moment we walked through the door – even though the mortgage was really more than we could afford. Generous friends gave us enough money to build an extension, which we called the Prayer Room, and a large wooden building at the bottom of the garden for our office. Tony was in his element, doing most of the building himself, and when he finally finished the courtyard and the fountain it was so perfect that anyone would have thought *he'd* been the one to see the picture!

We moved in at the end of January 1995 full of happy plans for our new mini healing centre, and the first morning, when I sat up in bed and heard the silence of the country all around me, I felt my soul had come home again.

★ ★ ★

But happiness has a strange way of trickling through your fingers just when you feel it's safely in your grasp. Tony was still in the middle of building the Prayer Room when his mother, whom we always called Gan, had a stroke and needed to come and live with us. We both felt this was right, but her arrival meant we could no longer travel together because she needed one of us there to give her constant care, day and night.

By this time Tony had taken over as the administrator for all the work of the Hildenborough Trust, as well as running our own conferences and breaks, so he felt he should leave most of the travelling to me while he developed our vision for the centre and looked after his mother and Richard (Duncan had left for university by then). Tony continued to come with me to run the conferences and breaks, which were his passion, but he seemed genuinely happy to stay at home for the rest of the time. He had never enjoyed life 'on the road' very much, and it also seemed as if the Lord was moving me into more of a prophetic, inner-healing type of ministry. While Tony encouraged me in this, he did not feel gifted in that direction himself.

'I prefer a practical ministry,' he would say. 'Admin, counselling and creating a garden for others to enjoy, all that's just as important as the upfront stuff.' He was right, but after Gan came to live with us all the fun went out of life. That was definitely not her fault, but Tony and I missed each other enormously and I found travelling alone increasingly exhausting and stressful. Coming home was no better, because I obviously had to take my turn to nurse Gan, which brought back all the awful memories of caring for Otty.

'This isn't fair, Lord,' I remember thinking one morning as I struggled to get Gan dressed. I had been up most of the night trying to shift the mountain of post which always accumulated on my desk when I had been away on speaking tours. Before I could face all the housework and shopping I slumped down on the sofa and burst into tears. 'Lord, you anointed me to serve you, so couldn't you make life just a little bit easier?'

At once I saw a picture of a big juicy orange being cut in half by a sharp knife and the Lord seemed to be saying, 'Oranges are no use to people until they are cut open, exposed and then squeezed; that's when the juice trickles out to refresh and nourish other people. Your life is like this orange.'

I dismissed the incident by replying, 'Thanks a lot, but I'd much rather not be squeezed any more!' I did not realise that once again he was warning me of events to come.

It is all too easy to allow the things we do for God to rob us of time to *be with* him – just to enjoy him for himself alone. While I still used to get up early in the morning to pray, these appointments had become more like committee meetings when I prepared talks, planned conferences and juggled my diary. Being busy in ministry does not always mean that our 'Martha' side has got the upper hand; we can stay fresh serving the Lord as a busy

Martha so long as we let our 'Mary' have regular times just to sit with him. Now that our home had ceased to be a place where we could relax and be still in God's presence, my poor Mary was fast being suffocated by activity.

With hindsight it is easy to see that I should either have given up my speaking ministry for a time or made other arrangements for Gan; we both felt sure families come first in God's economy, but perhaps I loved itinerant ministry too much to let that go. When Tony and I first set out 'on the road' together I think our hearts were so full of gratitude that, like Paul, we were compelled by the love of Christ (2 Corinthians 5:14). In other words, we felt urged, compelled, driven along by the Lord's love for a suffering world; but now I can see that was not my only motivation. Whatever we do for God, the job has spin-off effects that gratify our own human needs, whether we are arranging the church flowers or preaching to large congregations. After those eight years of illness, hidden away, restricted and often scorned by other Christians because I did not have 'enough faith to be healed', I had suddenly been catapulted out into the sunshine of so much affirmation, encouragement and even admiration. The hidden engine that drove me towards seeking the approval of others had gradually begun to kick back in.

'You'll have to work harder than the others', the words my mother spoke when she was told I was educationally retarded, also rang in my ears, albeit subconsciously, making me feel I could never say no to speaking invitations or fall behind with correspondence. So many of us who grow up feeling a failure push ourselves to the limit when we go into full-time ministry – trying to appear superhuman! If we once realised that the only qualification for serving God is to know our own total *inadequacy* and recognise his complete *adequacy*, we wouldn't keep on pushing ourselves like hamsters running on an exercise-wheel!

Guilt was probably another cause of my workaholism. Whenever I saw someone in a wheelchair I felt so bad: I would think,

'Why was I healed and not them?' Did I want to pay God back for what he had done? How ridiculous! Of course he knows all about our human agendas, and if he waited until all our motives were pure he could never use any of us. Perhaps whatever we do for God, we are all driven by several engines at once – rather like a jet plane. St Paul understood this problem but had no engines or planes to use as illustrations! So he told us the work we do for God will one day be tested by fire which will burn up everything we did to satisfy our own needs (he calls all that 'wood, hay and stubble'), but the things we do purely for the love of God (Paul calls that 'gold and silver') will be left unharmed by the fire (1 Corinthians 3:12–15). When we have set our sights on intimacy with God we simply cannot afford to wait until the Day of Judgment to discover whether we are pure of heart, because we want to see God here and now (Matthew 5:8). So, although I had no idea at the time *why* I was working so hard, towards the end of those six years God began to allow me to have the uneasy feeling that the job I did for him had become more important to me than he was himself.

However, when the 'exercise-wheel' is spinning too fast the hamster finds it hard to know how to get off. Tony was horrified when I said I wanted to do less speaking; instead, he urged me on and did everything possible to support me. So in the end it was a cancer scare after a smear test that finally slowed the 'wheel'. Just a month before, I had written these words in the front cover of my Bible:

1 January 1996
During communion I felt the Lord say, 'This year I am asking you to walk with me to Calvary. You will be broken but not lost – crushed but not defeated.'

As my life reverted to the all-too-familiar round of hospital appointments, procedures and treatments, I thought this was the 'Calvary' the Lord had been warning me about, but I was wrong.

Tony and I both found it hard to face more illness after we had been so amazingly set free, so when he became gloomy and withdrawn I thought at first he was worrying about me. However, as he became increasingly tired and listless it was soon *me* who was doing the worrying! He also seemed to be going through some kind of a faith crisis and I began to wonder if the strain of being his mother's carer was making him depressed. When I suggested she might go into a home, however, he doggedly rejected the idea. Soon we were living inside two separate bubbles of silence, but all my efforts to discover what was troubling him only seemed to widen the gap between us.

'Let's give up ministry and go off into the blue,' I suggested, 'run that bed and breakfast we used to talk about,' but he did not seem to hear. For thirty-five years we had been so close we could read each other's thoughts, so the pain of feeling disconnected was enormous.

★ ★ ★

By September I was desperate. We took one of our little groups to Keswick that month so, early one morning long before our guests were awake, I walked to Friar's Crag and stood on the same little beach where I had once sat in my wheelchair in the rain. I took my journal with me because I wanted to have a written record of what I was going to say to the Lord that morning.

16 September 1996
Lord, I came here seven years ago and asked you for an anointing for ministry. But I've come back now to ask you to take it away again. I want out! You knew I wouldn't be able to handle it so you just said: 'All you need is me.' I wanted power to serve you, but I should have asked for YOU, and you ALONE. I'm so sorry! If my ministry has become an idol then take it away – give me you and you alone – whatever the cost!

Three weeks later, Tony packed all his possessions into four black bin liners and drove away down the lane.

10

When my soul was embittered,
when I was pricked in heart,
I was stupid and ignorant;
I was like a brute beast towards you.
Nevertheless I am continually with you;
you hold my right hand.
You guide me with your counsel,
and afterwards you will receive me with honour.
Whom have I in heaven but you?
And there is nothing on earth that I desire other than you.
My flesh and my heart may fail,
but God is the strength of my heart and my portion for ever . . .
for me it is good to be near God;
I have made the LORD God my refuge,
to tell of all your works.

Psalm 73:21–8, NRSV

My very worst fear had always been that Tony would die. I often prayed, 'Lord, I could cope with anything except *that*.' The thought of losing him another way simply never entered my head. We had gone through so much together during all those years that I thought our marriage was cast-iron safe. Nowadays no marriages are safe.

Just before the time when I first noticed Tony was withdrawing from me behind his wall of silence, he had led one of our breaks on his own while I took my turn to stay home with the family. It was during that holiday week in Corfu that he had met someone, and they had fallen deeply in love.

A few weeks later, when I accidentally found out, we both tried desperately to save our marriage; we went to counsellors, took a holiday alone together and I cut down my speaking engagements drastically. By the following September, when we ran that break together in Keswick, I was still hoping that he would make the choice to stay with me, but poor soft-hearted, gentle Tony was caught between two women who both loved him and the pain of that was nearly killing him. After a sleepless night in early October he suddenly said, 'She needs me more than you do because you've got the Lord to take care of you.'

As he packed his things I followed him round the house frozen, too shocked to speak. We certainly didn't quarrel. He even gently kissed me goodbye on the front doorstep, and prayed that Jesus would take care of me before the car door slammed closed between us. I have often thought he might have stayed if only I'd cried, had hysterics or threatened to top myself, but I just stood there, like a zombie devoid of emotion, gazing after the car until the last sound of the engine died away.

At my feet on the drive I noticed the mangled body of one of our collared doves, the shy, peace-loving birds that seem to love nesting in our garden. I remember feeling furious with the neighbour's cat, which must have caught it and torn it apart with its sharp teeth and claws. Somehow it felt safer to feel upset over a bird rather than face the horror of what was happening to Tony and me. 'Satan's like that cat,' I thought vaguely, 'he's done just the same to us.' Gan's little silver bell was ringing violently so, mechanically, I walked back into the house telling myself I couldn't put all the blame on the Devil, or on Tony, for something which was every bit as much my fault as theirs.

'Where's Tony gone?' demanded Gan querulously. I knew he

had told her he was leaving me just before he drove away, so I simply said, 'I'll make a cup of tea, Gan.'

For some odd reason, as I stood gazing at the kettle I was remembering all the talks I had given on forgiveness all over the world – I'd even written a book on the subject! 'That's the first thing I've got to decide to do,' I thought, and it seemed quite easy then, because I wasn't feeling any pain at all, my heart was anaesthetised. Little did I realise I was only taking the first step of a journey that will last the rest of my life!

'When's Tony coming back?' asked Gan as I stirred the tea for her, and then watched as she dribbled it down the front of her clean nightie.

'I'm going to clear out the garage, Gan,' I said in a flat, dull voice. 'Ring if you need me.'

For the next week I did nothing else, day and night, but clean and tidy compulsively. When the garage was done I started on the attic, then the garden shed, office, kitchen, wardrobes and drawers. The sense of powerlessness was suffocating. I could do nothing to control the chaotic mess in my life but I had to bring order to something, somewhere.

Late that first evening, once Gan was finally settled, I rang a friend called Jill; she drove straight over and gave me a verse she had written out on a card. She didn't ask intrusive questions or swamp me with advice, she just prayed a short prayer, hugged me and left. Such friends are beyond price. I stood, watching her drive away as I had watched Tony earlier in the day, and then looked down at the words she had written out for me:

Who is among you who reverently fears the LORD, who obeys the voice of His Servant, yet who walks in darkness and deep trouble and has no shining splendour in his heart? Let him rely on, trust in, and be confident in the name of the LORD, and let him lean upon and be supported by his God.

Isaiah 50:10, AMP

At that moment I certainly had no shining splendour in my heart! I felt totally unable to connect with God or anyone else. The words did not really mean anything to me but I sensed they were important, so I found a bit of Blu Tack and stuck the card up on the wall above the kettle. Then I went back to sorting the attic.

For days I went round wearing that 'thousand-mile stare' which you so often see on the faces of people in shock. Although I often found Gan infuriating, I think it was caring for her which actually helped me more than anything else. Richard, the last of our brood, had gone off to university only two weeks before Tony left, so after years of managing a large family Gan was suddenly all I had left. She felt just as abandoned as I did, and because the shock made her more confused than ever she absorbed all my time – when I wasn't clearing cupboards. I had no job any more, either; wisely, our trustees insisted that I cancelled everything in my diary for the next six months, but we all doubted that I would ever go back into ministry again. Who would ask me to speak after this? Fortunately, my closest friend, Barbara, came round every day to make sure we were fed; Gan and I kept forgetting little things like food.

Friends sent flowers and cards as if Tony had died, but there was no funeral to plan, nothing to mark the end of all the happy years we had spent together. In some ways it might have been easier for me if he *had* died, because I could have pictured him happily in heaven, waiting for me; but he was alive and well, living with somebody else.

Sleep was totally impossible; I blamed Gan, who often rang her bell during the night, but I doubt if I would have slept anyway. I couldn't face our double bed without Tony so I camped out in Richard's room, but even his narrow bed felt half empty. About four in the mornings I used to go and sit in the Prayer Room and curl up in my favourite rocking armchair, gripping a mug of tea like a drowning man clutches driftwood. I couldn't pray but scribbled endlessly in my journal. At the time, writing was merely a way of expressing pain, but now that I have safely emerged on the far side of that dark tunnel of grief I really treasure that battered old notebook. In the darkness I often felt abandoned by God, but my journal shows how he kept on lighting little candles to show me the way through. Perhaps it was a verse someone sent me, the words of a song or the kindness of a friend: little things that could so easily have been forgotten had they had not been recorded.

The children were wonderfully supportive. They each did their best to persuade Tony to come home but, perhaps because he was hurting so badly, he built a wall around himself that excluded them for several years. In spite of grappling with their own grief and sense of rejection they were a great help to me. Duncan, who was then in his last year of university, came straight home during that first week and marched me off to the bank to open my first account. Tony had always looked after every detail of the business side of things; he generously gave me all the cash I needed but never saw the necessity of arranging for me to have a banker's card.

'You just slide your bit of plastic into the slot in the wall outside the bank,' explained Duncan patiently. It seemed a great idea to me – at first – but it was not long before my new card brought forth no money at all!

'I'll teach you how to keep accounts and budget,' offered Naomi kindly. I accepted their help mechanically; it never occurred to me that parents are supposed to teach their children that kind of thing, not the other way about!

My brother Justyn flew back from Canada hoping to talk Tony into a reconciliation, but I can scarcely remember his visit. Most of the time I was hardly aware of any of the people who came and went, but I definitely saw an angel and described it in my journal.

Richard home for weekend, so hurt. Took him to the Artichoke [local pub] to get him away from Gan's endless lamenting. Said he feels his security has been shot away. He was crying helplessly when I saw an

*angel (his guardian) standing beside him, head bowed and wings all
bedraggled like hens when it's raining hard.*

Because I was so firmly convinced that Tony would come home
at any minute, my first instinct was to keep quiet and tell nobody
that he had gone. However, that kind of privacy is not so easy
when you are in full-time ministry. We had over 2,000 people
who supported our work by prayer and regular gifts. They had a
right to know I was cancelling all my engagements, and needed
some kind of explanation.

*Terrible day: got up early: had to sign, pack and send off letters to
supporters; said Tony was having a faith crisis and had gone away for
a bit. I'm scared they'll guess.*

They guessed all right! As soon as those letters arrived at their
destinations the rumours began to reverberate around the country,
becoming more exaggerated and distorted each time the story
was told. The phone never stopped ringing, nor did the doorbell,
and I felt utterly exposed and vulnerable. Whenever I went out
shopping I kept bumping into people I knew, and behind their
smiles I was sure they were thinking, 'She must have been
impossible to live with or a nice man like that would never have
left her!' The word 'failure' seemed to be written in red across my
forehead. When you live in the public eye everyone seems to feel
they have the right to dissect you, so people I had not seen for
years used to ring up and ask searching questions; one even wanted
to know if our sex life had been satisfactory!

In spite of all this, for a while after Tony left I felt closer to God
than I have at any other time of my life.

*I seem to have lost everything: my children after twenty-eight years of
motherhood; my husband and the security of his love; my job, my
reputation and I'm likely to lose my home; I've lost my freedom too —
I'm stuck here with Gan. But at Keswick last September I prayed,*

'Lord, give me you and you alone – whatever the cost!' and now I really do have him! He is all I have left. If he's willing to take everything from me, simply to get my attention/company/time – wow! I must be so precious to him!

Since then I have met many people who, after a major shock or loss, live in that kind of delightful euphoria for a while. Everyone says, 'What wonderful faith!' but actually it is only a transient part of the grieving process, which always seems to wear off when real grieving begins. Perhaps it is like hitting your thumb with a hammer; at first you are surprised to find it didn't hurt at all, but once the numbness wears off you quickly realise it did!

This has all the pain of a bereavement but to all the other emotions add confusion, guilt, shame, rejection – so much more.

Spent yesterday in hospital, they had to do an anaesthetic to do the test so they needed a consent form. Couldn't bring myself to tick 'separated' in marital status box and cried over the 'next of kin' bit. This 'aloneness' thing is getting to me. Please show me what you meant by saying 'All you need is me.'

If I'm such a vile person that Tony had to run away from me like this then I might as well be dead. Please let me die soon.

During the following months the entries in that journey contain an awful lot of references to death, and I remember crying with disappointment when the hospital rang to say the latest batch of tests had shown no further cancer.

Drove along the by-pass, screaming until my throat hurt. Aimed for a tree in the distance and put my foot down hard. No one around. Wanted to die. Thought of Richard so didn't.

Going to church presented a major problem. Again Gan was my excuse, but I doubt if I would have gone even if I could have found someone to sit with her. Tony had been a much-loved elder for years; I simply could not face walking in and having to sit alone in our usual, once crowded, pew. I guess most people just didn't know what to say, so very few of them made contact. Had Tony died I would have been surrounded by so much love and support from my church, but losing a husband this way is a very different matter.

Horror! Going to the solicitor today. Tony has drawn up a deed of separation. Have to sort the house etc. Thirty years of marriage can't end in such a sordid way as this!

'Are you considering divorce?' asked the solicitor.

'Oh *no*,' I replied. 'This is just a little temporary fling – he'll be back soon.' She gave me an odd look and murmured something about being 'in denial'. I felt rather sorry for her: after all, she was not a Christian so how could she know that God was *bound to intervene* when there was so much prayer going up all round the country?

In order to make it easy for Tony to come home I sent the door key, which he had left behind the day he left, adding a note pleading with him to use it – soon! I was so convinced he would come back I kept glancing out of the window, watching for his car. Then, one evening, I saw him walking towards the house. I shot up like a rocket to fling open the front door, arms wide open, only to find a stranger on the doorstep, canvassing for the Conservatives. He must have found my welcome exceedingly encouraging!

★　★　★

The experts tell us that grief is a journey, and you walk from one end to the other through stages such as denial, anger, guilt, anxiety, isolation, despair and a whole clutch of other nasties. To me it did not feel like a walk through a straight tunnel; it seemed to twist in endless circles like a spiral staircase. I went round and round, experiencing the same stages many times over – and sometimes several of them at the same time. So from this point onwards I won't try to tell the story in chronological order.

According to those experts, anger is usually the first nasty to hit after a marriage break-up, but for me that came later – and with a vengeance! My journal shows it was guilt and remorse that swamped me during the first couple of months. I was quite convinced that my ministry had destroyed our marriage. I am not sure now that I was right to put all the blame on that, because up until the time when Tony met someone else he was one hundred per cent with me in the work, and he has never ever, at any time, said that he resented my being away from home so much. But at the time I felt convinced the whole thing was entirely my fault.

Bad day. Found the stilton cheese with apricots that Tony likes in the back of the fridge, felt overwhelmed by the thought he won't be coming home to eat it. If only he'd said he wasn't happy in ministry – if only I'd noticed he wasn't!

Left Gan with Barbi and went to see Jill, got home late but no Tony to come out to meet me as I turned into the drive. Always loved the way he waited up for me. He must have hated me being out so much.

For a long time I was also convinced I did not deserve ever to be allowed to serve the Lord again and was not surprised when letters began arriving from Australia, New Zealand, Canada and all over the UK saying, 'In the circumstances it might be best if you did *not* come and speak at . . .'; and they were referring to conferences or events that were scheduled well after the six months set by my trustees. Some of the other letters that flooded in each morning also increased my sense of condemnation, because complete strangers used to write and tell me *exactly* why they thought I had ruined my marriage. Of course, there were far more letters that were full of loving support, but somehow it's always the painful ones you remember!

'There is no such thing as "an innocent party". He may have gone off with someone else but have you asked yourself *why*? Or *what* you could have done to keep him?'

'I hope you have repented for your side of this failure.'

'If you had been close to Jesus he would not have allowed this to happen.'

'. . . you are no longer qualified for ministry.'

'I blame all that speaking, your healing went to your head.'

'You will have to be prepared to change yourself drastically before he'll come home.'

'We could see it coming a mile off, women should not be in ministry, God created them to stay home and look after their families.'

These letters hurt all the more because they exaggerated my irrational feeling that everything was all my own fault. Other letters were just as scathing in their comments about Tony, but actually it is pointless to put all the blame on one partner when a marriage breaks up: both have to face up to their part in the failure. There is no such thing as a 'perfect wife' or a 'perfect husband'; we all fail to love, affirm and respect as much as we should. When your ministry is taken away you also have to ask yourself searching questions, so for me this was a double whammy. Unfortunately I totally lost the ability to be objective over either and positively wallowed in remorse, pouring out into my journal pages of endless regrets and 'if onlys'.

Then one evening a lady called Helen, who is widely known as a conference speaker, asked me round for coffee; Barbara was willing to 'Granny-sit' so I went. It would have been useless for Helen to try and cheer me up by talking about other things; all you can do at first is talk about the *same things* over and over again. It is exhausting for everyone else but very healing for you! After I had replayed all my failures several times over she said, 'Jen, do you believe Jesus died for you on the cross?'

I gazed at her, quite astonished. 'Of course I do!' I said at last. 'I've been preaching about the cross for years!'

'Preaching is one thing,' said Helen firmly. 'But if you *really* believe it for yourself, why are you carrying all this weight of guilt?'

'I don't feel I deserve to be free of it,' I replied simply.

'Then don't you think you could be insulting the Lord by not accepting his offer of freedom?'

I sat gazing at her, too stunned to speak; but overnight I wrote a lengthy list of all the things I regretted doing or saying, or failing to do or say, throughout our marriage. It took up several sheets of paper! At first light I went down to the office, photocopied my list, and then walked on down to the bottom of the garden where there is a large wooden cross. I burnt those sheets of paper one by one, asking the Lord to forgive me. Then I sent the copy to Tony, asking for his forgiveness too. He never replied, but sending it proved to be very healing for me. Sad to say, repentance does not always wipe out the *consequences* of past sin but it does make it possible to move into the future with peace.

Obviously a holy lifestyle is vital for anyone who longs for intimacy with God (Psalm 24:3–4), but all those years of trying to be 'very very good' had only made me conscious of how totally I fail in my own strength. Standing there at that cross, early in the morning, I realised with huge relief that you do not have to be perfect to journey into God's heart: holiness simply means the willingness to repent – often. We can't make *ourselves* holy; he does this for us – so long as we'll let him (1 Thessalonians 5:23–4).

★ ★ ★

Fear soon took the place of guilt and shame, particularly as my bleak financial position became more obvious. Had Tony died I would have had a widow's pension and his life insurance to pay off the mortgage.

'Sell the house and get yourself a job,' he told me coldly on one of the rare occasions when he rang, after which I wrote in my journal:

What sort of a job could I do while Gan needs twenty-four-hour care?!

I used to sit at my desk looking at the piles of forms that came flooding in with every post. All the direct debits and banker's orders had to be changed into my name, but I didn't have the faintest idea what those mysterious things were! Forms terrify dyslexics so Tony had always filled everything in for me; now I just sat at my desk, endlessly rearranging the piles of paper but never quite getting round to dealing with them. Then there were the bills!

One terrible night it rained so hard the roof leaked. As I ran round placing buckets in strategic places I panicked: 'How much is it going to cost to get all this repaired?' The toilet had refused to flush properly for days and I knew it would be £50 just to call out a plumber to take a look. I had never appreciated Tony's abilities as much as I did that night! Cold, tired and miserable, I finally went to bed, but then came the worst disaster of all. Inside the wardrobe I distinctly heard a scuffling noise. If it had been a burglar or even a serial killer I would not have been nearly as terrified as I was of that mouse!

Pulling the duvet off the bed I ran out of the room, slamming the door behind me. Still shaking with fright I curled up into a foetal ball on the sofa, where the Lord had once shown me a picture of a crushed orange, and pulled the duvet right over my head. I've since christened the way I felt that night 'the Abomination of Desolation', but even that is an understatement. Hiding under the duvet, there did not seem to be the slightest ray of light left in the whole world. The sound of the drips plopping into those buckets seemed to grow louder as the hours dragged by. I considered getting up and making a cup of tea, but there might be more mice in the kitchen so I stayed where I was.

On the coffee table beside me lay a card. I had snorted with disgust that morning when I read what a friend had written inside it: 'Take a look at Isaiah 54.'

'She must be joking!' I had muttered crossly. 'Read a whole chapter from the Old Testament – at a time like this?'

For weeks I had not been able to read the Bible: I just picked and snacked on verses I knew well or simply sat holding the scriptures in my lap. Perhaps because I had nothing better to do at three in the morning I finally turned to the offending chapter. It sounds corny to say the words of verse 5 jumped up off the page and hit me in the face – but corny or no, that is what they did!

'Your Maker is your husband.' Suddenly all my attention was riveted on that one phrase. During my journey into God's heart I had already learnt to relate to him as my creator, father, master (boss), friend or even lover, but why had I never realised he also wanted me to see him as a husband? And, being God, he would obviously be a perfect one!

So what *was* a perfect husband? Tony had come very close to the mark, but surely absolute perfection would be a husband who took full responsibility for his wife, not only when she was young and active but *always;* he would care for her tenderly, provide financially, protect her from all danger, cherish her and meet all her needs, both practical and emotional. Was God really offering me all this?

When you are given a sudden insight it takes weeks or even months to think it all through, rather as you might examine the gift of a huge diamond, holding it between your fingers, slowly turning it so that each facet can reflect the light in turn. Initially, all I could think was, 'He's offering me yet another of his choices!' Either I could trust him to be all that Tony had been to me – and far more – or I could go on lying in a ball with my face to the wall for the rest of my life. It was a simple yes or no decision – but at first I was not sure which option to choose. When you have been badly hurt, sometimes the only comfort for the pain is to hold on to the pain itself and cuddle it to your heart. I had also been so profoundly shaken by Tony's sudden rejection that I now struggled to trust anyone's word ever again – even God's.

As I glanced back down at that chapter in Isaiah, other verses began to spring out at me which also seemed to have been written just for me:

> 'Do not be afraid; you will not suffer shame. Do not fear disgrace; you will not be humiliated . . . The LORD will call you back as if you were a wife deserted and distressed in spirit – a wife who married young, only to be rejected . . . Though the mountains be shaken and the hills be removed, yet my unfailing love for you will not be shaken nor my covenant of peace be removed,' says the LORD, who has compassion on you.
>
> Isaiah 54:4–10

The one thing that I craved most was faithful, never-ending love, and here was the Lord telling me that even if the mountains collapsed the promise he was making to me here and now on this sofa could never be broken.

'I can take it or leave it,' I muttered as I crawled out of the duvet to look for a pen and paper. 'After all, what have I got to lose?' As I wrote out those verses it felt as if I was drawing up a marriage certificate, so at the bottom of the page I signed it and, braving the mice, walked out into the kitchen to stick it up on the fridge.

I would hate to give you the wrong impression; I may have made my choice as I signed the contract that night but I went back on it dozens of times afterwards. I still had to endure lengthy bouts of suicidal depression, months on antidepressants, endless times of spiritual darkness, counselling sessions galore and many different kinds of prayer ministry. Underlying all that, however, was the knowledge that he wanted to give me all the security, status and benefits of an adored wife.

Because I had always had such a good earthly husband I had

ignored all the references in both Old and New Testaments to God as a bridegroom and husband. I had vowed to *know* God but I had never realised the significance of that word. We use it in several different ways. I can say, 'I *know* the Queen,' but I mean I know certain things about her; I can say, 'I *know* my friend Barbara,' because she and I spend so much time together; but the Bible word which is translated 'know' is the word used when a man and woman are joined physically in marriage. *'Adam knew Eve his wife; and she conceived and bare Cain'* (Genesis 4:1, KJV). God wanted to use the closest relationship possible between two human beings to illustrate the depth of intimacy he desires to have with us.

Of course, I thought I had been trusting him for years. Like so many of us when we are fit, fulfilled in a career, comfortably off and surrounded by the people we love, it is so easy to *think* God is our security when actually all our needs are being met in all these other ways. When all the props are knocked away and we find we only have God left, *only then* do we know for sure where our dependency lies.

The morning after the dreaded Night of the Mouse a friend and her husband came in for a coffee. After he had answered the call of nature, he came out saying, 'Did you know your loo won't flush?' When I told him, witheringly, that I was *fully* aware of the problem, he said, 'I can easily fix that for you,' and a few minutes later he had!

Another friend (with a degree in English and Economics) helped me fill in all those forms, and miraculously there was enough money in my bank account to pay the menacing bills. Best of all, Tony's brother Peter kindly arranged to pay the mortgage for a few months to give me breathing space. The following weekend Richard came home, climbed on to the roof with a thick roll of waterproofing material he found in the garage and it has never leaked since. And the mouse? I am not sure if an angel removed it to the garden by its tail or frightened it away by appearing in the form of a ferocious cat, but I've never had another mouse in my bedroom!

It was not only the practical things that 'my husband' sorted out for me. In one sense they were not the most crucial needs that I had right then. When some marriages break down there can be a feeling of relief, perhaps after years of rows, betrayal or neglect, but Tony and I had been inseparably close, best friends, work colleagues as well as a long-time married couple. Without him I felt utterly lost, abandoned and alone; I had no desire to live, no purpose in life and no confidence to face the world. God did not meet all those deep emotional needs in one go as I lay on the sofa that night, but over the years since he has met every one of them in full.

★ ★ ★

'You won't get over this until you let yourself get in touch with your anger,' said my GP. She had already given me a book on 'handling bereavement', which talked about 'the anger stage', and she obviously thought I ought to have reached it by then. 'It's perfectly normal to feel angry,' she continued. 'Everyone does after such a major rejection.' I knew she was right but was too embarrassed to tell her that I had already written a book about anger and forgiveness (*Turning Point*, Hodder & Stoughton, 1994)! But knowing things in theory does not always help.

'I'm sorry,' I said miserably. 'But I don't seem to *feel* angry.'

Actually I think I was afraid of anger. Perhaps this was because of my upbringing, but I had also seen so many people become prickly as hedgehogs after a bad experience. I could also remember how anger had distorted my life before I fell in all that cow dung, and I was determined not to let that happen again. Perhaps I had spent so many years forming the habit of burying my anger that even when I *wanted* to feel it I simply couldn't any more. I knew it must be there, but I simply could not access it.

During lunch one day soon after that uncomfortable visit to the doctor, Gan made a sour comment about my cooking; I said nothing but suddenly something erupted like a volcano inside me. I flew out into the kitchen and began hurling crockery at the stone tiled floor. If Barbara had not stopped me I might have demolished the entire kitchen!

When I finally came back to the lunch table Gan was still chewing her food. 'Dear, dear, dear,' she said mildly, just as Tony would have done. At that moment I could have killed her – and Tony as well! Once I had calmed down I was very ashamed of myself, but then I suddenly thought, 'Good! At least that's got my anger stage over and done with.' I did not realise there was still an awful lot more where that came from!

Perhaps many Christians share my problem over anger because we have a sneaky feeling that it is sinful; so when we are recovering from major loss we suppress what is actually a very normal part of the grief package. We forget that Jesus was often angry. He did not smoulder away silently for days (Ephesians 4:26): he harnessed it to provide energy and courage to change situations (John 2:14–16). Anger is only wrong when we let it boil over, unrestrained, to damage others, or when we hang on to it so long it turns to bitterness. Nowadays I spend a lot of my time helping other people to recover from rejection, and I've discovered that those who are able to express their strong, negative feelings in appropriate ways recover far more quickly than I did.

After Christmas my trustees unwittingly brought a lot more anger to the surface when they firmly told me they were sending me away for ten days' intensive counselling from a woman who had been highly recommended to them because she was 'very good in this type of situation'.

Why are they doing this to me? It's Tony who needs counselling! I don't know anything about this woman, Jean. Don't trust her! Don't like her voice on the phone! If I tell her how I really feel she'll report it all back to the trustees. It's inhuman! Outrageous!

No one likes to feel that other people think they need counselling! So I presented every possible objection: 'I can't leave Gan or

Brodie and I'm not up to going away on my own yet.' When Tony's brother offered to have Gan to stay and Jean said I could bring Brodie with me, and Barbara for support, I felt everyone was ganging up on me. So with my anger safely hidden once again I set off to face my fate – and soon discovered it was the best thing my trustees could possibly have done! Jean systematically took me apart and then gently put me back together again. I now firmly believe that everyone who has experienced a marriage break-up, for whatever reason, needs this kind of help if they are ever going to recover. During the following three years I went back to see Jean on many occasions and she has now become a close friend.

She was not deceived by my bright assurances that I was 'safely over the anger state'; she just smiled and waited.

'I think I'm depressed,' I told her when I went back to see her four months after my first visit.

'I don't think you are,' she said, 'I think you're angry.'

'No,' I assured her sweetly, 'I've been depressed before so I ought to know what it feels like.'

'Depression can be caused by anger we won't allow ourselves to express,' said Jean. I was still politely unconvinced so she continued, 'I want you to go off by yourself now, and write out a complete list of everyone who has upset you, failed you or damaged you since your wedding day; then bring it back here to me tomorrow morning.'

'That won't take me long,' I muttered. 'I've led a charmed life.'

I was wrong! Once I let myself go, I sat with my laptop on my knee, adding to my list throughout the night; and every time I tried to sleep I remembered something else. It was not just the two central characters in my drama who had hurt me, but tactless friends, unsympathetic colleagues and intrusive strangers. I finally returned to Jean with a pile of papers that resembled a manuscript.

'Right!' she said, pointing to a chair she had placed at the far end of the room, 'imagine that is God's Judgment Seat. We're going to sit in front of his throne on these two chairs and you're going to read out your accusation against all those people.' I felt such a fool as I began reading my list out loud, but as I turned each page I heard my voice becoming louder and more aggressive. By the end I was puce in the face and shaking violently, fists clenched, gasping for breath.

'Good,' said Jean. 'Now, what do you want the Judge to do about all those people? It's up to you.'

I felt like a pricked balloon as I muttered, 'Forgive them, I suppose.'

'What about the two in the middle?' asked Jean, 'Do you want them to be let off, too?'

I sat gazing at the 'Seat of Judgment', realising I wanted justice for myself, not mercy for them. I wanted them to be mutilated, killed slowly, painfully, agonisingly; but suddenly I saw Jesus on the cross as clearly as I had seen him that day in the London hospital when I was being raced along corridors in a wheelchair. I saw how his body was mutilated, how he was dying slowly, painfully, agonisingly. He had died like that for me, but he had also died like that for them.

'But they're not even sorry,' I protested.

'Doesn't make any difference,' said Jean mildly. 'It's your *willingness* to forgive that sets you free from them.'

It took Jean several days to help me recover from the shock of discovering just how much anger I had been burying for so long. Obviously I had to ask the Lord to forgive me for hoarding it, and I also needed prayer for healing from all the damage it had done to me, physically, mentally and spiritually. It was a major turning point in my recovery, even though I still had to go on down through countless layers of forgiveness – and probably I'll have to keep at it a lot longer yet.

After that imaginary courtroom session I was determined to take St Paul's advice and *'get rid of all bitterness, rage and anger'* (Ephesians 4:31) as soon as I possibly could, rather than denying its existence. Two simple little things that I began to do around that time helped me enormously with this problem. The first is spitting! Every time I felt anger rising up inside, rather than counting to ten and then swallowing hard, I spat it out – literally. It was easier when I was gardening or out walking the dogs; indoors I had to use a tissue! It must sound silly, but doing something tangible really helped me to release the anger harmlessly and it also made me laugh, which is a marvellous antidote to rage.

The other thing was equally simple: I found two egg-sized stones on my favourite beach in Devon and every morning, when I went to pray in my rocking chair, I held one stone in each hand, lifting them up in God's direction. Then, out loud, I released forgiveness to the two people those stones represented. Afterwards I placed them on my Bible, leaving them there all day beside a little wooden cross. On bad days, when anger kept boiling up constantly, I had to go back and hold them out like that several times over.

* * *

Unfortunately, releasing all that anger did not cure my depression straight away, and without Prozac I would probably have had a complete breakdown; but medication kept me functioning – more or less. My journal during the following months makes dismal reading, but even among all that black despair God still lit the occasional candle.

Went to new house group alone – only single person there, all the rest couples. Came home in the car alone, they all went off in pairs. No one to chat it over with – felt terrible. 'I'll always have to go home alone now,' I thought, then heard the Lord say, 'You are never alone, why not chat it over with me!' Felt so flooded with joy I danced all round the house when I got back.

Went to dinner with Tim and Nancy. Adrian and Bridget Plass were there. Didn't want to go alone and face them. [Tony and I had

251

worked with Adrian quite often in the past.] *Felt embarrassed when I walked in, didn't know what to say, but Adrian didn't say anything or ask nosy questions, he just stood holding my hand and when I looked up he was crying. Felt so comforted.*

Brodie was also an enormous help; she sensed my misery and followed me about even more closely than usual.

Brodie now sleeps in my bedroom, but snores even louder than Tony used to; but when the noise wakes me up it feels nice to know I am not alone!

One of the grief stages that I found most difficult to handle was the restlessness. I just could not sit still or concentrate on anything for more than a few moments. Whenever I went to my rocking chair to spend time with the Lord I felt as if a swarm of bees were buzzing round inside my head, rendering prayer and stillness totally impossible.

This inner restlessness is terrible! I was getting ready to take Brodie out for her walk yesterday evening and she was making it so difficult by jumping round in circles, barking and generally getting under my feet. In the end I had to say, very firmly, 'Sit! Stay!' and make her wait until she had calmed down. Lord, I realise that I need to hear you say, 'Sit! Stay!' like that to me!

It took at least a couple of years before that prayer was answered and I could find that inner peace once again.

Sometimes, when you are struggling up this spiral staircase of grief and you feel you are making progress at long last, something trips you up and sends you slithering all the way back down again. Often it is something ridiculously small, like finding Tony's gardening gloves in the shed or opening a case in the attic and discovering our wedding album.

As I took communion I realised that when I die I won't be buried in the same grave as Tony. That hurt. I always wanted to be buried with him.

It's Mother's Day. Will Tony have helped her *children to buy* her *presents today?*

St Valentine's Day! Back here at Stillmeadow for a couple of weeks. How could Tony and I have been here, just months ago on our thirtieth wedding anniversary with all the cards up on that shelf, walking, eating, laughing, together! And now – I'm alone, silence, nothing.

For some reason, during those two weeks I became absolutely convinced that if I could only see and talk to Tony, I could persuade him to come home and the nightmare would be over. He was living quite near so it felt logical to try and see him before I went home. After fasting and praying for three days like Queen Esther (Esther 4:16) I plucked up enough courage to dial his number.

Lowest day yet. Rang Tony and asked if we could meet. He said no; because there's no hope for our future and he needs to move on into a new life. He said I should start writing secular books and earn my own living. Went out on to the beach where you said, 'All you need is me,' and cried and cried and cried – then drank a whole big bottle of Devon Scrumpy until nothing hurt any more.

But my head certainly did, when I woke the following morning! In spite of the disappointment I doggedly refused to accept that our marriage was over, and the many letters that arrived from all over the world fuelled my faith. They were written by people who felt they had received words from the Lord that Tony would definitely come home and promised to go on praying until he did so. 'No one could possibly pit their will against so much combined faith,' I told myself. 'He's *sure* to come back!'

In spite of all God's many reassurances, my journal shows clearly that my main problem, during the first six months, was trusting him over the future. The Hildenborough Trust kindly kept me on during that time, treating it like a sabbatical, but I was sure I would be out of a job by the spring.

Went for a sploshy walk over fields with Brodie, fighting my doubts all the way.

Lord, I can't pay off such a huge mortgage now Tony won't pay any more towards it. I'm badly short each month.

Spent most of the night in the Prayer Room. Saw myself putting everything I have on an altar, everyone and everything, ministry (again), this home, the vision I had for this Prayer Room being a place of healing — everything. Then read Job 22:23–30:

If you return to the Almighty, you will be restored:
If you . . . assign your nuggets to the dust,
your gold . . . to the rocks in the ravines,
then the Almighty will be your gold,
the choicest silver for you.
Surely then you will find delight in the Almighty
and will lift up your face to God . . .
He will deliver even one who is not innocent,
who will be delivered through the cleanness of your hands.

How I would love to have been able to see people coming to this room for prayer.

Yesterday morning, after I'd prayed all night, I felt it right to pray with Violet and Liz Piz (my two closest prayer partners) that God would send someone to pay off the whole mortgage. Knelt in the Prayer Room as I prayed with them. Show me, Lord, if you want me to go on developing this place as a healing/support centre — I thought that was what you wanted, Lord, but perhaps I should sell up and find a small, affordable place and abandon the vision.

Later the same day that I had written those words, I sat down at my desk to open the post. One of the letters was from Timmy. I had known and loved her as a teenager when she often stayed at Hildenborough Hall back in the 1940s and 1950s. Our friendship had continued over the years and she had been a great support to Tony and me in our ministry, as well as being a willing Granny-sitter. I glanced at her letter, still bleary-eyed from that sleepless night. I knew Timmy's husband had just died and she was soon moving back to Australia to be near her children.

'The house is sold,' said her letter, 'but also some land next door that I didn't realise was worth anything. I want you to have this with my love . . .'

I picked up the cheque, which had fallen out of the envelope. 'How kind,' I thought, glancing at it sleepily. Then, as I looked again, I noticed all the noughts! I felt dizzy and breathless as I picked up her letter again.

'I want you to be able to keep your home. No strings, you don't have to use it for the ministry, just enjoy it and be safe in it. I decided to do this because I was reading Job 22:24 so I'm sending my gold nuggets in your direction.'

God had taken us, quite separately, to the same passage! My journal goes on for days, 'lost in wonder, love and praise', but I honestly could not find enough words to thank Timmy or the Lord!

Spontaneously, without me mentioning that I had financial needs, several other people gave me the rest of the money to pay off the mortgage. 'But,' said my solicitor gloomily, 'your husband could well demand half, you know.' The thought hung over me for several months but Tony, generous as always, waived his rights and gave me the house in lieu of any maintenance and pension rights. My 'new husband' had provided me with the home I loved.

When Gan decided to go and live permanently with my

brother-in-law Peter, everyone started asking what kind of a job I intended to get – now I was free. 'The world's your oyster,' they told me, and gave me a whole range of suggestions; but inside I knew there was only one thing I wanted to do.

I know I gave you back my ministry at Friar's Crag but this verse screamed at me today, 'But my life is worth nothing unless I use it for doing the work assigned me by the Lord Jesus – the work of telling others the Good News about God's wonderful kindness and love' [Acts 20:24, NLB]. Lord, I'm not asking you to let me go off round the country, speaking again, but that picture you gave me of all those people coming here for prayer just haunts me.

I was beginning to get letters from other people whose marriages had also broken apart. Many of them said, 'Couldn't we get together and talk? People who haven't had this happen to them just don't seem to understand.' After three such letters arrived in one day I began to wonder if the Lord might actually be able to use the mess I was in for the benefit of other people. When I found this prayer in one of Leanne Payne's books I pinned it up on the kitchen wall: 'Lord, transform this anguish into healing grace for others' (*Listening Prayer*, Kingsway, 1995). Gradually I was beginning to realise that when we give the Lord something which is precious to us, as when he asked Abraham to give up Isaac, he sometimes gives it back when he is sure we are ready to put him first in our lives (Genesis 22:11–13). The fact that he had given me the house so miraculously did seem like an indication that he still wanted to use it after all. Yet I had no idea how I would support myself now I could no longer work for the Hildenborough Trust, which I had just heard was disbanding.

'It's easy, Mum,' said Duncan when we were out walking Brodie together on the hills. 'You just get all your friends to club together and form a small trust.'

'I'm not the sort of person who forms trusts!' I laughed. 'I've got dyslexia, remember? It was Dad who had all the brains.' I was somewhat startled, however, when I next went to see the couple who had been our mentors, or spiritual directors, for the previous eight years – the Rev. Leslie Edgell and his wife Shirley.

'You should form your own trust,' they told me enthusiastically, 'to support what you feel the Lord wants to do.' By that time several other friends were also egging me on and promising their support.

Lord, what are you doing??!!! Do you want me to go for this? But how will Tony feel when he comes home? Wouldn't it be best to sell the house – go and live on a Welsh mountain and write secular novels? Would that bring him back?

In the end I made it clear to everyone that the moment Tony showed even the slightest interest in coming back, I must be free to sell the house so we could start all over again somewhere else. I wrote and told Tony that, too, and explained I was just doing something to fill in the time while I waited for him. Still, the thought of launching *anything* without him terrified me – with such a capable husband, and parents who were both high achievers, I had never had to do anything on my own; but I guess the Lord was teaching me to trust him instead!

Woke up terrified. Can't do this! I'm stressing myself out trying to learn all this computer stuff!

When Richard had come home for the weekend from university, he told me firmly,

'Mum, if you're going to run a charity you'll have to learn about databases, spreadsheets and mail merges – not to mention desktop publishing.' He soon installed all the software and then patiently began teaching me how to use it.

On paper, I must be the least likely candidate the Lord could possibly have found to organise a charity, but '*the people that do know their God shall be strong and do exploits*' (Daniel 11:32, KJV), and this is not because of *what* they know, it is *who* they know that counts! Like so many other women after the break-up of a long-standing marriage, I faced the need to support myself just when my self-confidence was at its lowest ebb. 'I feel like dog shit' is a phrase that occurs often in my journal, but that is just how you feel when the person whose love you have relied on for years suddenly rejects you. It had been Tony who had built my self-esteem over the years, and his opinion of me had always been far more important than anyone else's; but I now had to learn that God's opinion was the only one that mattered. 'I am defined as a person (who I am and what I am) because of who loves me,' says Christian writer John Powell, but the realisation of just how much God loved me took a long time to sink down into my soul. Only when it was firmly embedded there did the candyfloss finally slither off for good!

Perhaps I was also afraid of going back into ministry, in case those less worthy 'engines' started to drive me again. About that time Jean was helping me become aware of the massive power that childhood vows can have over our future life. I longed to fulfil the most important of the three vows I had made, to be one of the 'small handful of people who follow on to *know* the Lord', but how could I be sure that the other two did not still have a sinister hold over me?

'You can be rid of them easily,' said Jean during my next visit to Shropshire. 'You just have to revoke them and then sincerely repent of ever having made them in the first place. After that,' she added confidently, 'you need to keep on asking the Lord to show you the "wood, hay and stubble" the *moment* they start swamping the gold and silver' (1 Corinthians 3:12–15).

In spite of all these misgivings it was not long before I had a new set of trustees and Leslie became the chairman of our new little charity. He christened it Beauty from Ashes because, he said, 'The people who will come to you are broken hearted and imprisoned by all kinds of things; but the Lord said he had come to give people like that a crown of beauty instead of the ashes of their ruined lives' (Isaiah 61:1–3).

The Hildenborough Trust gave us a grant to start us off and also kindly paid for me to do a year's Christian counselling course. Since then I have done secular courses, too, in spite of my terror at feeling I am back at school! Gradually I also began to take speaking engagements again, and to my astonishment I soon discovered that the Lord was giving me a new and deeper anointing than ever before. Because I knew I must preserve this at all costs I was careful to give my 'Mary' side daily space, as well as carving out longer periods of times from my diary when I could get away to be alone with him at Stillmeadow.

One thing still bothered me, and that was the fountain in the courtyard that led to the Prayer Room. Strangely, the day Tony left, its inner workings had mysteriously seized up, so after a few unsuccessful attempts to get it started again I had filled it with soil and planted pansies.

'The fountain's a vital part of your vision for this place,' said my brother Justyn when he came to visit me that summer; and after a lot of hard work, and even more patience, he had the water flowing again.

*　*　*

All this sounds as if I was happily over my grief by the end of the first year. Sadly, I've discovered that grief always takes longer than you think it will and a *lot* longer than others think it should! The last stage of the grieving process is acceptance, and the experts dangle it in front of us like a magical finishing line. I wanted to get there and often thought that I had, only to find myself revisiting all those previous stages yet again. Acceptance is the point when we are able to let go of the past in order to embrace a new kind of future, but that was my sticking point; I did not want to accept a future that did not contain Tony.

'We're all so glad to see the way you've been able to move on with your life,' beamed the rather too cheerful friend I met in the High Street almost five years after Tony had left. I looked at her sourly as I thought how much I hate that phrase 'move on with your life'; I honestly did not believe I was at liberty to do so until Tony came back, even though on the outside my life probably looked delightful.

By then, Beauty from Ashes had attracted a group of very special people to help me carry the load. We began running healing days in the garden here and holiday breaks for people recovering from loss of all kinds; but, best of all, a constant stream of people kept on coming to see us in the Prayer Room, looking for a touch from the Lord.

Yet, in spite of all his kindness and provision, I still felt empty and incomplete. Five of our children got married during the first three years after Tony left, and I found it agonising to sit next to him during each of those weddings, listening to the solemn vows we had once made ourselves.

'You won't get over this until you let Tony go': that was another oft-repeated phrase I came to loathe. Inwardly I would scream, 'Doesn't anyone nowadays remember that marriages are supposed to last for life?' I had promised in front of a thousand wedding guests that I would *never* let Tony go, come poverty or wealth, sickness or health, until death parted us – so why did everyone expect me just to switch love off like a light bulb? If you lose a husband through death you have no choice but to accept he has gone and will not be coming back in this life. Being separated leaves you suspended in a strange kind of vacuum: you are not married but neither are you single. The fact that Tony never mentioned divorce kept alive my hope that he would come back, so I did not want to make plans for the future that did not include him.

People continued to write encouraging letters telling me how their marriages had been restored by all kinds of supernatural interventions, even after many years of separation or divorce, while others said they still felt burdened to pray and fast for Tony's return.

'He'll be back!' I told them all confidently. 'Believing prayer always prevails in the end.'

★ ★ ★

Five years and two weeks after Tony left I was sitting at my desk opening the post one October morning. 'This one looks a bit dull and official,' I thought as I slit open a brown envelope. It was official – but definitely *not* dull! As I read the typed letter inside I found I couldn't breathe for the pain, which suddenly grabbed and squeezed my chest. The brief sentences on the page were lost in swirling black dots once I realised they told me that Tony was going to divorce me in order to marry again. They also informed me that because we had lived apart for five years, there was nothing I could do but accept the inevitable.

It was not the final death of my marriage that devastated me, but the feeling that God had let me down – *totally!*

For what seemed like hours I just sat there, holding the letter, unable to move. Divorce! How I had always dreaded that horrible D word! The Bible says God also hates divorce (Malachi 2:16), so how could he let it happen to me when I had trusted so completely in his power, and desire, to restore our marriage? Had all that prayer, faith and fasting just been wasted effort? If one man could withstand all the powers of heaven, then what was the point of praying about anything – ever again?

As I clutched the arms of my office chair for support I thought about all those Bible promises I'd stuck up round my kitchen walls, which confidently described the rewards of persistent faith. I also wondered why I had been so sure that if I repented long enough and hard enough for all my mistakes God would give me a second chance to be a better wife to Tony. In the end, all that had made no difference whatsoever. And what a farce all that spiritual warfare had proved to be! I felt so utterly disillusioned I could hardly speak to anyone for days. I knew I was spiralling down into the worst black hole of doubt that I had ever experienced; but I was too hurt and angry to care.

'*This time, God, you've gone too far!*' I felt like that because the solicitor's letter had arrived on top of a whole series of other losses. In the space of a few months my three closest friends had died, two of my children had emigrated, and several other painful situations had occurred that I could not describe without damaging other people. Now, all these other disasters paled into insignificance beside the harsh finality of divorce – and Tony's remarriage. The realisation that he was never coming back cut very deep, and I felt like the man who wrote Psalm 73: *'my soul was embittered, when I was pricked in heart ... I was like a brute beast towards you.'*

For months I floundered on, trying to act normally, relying on my 'Martha' side and all her busy activity to keep me going while my 'Mary' sulked in a corner (John 11:20). I kept trying to make fresh teeth-gritted, act-of-the-will decisions to 'trust the Lord anyway' but those doubts kept returning, and I can see from my journal that fighting them became a daily battle.

> *It is such an odd feeling to know that there is no one in the world who loves me best. Some people do love me but they all have someone else they love more. Feel as if God isn't there for me either; that is a lie and I reject it utterly. Still feel it though.*

Perhaps I could have regained my equilibrium faster if still more disasters had not kept on arriving with bewildering speed; the serious and medically incurable illness of a much loved granddaughter was diagnosed, followed soon afterwards by the death of her little sister. Furiously I scrawled in my journal,

> *Everything I pray for, you seem to do the exact opposite! I'm just not going to risk praying for anything from now on!*

However, the worst moment of my *annus horribilis* was when I stood helplessly outside the door of Intensive Care while staff battled to save the life of my eldest daughter, Sarah, who had collapsed one day when we were out together. They did manage to resuscitate her eventually, but the 'horror movie' replayed endlessly in my mind for weeks afterwards and Sister's voice kept on ringing in my ears, 'Get the husband here – *FAST!*' while I frantically tried to reach Paul on his mobile phone.

I am not trying to make excuses for myself, but prolonged stress and a whole series of shocks and losses can have the strangest effects on people, and by the time I arrived at that surprise birthday party my faith had really taken a battering. It was not that I had stopped believing in God's existence, but I struggled to go on believing he was good or kind – at any rate to me.

Now, looking back, I can see that from the day that solicitor's letter arrived I had been furious with God because he had not done the one thing I most wanted him to do. I felt like shaking my fist in his face and screaming, 'You messed up! I could have done a much better job of looking after things than you have!' Of course, I did not realise at the time that this kind of anger towards God always has its roots in pride; and pride impedes our journey into God's heart like nothing else. To know God is to trust him enough to let him do anything he wants to do with our lives, even when that means refusing our most urgent requests, simply because we know his only desire is that everything should ultimately bring us good (Romans 8:28). All my sulking only demonstrated how far I still had to travel on my journey, but at the time I certainly would not have admitted it.

Perhaps I had been so busy trying to forgive Tony, and myself, for the break-up of our marriage that I had not faced the fact that I still needed to forgive God for not mending it. Forgiveness is defined in my dictionary as 'ceasing to blame', and I definitely blamed him because I knew without any doubt he had the power to answer my prayers. Perhaps I spent so long groping about in those shadows simply because I was not willing to forgive.

One day I became so desperate I emailed Sarah, who had just returned to work in her Oxford college. 'Help! I've stopped believing that God is kind! How could he let so much go wrong?' She replied hastily between tutorials:

Since losing Cerian I've realised that the biggest pain of all is the pain of 'God, where were you when it happened?' That is a far bigger pain than any other because you love God more than any other. But it was through losing Cerian that I came to know for sure that God is kind. Please don't stop taking all this pain to the Lord, let it all out at him. After you have cried yourself to the end of the pain, I know that you will find that he is there. In this place you could choose to turn away and to learn to hate him or you can keep on pressing in and pressing in – until your own love for him is greater than your desire for him to love you.

It is very humbling when you realise your own children are closer to God's heart than you are yourself! I wanted to hear what she was saying but I still felt as if I was wearing spiritual earplugs.

But God always has his reasons for allowing us to plunge into a 'dark night of the soul'. I certainly do not believe he *arranges* the harsh situations that often precipitate them, but he does use these circumstances when they occur naturally. What he wanted me to discover in all this misery was just how much my long-held desire for intimacy really mattered to me. You can only know God to the degree to which you are prepared to trust him. He had brought me to the place where I relied on him as a perfect husband, but the depth of intimacy I had always longed for required an even closer bond than the union between a husband and wife. It is the place when we *'live and move and have our being'* (Acts 17:28) right inside his heart, as utterly dependent on him as an unborn baby in the womb who relies on its mother for *everything* – nourishment, oxygen, warmth, comfort, even life itself. I could not reach that place of total connectedness while there was still a part of me that depended on Tony.

How anxiously God must watch us whenever he makes an attempt at drawing us deeper into his heart because, of course, he actually risks losing our friendship and trust for good. So many of us do give up at this point, and not all of my special 'handful' of people had managed to *'follow on to know the LORD'* (Hosea 6:3,

KJV) right to the end of their lives; perhaps I have to include my own mother in that category.

One evening when I lay soaking in the bath after a long hike with the dogs, I dimly realised that both Satan and God had their own agenda for my present situation. Satan, who loathes anything that gives God pleasure, hoped he could use the impending divorce to destroy my desire for God once and for all. He also planned to steal my belief in prayer, make me bitter and resentful and so discouraged that I would stop serving the Lord entirely.

On the other hand, God had allowed all this because he hoped it might make me cling on to him as tenaciously as a baby koala adheres to its mother – even when he didn't give me what I wanted or even offer me an explanation.

As I lay in the soap bubbles I remembered what Mr Luff, the old man I had loved as a teenager in Frinton, used to say so often: 'Seek the Lord for himself, not for the power to serve him, or for the things you want to make your life comfortable. Seek him for himself alone; look at his face and not his hand.'

I knew I had not been doing that. For the last five years I had been waving my faith at the Lord like a demand notice. 'Give Tony back – or else!' Perhaps it had not been faith at all, but just pig-headed stubbornness. I was facing another of those choices: either I would let Satan get what he wanted out of this divorce or I would allow God's plans to work for me. It would be simplistic to say I leapt out of the bath victoriously, with my faith and desire for intimacy totally restored, but my cold-blooded decision to trust – whatever might happen – was definitely a step in the right direction.

* * *

'Don't go!' said all my friends and family, as the time came for my annual retreat at Stillmeadow.

'You're in no fit state to be alone for so long,' added my spiritual advisor; but I went anyway!

'Help me!' I screamed at the Lord into the teeth of a gale out on the cliffs one morning. 'I miss your presence so badly!' When I had calmed down with a mug of tea and some dry clothes I realised I was sitting in the same room where I had first 'met' Anna the prophetess (Luke 2:36–8), twenty-two years before. I could not help wondering if, at first, she had argued with God when he allowed her husband to die just seven years after they were married. Yet, in the end, it was *because* she was a childless widow that she had the opportunity to spend all her time with God, undistracted. The thing that she may have felt was a catastrophic disaster at the time had become God's greatest gift. So perhaps I should also see my singleness as an asset.

It was that morning that I discovered a quote by one of my favourite authors, Oswald Chambers: 'The root of sin is doubting that God is good.' I knew I had been weighed down by all that pride and resentment I had been holding against God for far too long, so I hurried back down on to the beach and put the biggest rock I could lift into my rucksack. Then I staggered with it on my back right up to the highest point on the cliff path. As I heaved it over the edge, down into the boiling waves below, I felt an even bigger weight lift off my shoulders.

That evening my Bible portion was Daniel chapter 3, and as I began to read I suddenly saw myself as a child of six, back in our nursery at Hildenborough Hall. Nanny was making toast for our tea, holding the bread against the bars of the gas fire with a long toasting fork, while Otty told us the story of Shadrach, Meshach and Abednego.

'Make the fiery furnace *even hotter*,' Otty was shouting as she stood on her chair impersonating the Emperor Nebuchadnezzar – with a tea cosy on his head. 'And you three will be thrown into the flames if you don't bow down and worship my gods! Forget your silly old God, you'll soon see he won't be able to deliver you out of my hand.' By this time our eyes were round with awe while Nanny let the toast burn.

'Our God *can* save us,' replied Shadrach, Meshach and

Abednego. '*But if not* (even if he doesn't) we'll still worship him and no one else!' Of course, we knew exactly what would happen next because we asked for the story so often, but we still savoured its delicious end. 'Even though they were thrown into the fierce heat, they walked about in the flames without even being singed, not even their "tunics, trousers and turbines" because . . . [pause for effect] . . . there was someone else in the furnace with them!'

'It was *Jesus!*' we shrieked.

'Don't ever forget the bit where they said, "But if not",' Otty always concluded. 'God is powerful enough to save us from all the horrid things of life, *but if not* (even if he doesn't) he is always there with us, right in the hottest part of the fire.' As my memory faded Otty was still wagging her finger in my direction and saying, 'Don't you ever forget that, Jen-Jen.'

But I had forgotten! I'd been so busy trying to force him to take the flames away that I had missed the joy of his company *in* the flames! I finally went off to bed revelling in a God who still loved me, and wanted to use me, in spite of all that sulking! '*If we are not faithful, he remains faithful, because he cannot be false to himself*' (2 Timothy 2:13, GNB).

Before I came home from that retreat I thought a lot about the 'handful' of people my mother had told me I would meet throughout my life. As I listed them, I asked myself what made them stand out from other Christians. Although they had all been very different, three things characterised them all: joy, peace and humility. It was joy which made their faces beam back at me from my memories; because they had all been so much in love with the Lord they thanked him constantly, seeing everything he brought into their lives, both good and bad, as sent from him in order to draw them still further into his arms (Romans 8:28). Like Brother Lawrence, the monastery cook, they had trained themselves to be continuously aware of God's presence until he was far more real and enjoyable than any human relationship. They were full of peace because worry was unnecessary; they knew he would take care of everything that concerned them so they were free to relish the tiny details of life.

They were also very humble people. Not one of them felt they had 'arrived' – in fact, they were deeply aware of their failures. Perhaps the closer we get to God the more conscious we are of our sin – and the need for his continuous forgiveness.

As well as travelling deep into his heart they had also opened their own hearts to him, until he had infiltrated every aspect of their thoughts, feelings and desires. In fact, they had reached a point where they no longer knew themselves apart from him (Ephesians 3:17). Thinking about those special people made my months of whingeing feel even more embarrassing, but it also sent me home determined to live very differently.

★ ★ ★

That final stage of the grief journey, acceptance, had certainly taken me a long time to reach, and it seems ironic to say that the event which helped me most to cross that elusive finishing line was actually the thing I had most dreaded – the divorce.

The date 6 February, 10 a.m., was marked in red on the kitchen calendar and filled me with dread as it approached. It was the time when our divorce case was going to come up in a Taunton court. I didn't have to be there, as there was nothing to contend, but I felt I had to do something to mark the end of our marriage and bring about some kind of closure. It seemed a good idea to do that in Otford parish church, where we had been married thirty-five years before. Since Tony had left I had often made a pilgrimage there on 6 August, our wedding anniversary, to ask the Lord to heal our marriage; there was no more point in doing that, but it seemed the 'right' place to go while the court hearing was in progress.

I arrived well before ten, and stood on the chancel steps reading aloud the marriage service we had used when the church had been full of smiling friends and relations. Again I repented for the times when I had not 'loved, served, obeyed and honoured' as fully as I should. I was just asking the Lord what he wanted me to do with my wedding ring when I heard the latch of the church door click. Rather crossly, I retired to a dark corner while I watched several old people shuffling in on sticks and zimmer-frames, ready for their mid-week communion service. It was their church, but I still resented them being there because I wanted to be alone when ten o'clock finally struck.

As the bell began to toll, high above our heads, I felt the Lord was asking me to take off my wedding ring, as a way of marking the end of our marriage. I had never removed it once since the day Tony had placed it on my finger, here in this church. I was astonished to find how hard it was to do; everything in me wanted to leave the ring where it was, but I also knew that peace only comes through obedience. An enormous surge of grief nearly choked me as I pulled it off and sat clutching it in my palm while the service progressed. It was still there when I walked up the aisle, with everyone else, to take communion, and knelt on the spot where I had once made my wedding vows.

'Will you give Tony to me – finally?' I felt the Lord ask, and as a tangible way of saying 'yes' I held the ring out on my hand.

As I thought about the guests who had once packed into the pews behind me to witness our wedding, I felt such a sense of shame at the thought of how we had both failed to keep our vows. So as I held out the ring on my hand I knew I was not only giving Tony to the Lord, but I also wanted him to take all the mess we had made of our marriage.

The retired vicar who was ministering the sacraments did not know anything about me, and he was so elderly he may not even have seen the ring on my palm, but he just put the wafer down on top of it. When I opened my eyes the ring was hidden; all I could see was the cross on the white wafer. At that moment it felt as if Christ was coving our mess with his own dazzling white purity.

I have never put that ring back on since. For a few weeks it lay on the Bible next to my rocking chair in the Prayer Room, but as the date for Tony's wedding approached I felt the Lord was asking me to send it back to him. Once again I fought the idea vigorously, but sometimes obedience is like taking a very unpleasant medicine – you just have to hold your nose and get on with it! So I wrapped the ring in tissue paper and sent it to Tony with a note.

I am not sure that I totally meant what I wrote at that time but I genuinely wanted to *want* to mean it!

Dear Tony
Thank you for being such a wonderful husband and father for those thirty years. This ring has probably been my most precious possession but I felt I should send it back as a way of showing you that you are free to be happy in the way you have chosen. I wish you both well and hope you will be happy.
All my love as always,
Jen

Tony and his new wife now live on a Greek island, but last summer, two years after their wedding, they were in England visiting the family. So I wrote asking them both here to tea. I realised it was inevitable that the three of us would have to see each other at future family occasions, so I guessed it would be less embarrassing to meet for the first time in private. However, as I sat waiting for them to arrive, the idea suddenly did not seem quite such a good one!

'Whatever have I done?' I asked myself; it felt even more terrifying than going to see Miss Mitchell, my old schoolteacher! When the bell finally rang, I could see them, through the glass front door, waiting on the step where Tony had kissed me goodbye the day he left. For years I had daydreamed about the moment when I would find him standing there again, ready and willing to restore our marriage. Now he was there at last – but his new wife stood beside him. I wanted to run away in the opposite direction and hide at the far end of the garden, but I noticed how nervous they both looked too – and she seemed so vulnerable.

'Fill me with *your* love, just as if I were your gloves,' I whispered as I opened the door.

For two hours we sat in the Prayer Room that Tony had built all those years before and chatted happily about our children and grandchildren. It was one of the most healing experiences of my life. He looked well and they were obviously both still very much in love. I am not condoning divorce – far from it. God has good reason to hate it because of the agony it causes to everyone concerned, but when there was nothing more I could do to prevent it, acceptance was the only way to find peace. The three of us are now on comfortable terms and Tony even went through the manuscript of this book with his red pen; after marking a host of spelling mistakes he said he was happy for me to go ahead and publish it.

That tea party brought me healing on a very deep level; soon afterwards I realised to my surprise that I am happier now than I have ever been before. There really is life after divorce – not just a bleak existence but life in all its abundance, just as Jesus intended for us (John 10:10). He really is enough to meet every single one of our needs, provided we let him give us as much of himself as we are capable of containing! *'You're blessed when you feel you've lost what is most dear to you. Only then can you be embraced by the One most dear to you'* (Matthew 5:4, *The Message*).

Brother Lawrence proved that it is possible to have intimacy with God when you share your life with crowds of people, but personally I find it far easier when it's just 'him and me'. I talk to him out loud all the time, so it is a good thing I have no close neighbours! I fall asleep in the middle of a sentence and finish it next morning as I wake up (Psalm 139:18b). Being alone does not necessarily mean being lonely; he comes with me when I walk the dogs and we enjoy the beauty of the countryside together, and if I see something funny I often laugh out loud, feeling as if we are sharing the joke. His words, 'All you need is me,' have finally become a reality.

However, intimacy does not mean living the life of a hermit. Like Anna, I can move peacefully out of that secret place (Psalm 91:1, KJV) in order to enjoy the people he brings in and out of my life. I love talking to them about him and talking to him about them! That, after all, is the essence of any kind of ministry. I may finish up as old and gnarled as Anna herself, but the glorious fact is that the journey into God's heart continues even after death, and I have the rest of eternity to discover yet more vistas of his character than a mere human mind could ever comprehend. After being as angry with God as the man who wrote Psalm 73 (vv. 2–17), I had finally made the same discovery:

> *Nevertheless I am continually with you; you hold my right hand*
> *. . . there is nothing on earth that I desire other than you.*
> *My flesh and my heart may fail, but God is the strength of my heart*
> *and my portion forever*
> *. . . for me it is good to be near God; I have made the LORD God my*
> *refuge, to tell of all your works.*
>
> Psalm 73:23–8, NRSV

> *I want to know Christ … I do not consider myself yet to have taken*
> *hold of it. But one thing I do: Forgetting what is behind and straining*
> *towards what is ahead, I press on towards the goal to win the prize for*
> *which God has called me heavenwards.*
>
> Philippians 3:10–13

Epilogue

So what do I mean by intimacy with God? These days there is an increasing desire for a deep, personal relationship with the creator of the universe and many of us are pressing into his heart as never before. I believe this is his doing; he longs for us to know him infinitely more than we do! Just as we humans long to be known by someone else to the deepest possible level and then understood and completely accepted, God, who made us in his own image, also wants that kind of intimacy.

No one has ever loved us in the way we secretly long to be loved, not parents, spouse, friends or children, but once we know how much God loves us we find the deepest satisfaction we have ever known, and the more deeply we become acquainted with him the more of a delight prayer becomes. In the early stages of the journey we hurry up to him, waving lists of requests in the hope of making him agree to do what we want or prosper the plans we have already made. Later in the journey we learn to nestle up close to him and wait there long enough until we begin to sense what he is thinking about the issues that concern us: how he is reacting to them and what his desires and plans are for us in them. Then we can pray confidently with the current of his will. Prayer becomes a continuous occupation rather than just a rigidly defined slot in our daily schedule. Obviously we are not muttering away to him as we go round the supermarket and sit at our office desk, but we simply learn to live continuously in his presence, aware he is with us all the time, so even our thoughts become prayer. Wherever we go and whatever we do, see or read, we are open to him speaking to us through these ordinary things in the world around us: and every little thing we do each day becomes an act of worship. I think St Paul was defining this kind of lifestyle when he said: '*In him we live and move and have our being*' (Acts 17:28).

There are definitely a lot of things that make this way of life extremely difficult, but in spite of all the hardships of this journey into his heart there is nothing so completely satisfying, because his company, as you walk through life beside him, makes everything infinitely worthwhile. We never really find ourselves until we have completely lost ourselves in him.

But how can ordinary people nowadays know God to this intimate extent? Isn't this kind of relationship only possible for monks and nuns, or people who are rich enough to live above the pressures that occupy the majority of mankind? I believe knowing God is not about time or the freedom to sit for hours in contemplation and Bible study. Knowing God is an attitude of the heart, the goal that determines all our choices throughout life. It is a secret relationship that goes on underneath all the outside pressures, activities and involvements. In fact, it often thrives best when our outward life is under the most pressure. The only thing that really matters is that we *want* to know God; and the more of him we have the more we long to have!